Opening the Door to Retirement

Successfully Transitioning from the Workforce into Retirement

by Ray E. LeVitre, CFM

Opening the Door to Retirement
Cover Design by Caroline Norton
Edited by Suzanne Kimball and Michael Freeman
Graphic Images by Rani Hansen
Printed in the U.S.A. by Alexanderís Digital Printing

To order this title, or for further information about this book and related
subject matter, please call (801) 277-6280.

The information relating to investments and investment services contained herein is for
informational purposes only and is not a solicitation to sell or an offer to buy any securities.
The information is obtained from sources believed to be reliable; accuracy
and completeness is not guaranteed.

Library of Congress Cataloging-in-Publication Data

LeVitre, Ray E.
  Opening the Door to Retirement: Successfully Transitioning from the Workforce Into Retirement
  by Ray E. LeVitre
  ISBN: 0-9727882-0-4 (pbk.)
  Library of Congress Control Number: 2003093466

Copyright © 2003 by Ray E. LeVitre

DEDICATIONS

Dedicated to God who has blessed me with life, experience, opportunities, abilities and the desire to live a little bit better each day. I believe that God truly inspires us with thoughts and ideas to help us succeed on our life's journey.

Dedicated to my wife, Jana, whom I deeply love and adore. I love her for her never failing support and unwavering confidence in me. Without her constant willingness to endure my often overzealous, entrepreneurial spirit, this book would never have come to fruition. Jana, thanks for believing with me that even the loftiest goals can be achieved and for making me want to be better than I am.

SPECIAL ACKNOWLEDGMENTS

Ray and Judy LeVitre – Thanks for your encouragement and support. A special thanks for helping me over the hurdles that life has thrown my way. Life's challenges are much easier to face when your parents and family are always there for you. I love you for always believing in my dreams.

Gwen Remund – Thanks for your tireless hours of editing and feedback during the early and late stages of *Opening the Door to Retirement's* development.

Chuck L. Cutler – You are a rock-solid mentor and role model. Thanks for giving me a solid financial planning foundation. Without your help I would have missed out on many opportunities and would surely not be where I am today. I owe you a great deal.

Eugene Banks – Because you hired me and gave me the opportunity to work for the largest brokerage company in the world, I owe much of what I have learned in the financial services industry to you.

My Clients – A special thanks to each of you for placing so much trust in me as your financial advisor and for giving me the opportunity to help you develop a strategy to reach your financial goals. The strategies outlined in *Opening the Door to Retirement* are a culmination of my experience in working to develop fundamentally sound solutions to your unique financial situations.

And finally, I would like to thank the many companies that have invited me onto their corporate campuses and into their work sites to teach their employees how to manage a retirement plan distribution and develop a solid investment strategy.

Opening the Door to Retirement

*Successfully Transitioning from
the Workforce into Retirement*

TABLE OF CONTENTS

PART THREE: DEVELOPING A SUCCESSFUL INVESTMENT STRATEGY

PART FOUR: OTHER RETIREMENT CONSIDERATIONS

PART FIVE: RETIREMENT PLAN DISTRIBUTION GUIDE

INTRODUCTION: WHY YOU SHOULD READ THIS BOOK

*Successfully Transitioning from
the Workforce into Retirement*

Look into the future for a moment and imagine yourself on the day you retire. Will it be a day of joy or one that you don't quite feel ready for financially? Are you currently dreading the thought of it, or are you longingly dreaming about it? How well will you be prepared for the life that begins the day you give notice and leave your full-time working years behind?

If you're getting ready to retire in the near future, the pressure is on to make the right financial choices with your retirement money. The decisions you make at this critical juncture will profoundly affect your financial security and your lifestyle for the next 25 to 30 years.

Enormous amounts of money are riding on your decisions. To date, Americans have amassed over $2.7 trillion in various types of qualified retirement plans[2] and assets in 401(k) plans alone have almost tripled since 1993.[3] Over 42 million people participate in 401(k) plans. The amount of money in transition is staggering. For example in 2001, for every dollar contributed to a 401(k) plan, 83 cents was distributed to job changers and retirees.[5] About $200 billion of the money exiting corporate plans is rolled into IRA's each year.[6] These withdrawals are expected to soar to over $600 billion by 2005 as the baby boomers begin to retire.[7]

Because so much money is at stake and many of your financial decisions are going to be irrevocable, now is the time to prepare yourself to handle the many challenges you face. *Opening the Door to Retirement* will help you successfully transition into retirement. It examines the critical decisions you will have to make about your money when deciding to end a full-time working career. It will also help you evaluate your current financial situation and do some critical planning for the future.

Opening the Door to Retirement is intended to be a guide book and is not necessarily meant to be read chapter by chapter. Each of the five parts of the book explain various components of retirement planning, investment options and retirement plan distribution strategies. As you read, focus on those sections and chapters that are most pertinent to you at this particular time in your life — use the other chapters as a reference. For those about to retire or who have already quit working, you will find the whole book extremely useful and may want to read each chapter in the order it is presented.

Part 1, Retirement Planning, will help you assess what your current retirement situation looks like and determine whether you are on track to meet your retirement goals. This section also outlines the importance of having a *written* comprehensive financial plan, how to determine a safe withdrawal rate, and what to do if you plan to retire early.

In Part 2, Sources of Retirement Income, we'll explore the issues surrounding Social Security, teach you how to maximize your company pension benefits and how to avoid the most common investor mistakes so that you can be sure not to sabotage your most important retirement income source: your investment portfolio.

Part 3 covers important investment planning techniques. After all, reaching your retirement goals will depend largely on how successful you are as an investor. This section deals primarily with how to develop successful investment strategies, including asset allocation, proper portfolio diversification, choosing investments, ongoing portfolio management, how to protect principal while investing in the stock market, and how to handle company stock positions.

Other retirement issues, such as health and long-term care insurance, are covered in Part 4. Without these safeguards in place, you could prematurely deplete all of your hard-earned assets. This section will teach you how to evaluate how much insurance you may need and when to purchase it.

Part 5 is intended to be a retirement plan distribution guide. This section deals primarily with the issues and choices facing people who, at retirement, take a distribution from an employer-sponsored retirement plan. Before making any decisions about your money, be sure to reference this section for a very detailed analysis of your retirement options.

Opening the Door to Retirement explains, in basic terms, highly complex financial concepts that you need to understand in order to make appropriate choices. Use it as a comprehensive information source on retirement planning and successful money management techniques. *Opening the Door to Retirement* is an important resource that can help you build a financial strategy to guide you toward the retirement lifestyle you deserve.

Opening the Door to Retirement

PART 1

RETIREMENT PLANNING

Chapter 1
Retirement Planning: Are You on Track?

When it comes to retirement planning, too many people face a reality gap. According to a recent study of American workers and retirees, 70 percent were confident they would have enough money to live comfortably during retirement. Yet that same survey revealed that only 39 percent would actually have enough money saved to enjoy the kind of retirement lifestyle they envision.[1]

- Are you on track to reach your retirement goals?

- How much money do you need to accumulate in your savings nest egg to generate enough retirement income to last for 20, even 30 years?

- How well have you prepared for the life that begins the day you give notice and leave your full-time working years behind?

Answering these questions is vitally important. That's why this book begins with a chapter designed to help you take a good hard look at your overall retirement situation. It will help you evaluate where you are now and whether you are on track to get where you want to go in the future by asking questions about your short-term and long-term goals.

To answer these questions, you will first need a target. What is your retirement goal? When you add up all your financial assets on the first day of retirement (see Figure 1), what does your portfolio need to total in order for you to reach your retirement target? How far are you from that goal?

Of course, the amount needed at retirement differs for everyone and ultimately hinges on your answers to the following questions:

Figure 1

+ **Brokerage Accounts**
+ **IRA Accounts**
+ **401 k's**
+ **Insurance Cash Value**
+ **Annuities**
+ **Savings Bonds**
+ **Bank Accounts**
+ **Other Investments**

???

- When will you retire?
- What is your current income?
- What percentage of your current income will you need each year during retirement?
- How long do you estimate you will be in retirement?
- What will your income sources be during retirement?
- What will be the rate of return on your investment assets during retirement?
- What impact will inflation have on your retirement goals?

The best way to see if you're on track is to obtain a retirement analysis which is one critical component of your comprehensive financial plan (see Chapter 2). In order to develop a retirement analysis and see if your numbers add up sufficiently to meet your goals, you will need to answer the questions asked throughout this chapter. A case study (Ron and Linda Hansen) has been included with each question to help you evaluate your own retirement situation.

WHEN DO YOU PLAN ON RETIRING?

The average American retires at age 63.[2]

Worksheet Question #1:

At what age do you plan on retiring? _____

Case Study: Ron and Linda Hansen, age 50, plan on retiring at age 60.

WHAT IS YOUR RETIREMENT INCOME NEED?

As a general rule, most financial planners suggest having approximately 70 to 80 percent of your pre-retirement gross income in order to maintain your current standard of living. This, of course, can vary widely depending on your individual situation.

During retirement you will pay less taxes, save less, spend less on your children, and have less of a mortgage burden than you did while working. Consequently, you will be able to live on less money and maintain the same lifestyle. A person who earned $100,000 during their working years can live on $70,000 to $80,000 during retirement (adjusted for inflation). Of course, a more detailed analysis of your spending habits will yield a more accurate picture of your retirement income needs.

Be aware that some of your expenses will increase during retirement, even as others decrease. Figure 2 outlines some of the most common changes in spending during retirement.

FIGURE 2

Expenses likely to decrease	**Expenses likely to increase**
• Home Mortgage • Commuting • Financial Responsibility for Children or Parents • Work-related Clothing • Education Expenses • Life Insurance • Savings • Income Taxes	• Healthcare • Travel • Second Home • Further Education • Hobbies/ Recreation • Second Career

Also, the way you decide to spend your retirement years will have an impact on how much income you will need. How do you plan to spend your time? The following poll reflects the most common desires of retirees:

FIGURE 3

Poll Results

How do you want to spend your "retirement" years?	
Go back to school	2.1%
Travel the world	19.6%
Pursue creative passions	16.7%
Give back by volunteering	11.3%
Sit home with my feet up	10.1%
Spoil the Grandkids	4.2%
Keep working (I love my job)	3.4%
Keep working (I need the money)	9.1%
Launch my own business	3.6%
Start a second career	11.2%
Other	8.4%

Source: www.mygeneration.org

After deciding how you are going to spend your retirement years, you should consider some of the changes that may occur in your spending habits and prepare a realistic estimate of your annual retirement costs. Figure 4 shows a list of annual expenditures for the average American couple over age 65 (column 2). How your expenses match up to these figures depends on your lifestyle, family size and income.

In the column entitled, "Your Budget Now," estimate your current annual expenses. To make it easier, take your monthly expenses and multiply by 12. Then in the last column, "Your Retirement Budget," estimate what these costs would be if you were to retire today. This exercise will give you a rough idea of the expenses you will face during retirement.

FIGURE 4

Spending per year	Average Budget for a Married Couple 65+	Your Budget Now	Your Budget at Retirement
Food	$7,333		
Housing (including rent/ mortgage, utilities, and furnishings)	$16,348		
Transportation	$10,214		
Clothing	$2,520		
Entertainment	$2,784		
Personal Care	$541		
Health Care	$2,200		
Contributions	$1,201		
Miscellaneous Family Consumption	$4,723		
Insurance	$644		
Social Security	$4,658		
Total Spending for a Median Family in 1999	$51,186		

Source: Bureau of Labor & Statistics, 1999

Have you considered where you're going to live after you retire? According to the American Association of Retired Persons, only one in ten Americans age 55 and over is interested in relocating when he or she retires. However, if you do plan to move to another city, you must adjust your estimated retirement spending depending on the cost-of-living differences from region to region. The cost of living, for example, in San Francisco, New York and other large cities is much greater than smaller cities like Twin Falls, Idaho, or Charlotte, North Carolina.

Use a cost-of-living index as an easy way to see how your new home will affect your living expenses. Many online sources provide this information, free of charge. For example, *www.homefair.com* is user-friendly and will perform all of the calculations for you.[3] Another option is the American Chamber of Commerce Research Association's index (see Figure 13 located at the end of this chapter). This is another source of valuable information. For example, if you live in Austin today and estimate your annual retirement income needs at $100,000, the index shows that you will need $121,900, or 21.9 percent more income to maintain that same standard of living in San Diego. These facts can be determined by performing a relatively simple calculation, using the table in Figure 13. Find the number listed next to the city where you plan to live at retirement, then subtract that number from the one listed next to the city where you currently live. The result will be the cost of living change, in percentage points.

For example, let's assume you plan on moving from Denver (105.3) to Palm Springs (116.3). By performing the calculation, you can see that living in Palm Springs will cost approximately 11 percent more than living in Denver (116.3-105.3 = 11). So, if you planned on retiring on $75,000 per year, you will need to increase this by 11 percent, or $8,250 per year, to account for higher prices in Palm Springs.

Worksheet Question #2:
    What is your annual retirement income goal?_____
Case Study: The Hansen's retirement income goal is $75,000/year (today's $).

How many years will you be in retirement?

Most financial planners assume people will spend 20 to 25 years in retirement, roughly until age 85. These assumptions are based on average life expectancies (see Figure 5). For example, a man who is currently age 65 can expect to live to age 81,

FIGURE 5

Single Life Expectancy			
Male		Female	
Age	Life Expectancy	Age	Life Expectancy
50	27.7	50	31.7
55	23.5	55	27.3
60	19.6	60	23.1
65	16.1	65	19.1
70	12.8	70	15.4
75	10.0	75	12.1
80	7.5	80	9.1
85	5.5	85	6.6
90	4.1	90	4.8
95	3.0	95	3.5
100	2.4	100	2.7

Source: National Vital Statistics Report, 2002

while a 65-year-old woman can expect to reach age 84.

However, in your individual retirement planning, you may want to adjust these assumptions upward to account for any history of longevity in your family. You will also want to be conservative in your planning. In most cases, even though your family may have a history of shorter life spans, plan to be in retirement no less than the number of years listed in Figure 5. It is better to plan on a long retirement than a short one and outlive your money.

There are twice as many people — 70,000 in all — over age 100 today than there were just a decade go. By 2050, it's estimated that over 1.1 million people in the U.S. will be over age 100. And these figures grow closer to obsolescence every day. That's because people are living much longer due to advances in science, medicine, and nutrition.

Longer life expectancies present a dilemma in developing your retirement plan. Let's assume you and your spouse are planning to retire at age 65. If you assume that you will be in retirement for 35 years, until you reach age 100, you may have to settle on a dramatically-reduced level of income in order to make your nest egg stretch for so many years. However, if you assume you will only be in retirement until age 80 or 85, as mortality tables suggest, and you or your spouse live to age 100, you run the risk of spending too much in the early years of retirement and running out of money later. In fact, some people will spend more years in retirement than they did in the labor force. Consider the example of Anne Scheiber — Anne retired from her $3,150-per-year, IRS auditor job in 1943 and passed away in 1995 at the age of 101. She spent over 52 years in retirement.[4]

So, how do you plan to optimize your chances of making your money last?

Much like the investment decisions you have made, you must decide if you want to be a little more aggressive or a little more conservative in your planning. It is better to err on the conservative side. This can best be accomplished by adding at least five years to the life expectancy figures in Figure 5. For example, a married couple retiring this year, both age 65, should add five years to the life expectancies in Figure 5 when doing their retirement planning. Consequently, this hypothetical couple should plan to be in retirement for 24 to 25 years (19.1 years in the table, plus five) or until they reach age 90.

Worksheet Question #3:

How long do you plan on being in retirement?_____

Case Study: Ron and Linda are planning for 30 years in retirement.

WHAT SOURCES OF INCOME WILL YOU HAVE DURING RETIREMENT?

Now, let's take an inventory of your retirement income sources. For this exercise, exclude any income that you will derive from investments during retirement. Will any of these sources of income be adjusted each year for inflation? For example, Social Security has a cost-of-living adjustment. Your company pension may or may not adjust annually for inflation. If you own rental property, most likely you will increase the rents periodically to keep pace with inflation. This is an important element to factor into your retirement planning.

Worksheet Question #4:

What sources of income will you have during retirement? Complete the worksheet in Figure 6 to total your anticipated retirement income sources.

Case Study: The Hansen's are anticipating retirement income of $30,000 from the income sources outlined in Figure 6.

INFLATION

Simply put, inflation is a measure of the annual increase in the costs of goods and services. It's an unavoidable fact that the price of things you need in life will go up over time. During the past 70 years, inflation has averaged about 3 percent

FIGURE 6

Sources of Income Worksheet

Annual Income Sources	$	Inflat. Adj. %
Your Social Security	_____	_____
Your spouse's Social Security	_____	_____
Your pension	_____	_____
Your spouse's pension	_____	_____
Rental income	_____	_____
Income from continued work	_____	_____
Other income	_____	_____
Other income	_____	_____
Total	_____	_____
Total income sources (excluding investments)	_____	_____

per year, as it has since 1989 (Figure 7). However, during the past 30 years, inflation has averaged 5 percent. There have also been times when the U.S. economy experienced double-digit inflation, such as the period from 1977 to 1981, when inflation averaged a whopping 10 percent.[5]

If you fail to factor inflation into your retirement planning, you'll find prices rising while your income remains level, and eventually you'll be forced to lower your standard of living or deplete your assets. A fixed income in a rising-cost world is slow financial suicide. In Figure 8, you can see how the costs of various products and services have increased over time and what they could cost in the future if they continue on the same inflationary course.

Of course, you don't know what the inflation rate will be during your retirement, so you must make assumptions. Here again, you have a choice between aggressive planning, in which you optimistically assume a lower inflation rate

FIGURE 7

Inflation Since 1989	
1989	4.65%
1990	6.11%
1991	3.06%
1992	2.90%
1993	2.75%
1994	2.68%
1995	2.54%
1996	3.32%
1997	1.70%
1998	1.61%
1999	2.68%
2000	3.39%
2001	1.55%
2002	2.60%

Source: CPI

FIGURE 8

Cost of Living Comparison (1900-1997)							
Year	House	Car	Milk	Gas	Bread	Postage	Income
1900	$4,000	$500	$.30	$.05	$.03	$.02	$637
1910	$4,800	$500	$.33	$.07	$.05	$.02	$963
1920	$6,396	$500	$.58	$.10	$.11	$.02	$1,179
1930	$7,146	$525	$.56	$.10	$.08	$.02	$1,428
1940	$6,558	$810	$.51	$.15	$.08	$.03	$1,231
1950	$14,500	$1,750	$.82	$.20	$.14	$.03	$3,216
1960	$30,000	$2,275	$1.04	$.25	$.20	$.04	$5,199
1970	$40,000	$2,500	$1.32	$.40	$.24	$.06	$8,933
1980	$86,159	$5,412	$1.60	$1.03	$.48	$.15	$11,321
1990	$128,732	$9,437	$2.15	$1.08	$1.29	$.25	$14,777
1997	$119,250	$13,600	$2.41	$1.11	$1.62	$.32	$20,788
Average	House 3.56%	Car 3.46%	Milk 2.17%	Gas 3.25%	Bread 4.19%	Postage 2.90%	Income 3.66%

Source: www/seniorliving.about.com

Where prices are headed if past inflation repeats itself.

Year	House	Car	Milk	Gas	Bread	Postage	Income
2010	$187,912	$21,163	$3.18	$1.68	$2.76	$.46	$33,170
2020	$266,609	$29,737	$3.94	$2.31	$4.16	$.61	$47,519
2030	$378,264	$41,785	$4.89	$3.18	$6.27	$.82	$68,074

than the average, or more conservative planning, using a higher inflation rate assumption. Most financial planners assume a 3-4 percent rate in their planning.

If inflation remains at 3 percent during your retirement, you will need to increase your income by 3 percent each year in order to buy the same amount of goods and services you purchased the previous year. Essentially, you should give yourself a 3 percent raise each year in order to maintain your standard of living. For example, if you need $75,000 in the first year of retirement, you will need $77,250 the second year, $79,567 the third year, and so forth to maintain your purchasing power. At this rate, in the 20th year of retirement, you will need $131,512 to purchase the same items that can be bought with $75,000 today. Figure 9 shows the impact of inflation during retirement.

Figure 9

Year	Amount Needed	Year	Amount Needed
1	$75,000	11	$100,793
2	$77,250	12	$103,817
3	$79,567	13	$106,932
4	$81,954	14	$110,140
5	$84,413	15	$113,444
6	$86,945	16	$116,847
7	$89,553	17	$120,352
8	$92,240	18	$123,963
9	$95,007	19	$127,682
10	$97,857	20	$131,512

Equivalent of $75,000 today assuming 3% annual inflation

Because of inflation, your investment portfolio must be structured to provide you with a rising income stream during retirement. This is especially critical if your pension or other sources of retirement income don't have built-in, cost-of-living adjustments.

Worksheet Question #5:

What inflation rate would you like to use in your planning? _____

Case Study: Ron and Linda are using a 3.5 percent rate.

How much should you already have accumulated in order to reach retirement goals?

Do you currently have enough money set aside to be on track to reach your retirement goals? The chart in Figure 10 will tell you if you are in the ballpark. Simply multiply your current annual income by the factor that best represents your situation.

For example, if you are a "moderate investor" making $100,000 per year and planning to retire in five years, you will need approximately 7.73 times your current annual income to maintain your pre-retirement standard of living during retirement. In order to reach this goal you will need to have $773,000 already accumulated in your various investment accounts. This assumes you will spend 25 years in retirement, save 8 percent of your income each year prior to retirement, reduce your exposure to equities at retirement, experience 4 percent inflation, and exhaust all of your savings during retirement. (Figure 10 does not take Social Security or pensions into account.)

Alternatively, if you're an "aggressive investor" planning to retire in ten years and currently have a $50,000 per year income, you would need to have accumulated $231,500 by now to be on track, using the same assumptions as above.

FIGURE 10

Are You On Track?

Years to Retirement	Aggressive Investor	Moderate Investor	Conservative Investor
0	9.57	10.46	11.48
5	6.75	7.73	8.90
10	4.63	5.58	6.76
15	3.07	3.93	5.05
20	1.93	2.68	3.69
25	1.09	1.72	2.61
30	.48	.98	1.74
35	.03	.42	1.05

Source: Wall Street Journal

HOW MUCH DO YOU HAVE INVESTED?

How much do you currently have invested in stocks, bonds, cash, or other investments that you plan on using to finance your retirement? Are you on track?

Take an inventory of all your investments and group each into asset classes. The retirement computer programs used by professionals and those you can take advantage of personally will make interest rate assumptions for each investment you own.

Worksheet Question #6:

How much do you have invested? Complete the worksheet in Figure 11.

Case Study: The Hansen's have accumulated $500,000.

Their portfolio consists of 65 percent stocks and 35 percent bonds.

AT WHAT RATE WILL YOUR INVESTMENT PORTFOLIO GROW?

To determine if you are on track to reach your retirement goal, you must assign a reasonable rate of return to your portfolio. Forecast the rate of return you expect to achieve between now and retirement, and the return you anticipate after you begin retirement. In Chapter 11 we will examine, in more detail, the expected growth rates of various investment portfolios.

For our purposes here, let's keep it simple: Since 1925, stocks have averaged a 10.7 percent rate of return, bonds, 5.3 percent, and Treasury bills, 3.8 percent.

FIGURE 11

Retirement Accounts (IRA's 401k's, Profit Sharing Plans, Etc.)

Stocks or stock mutual funds $ _____
Bonds or bond mutual funds $ _____
Cash Equivalents $ _____

Non-Retirement Accounts

Stocks or stock mutual funds $ _____
Bonds or bond mutual funds $ _____
Cash Equivalents $ _____

Total Investment Assets (retirement and Non-Retirement Assets)

Stocks or stock mutual funds $ _____ _____ %
Bonds or bond mutual funds $ _____ _____ %
Cash Equivalents $ _____ _____ %
Total $ _____ 100 %

What is the sum of all of your investment assets $_____?
What percent of your portfolio is invested in stocks, bonds, and cash?

Stocks _____ %
Bonds _____ %
Cash _____ %

Figure 12 illustrates how different mixes of stocks, bonds, and cash performed, on average, from 1926 through 2001. Which portfolio most resembles your own? What is the expected rate of return? Now you need to ask the most important question: If your investments grow at this rate, will you reach your retirement goals? Developing a retirement analysis will answer this question.

You may find yourself behind in your retirement savings. If this is the case, you may need to reposition your investments to improve your long-term rate of return, save much more aggressively, or reduce your retirement income goal. If you are

FIGURE 12

Asset Allocation (Annual Returns 1926-2001)	
% Stocks/Bonds/Cash	**Average Return**
90/0/10	11.77%
80/10/10	11.06%
70/20/10	10.34%
60/30/10	9.63%
50/40/10	8.91%
40/50/10	8.19%
30/60/10	7.48%
20/70/10	6.76%
10/80/10	6.04%
0/90/10	5.04%

Source: Ibbotson and Associates

ahead of the game and don't need to seek a high rate of return, you may want to reposition your investments more conservatively. Why take additional and unnecessary risk if you are able to reach and exceed your goals without that risk?

What will your investment returns be during retirement? Most investors reposition assets during retirement in order to reduce risk. Although a 7-10 percent rate of return is possible, it is recommended that you remain conservative in your planning and assume a rate no higher than 7 percent per year.

Worksheet Question #7:

At what rate do you expect your investment portfolio to grow *between* now and retirement?_____

At what rate do you expect your investment portfolio to grow *after* retirement?_____

Case Study: Ron and Linda expect their portfolio to grow at a rate of 9 percent before retirement and 7 percent during retirement.

HOW MUCH SHOULD YOU BE SAVING EACH YEAR TOWARD YOUR RETIREMENT?

Hopefully you answered this question many years ago and have been saving aggressively toward retirement.

As a general rule, you should save no less than 10 percent of your gross income toward retirement; if married, 10 percent of your combined income. In most cases, you should work toward saving 15 percent. To accomplish this goal, control your expenses and strive to live within your means. The recent best-selling book, "The Millionaire Next Door," outlines characteristics of America's millionaires. The book's authors, Thomas Stanley and William Danko, conclude that the reason most millionaires accumulated so much wealth was due to their high savings rate and ability to live within their means.

How much would you guess the average American saves per year? Unbelievably the average savings rate is just over 1 percent of gross income. This is obviously far less than what is needed to enjoy a comfortable retirement. To be a good saver, you need discipline and consistency. The best way to do this is to set up a systematic savings plan, and have money drawn directly out of your bank account or paycheck and deposited into an investment account on at least a monthly basis.

Here's a simple rule: If you can't get your hands on it, you won't spend it. That's why company-sponsored retirement plans work so well, because the money is invested even before you receive your paycheck.

Worksheet Question #8:
    How much of your income (combined income, if married) are you currently saving each year? _____
Case Study: The Hansens save 10 percent of their income, or $10,000 per year.

WOULD YOU LIKE TO LEAVE AN INHERITANCE TO YOUR FAMILY OR A CHARITY?

It's natural to want to leave an estate to your heirs, or to an organization or cause about which you care deeply. Be sure to incorporate this into your retirement planning. Determine how much you wish to leave; this is the amount of your financial portfolio you will not spend during retirement.

Worksheet Question #9:
    How much of your total investment portfolio (financial assets) would you like to leave to your heirs or a charity? _____
Case Study: Ron and Linda are not planning to leave an estate to their heirs.

SUMMARY OF RON AND LINDA HANSEN'S CASE STUDY

How did Ron and Linda do?
- Ron and Linda, both currently age 50, are planning to retire in ten years.
- They need $75,000 per year of retirement income (in today's dollars).
- They will need this income for 30 years of retirement.
- They are expecting income from various sources to provide them with $30,000 per year leaving a $45,000 annual shortfall. This shortfall will have to be made up from their investment assets.
- They have accumulated a $500,000 investment portfolio made up of 65 percent stocks, 35 percent bonds.
- They save $10,000 per year.
- They've assumed an inflation rate of 3.5 percent per year and are anticipating their investments will grow at 9 percent annually between now and retirement, with a 7 percent growth rate assumed during retirement.

Based on these figures and assumptions, Ron and Linda are on track to reach their goal. In fact, if they choose, they could retire even earlier than planned, as early as age 58.

ARE YOU ON TRACK TO REACH YOUR RETIREMENT GOALS? LET'S CRUNCH THE NUMBERS.

Okay, now you have all the information you need to determine if you're on track to reach your retirement goals. There are a couple of ways to crunch the numbers.

The first involves simple linear equations in which you assume a constant rate of return on your investments throughout retirement. This approach is easy and works well, as long as you assume a conservative rate of return and you still have ten or more years until retirement. If you are investing for the long-term, chances are you will enjoy a rate of return that is close to the long-term averages.

The second is a little more complex. It involves probability calculations to determine the chances of reaching your goals, given the fact that rates of return will fluctuate from year to year during retirement. This approach is referred to as Monte Carlo analysis and is more appropriate for those on the immediate verge of retirement and those already retired, who do not have as many years to invest and who could be devastated by an unexpected and extended market downturn. Monte Carlo analysis will provide a more accurate view of whether or not you are on track, given the returns produced by hundreds of differing market conditions.[6]

Financial advisors have access to planning tools and software that can take into account the many variables that will change during retirement. These factors can include a spouse who plans to work several years after you retire, changes in tax rates, the impact of inflation on some income sources (which doesn't affect others), and different interest rate assumptions for each of your investment assets.

If you have a large asset base or if your financial situation is more complex, it is highly recommended that you seek the counsel of a professional financial advisor to develop a retirement analysis. Otherwise, you can simply utilize one of the many retirement calculators on the Internet — go to any search engine and type in key words like "retirement calculator" or "retirement worksheet." Whether you decide to work with a financial advisor or develop a retirement plan on your own, you will need the answers to the questions asked throughout this chapter to complete your retirement analysis. Following is a sampling of some Web sites that offer easy-to-use retirement planning calculators:

- Quicken: *www.quicken.com/retirement/planner/*
- Smart Money: *www.smartmoney.com/retirement/planning/*
- Kiplinger: *www.kiplinger.com/tools/retcalc2.html*
- NASD: *www.nasdr.com/retirement_calc.asp*
- T. Rowe Price: *www.troweprice.com*
- U.S. News: *www.usnews.com/usnews/nycu/money/moretcal.html*

Now back to the burning question: Are you on track to reach your retirement goals? If not, you may need to save more money each year, adjust your investment portfolio to obtain better returns, retire later, or retire with less than you had originally planned.

Determining if you are on track to reach your retirement goals depends on how honest you are with yourself in answering the important questions posed in this chapter. It also requires a long-term "big picture" view of your overall financial situation. Having the courage to look at where you are today and where you need to be in the future will go a long way to making your retirement all that it should be.

FIGURE 13 • Average City 100.0

AL

- Birmingham 99.1
- Huntsville 95.2
- Mobile 91.8
- Montgomery 92.4

AK

- Anchorage 125.9
- Juneau 136.2

AZ

- Phoenix 99.9
- Scottsdale 103.1
- Tucson 99.7

CA

- Bakersfield 106.1
- Fresno 105.8
- LA/Long Beach 122.0
- Palm Springs 116.3
- Sacramento 114.0
- San Diego 122.8
- San Francisco 144.7

CO

- Boulder 108.5
- Col. Springs 96.8
- Denver 105.3
- Pueblo 92.5

CT

- Hartford 121.8

DE

- Dover 101.5
- Wilmington 108.1

DC

- Washington, DC 132.0

FL

- Ft. Myers 97.2
- Jacksonville 95.4
- Miami/Dade Co. 104.5
- Orlando 97.0
- Pensacola 93.6
- Tallahassee 100.1
- Tampa 97.8
- West Palm Beach 104.7

GA

- Albany 90.5
- Atlanta 97.4
- Columbus 93.9
- Macon 95.1

ID

- Boise 102.7
- Pocatello 99.8
- Twin Falls 95.9

IL

- Bloomington 101.4
- Chicago (suburb) 121.6
- Jollet 108.7
- Quad Cities 97.5
- Rockford 103.6
- Schaumburg 123.3
- Springfield 95.1

IN

- Bloomington 98.6
- Fort Wayne 93.3
- Indianapolis 94.9
- South Bend 90.9

IA

- Cedar Rapids 100.7
- Des Moines 94.7
- Dubuque

KS

- Lawrence 95.1
- Wichita 94.8

KY

- Lexington 95.9
- Louisville 92.8

LA

- Baton Rouge 98.5
- New Orleans 94.5
- Shreveport 94.9

MD

- Baltimore 102.3
- Cumberland 102.0

MA

- Boston 136.8

MI

- Ann Arbor 115.1
- Grand Rapids 102.1
- Kalamazoo 108.6
- Lansing 102.9

MN

- Minneapolis 99.7
- Rochester 97.5

MS

- Jackson 94.3
- Laurel 90.7

MO

- Columbia 93.1
- Kansas City 96.1
- St. Louis 97.4
- Springfield 94.5

Source: American Chamber of Commerce Research Association

MT

- Billings 102.7
- Great Falls 102.5
- Missoula 101.8

NE

- Lincoln 88.8
- Omaha 92.3

NV

- Las Vegas 105.6
- Reno/Sparks 111.8

NH

- Manchester 108.8

NJ

- Morristown

NM

- Albuquerque 102.8
- Carlsbad 92.8
- Las Cruces 98.7
- Santa Fe 119.7

NY

- Albany 109.7
- Binghamton 97.3
- New York 226.5
- Rochester 110.4
- Syracuse 102.9

NC

- Asheville 100.0
- Charlotte 96.8
- Greensboro 97.5
- Raleigh-Durham 97.3
- Winston-Salem 97.8

ND

- Bismarck 99.9
- Fargo 100.8

OH

- Akron 96.3
- Cincinnati 101.1
- Cleveland 106.0
- Colombus 101.4
- Toledo 96.9

OK

- Oklahoma City 90.2
- Tulsa 89.4

OR

- Eugene 108.9
- Portland 107.3
- Salem 103.3

PA

- Allentown 104.4
- Erie 101.6
- Harrisburg 104.9
- Philadelphia 127.4
- Pittsburgh 113.3
- Wilkes-Barre 97.5

SC

- Charleston 95.2
- Columbia 94.2
- Greenville 95.9
- Myrtle Beach 97.4

SD

- Rapid City 100.2
- Sioux Falls 96.6

TN

- Knoxville 93.8
- Memphis 95.3
- Nashville 91.7

TX

- Abilene 91.8
- Amarillo 90.0
- Austin 100.9

- Corpus Christi 93.6
- Dallas 101.8
- El Paso 95.0
- Fort Worth 94.6
- Houston 96.8
- San Antonio 99.6
- Waco 92.1

UT

- Provo/Orem 96.3
- Salt Lake City 100.9

VT

- Montpelier 109.6

VA

- Norfolk 100.5
- Prince William 113.3
- Richmond 102.0
- Roanoke 93.0
- Virg. Peninsula 95.0

WA

- Bellingham 103.4
- Seattle 119.7
- Spokane 106.7
- Tacoma 102.6

WV

- Charleston 96.6
- Huntington 100.8

WI

- Green Bay 97.0
- La Crosse 98.5
- Milwaukee 107.5

WY

- Casper 101.4
- Cheyenne 96.0

CHAPTER 2
IMPORTANCE OF A COMPREHENSIVE FINANCIAL PLAN

In Chapter 1 you learned the importance of evaluating your retirement goals to see if you are on track to reach them. With this newfound awareness of your actual retirement situation, you may believe that you have your financial future all mapped out in your head. But without a *written* "map" to which you can refer often, it can be very easy to start down the wrong path and never arrive at your desired destination. In this chapter, we will learn the importance of having a written financial plan that will help you stay on track not only in your retirement planning, but in other important areas of your financial life as well. If you want to reach your long-range goals, here's one of the most important tips anyone can give you: Write them down!

Here's a proven fact: People who develop written financial plans increase their wealth. Whether you are changing jobs, retiring, or simply looking toward your foreseeable future, now is a good time to develop a comprehensive financial game plan that addresses every component of your financial portfolio.

These components include:

- Retirement
- Investments
- Taxes
- Liabilities
- Budgeting

- Insurance
- Asset Protection
- Estate Protection
- Children's Education
- Long-Term Care

A comprehensive financial plan will help you establish goals in each of these areas and outline specific strategies for accomplishing each of them.

The exercise on the following page illustrates the importance of having a strategy. Take a look at the numbers placed randomly from 1 to 100 in Figure 1. Time yourself for 30 seconds and see how many numbers you can find in succession, beginning with the number 1, moving on to 2, then 3, and so on.

Start timing yourself now....and go!

FIGURE 1

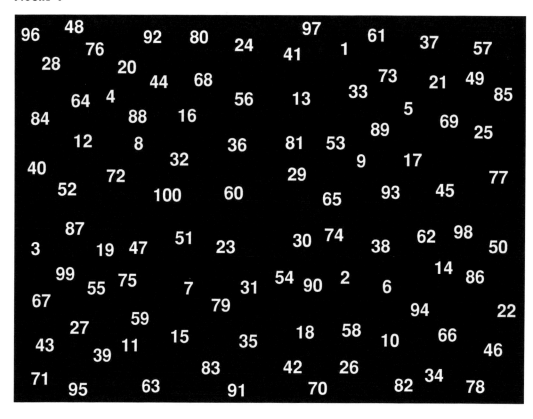

How far did you get? Remember your score.

Now, we're going to try the exercise again, with a strategy for improving upon your first score. The strategy is simple: In Figure 2 on the next page, a line has been placed down the center and across the middle of the chart, dividing it into four quadrants. The number "one" is located in the top right quadrant. The number "two" is in the bottom right quadrant. Number "three" is in the bottom left, and number "four" is in the top left. The numbers are sequentially located clockwise, moving from quadrant to quadrant.

Now, time yourself for another 30 seconds to see if you can beat your first score.

FIGURE 2

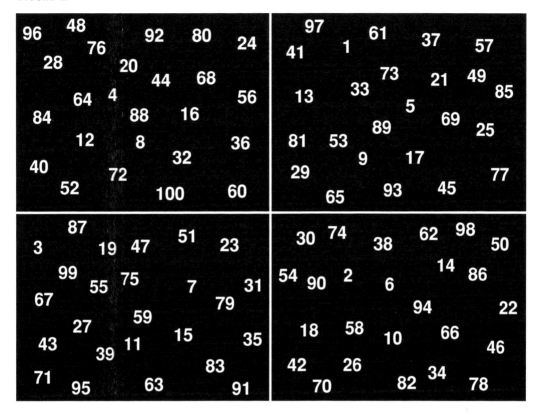

You improved, didn't you?

In many cases, people find they can double their score in the second exercise and it's all because they have a strategy. In the same way, having a financial strategy will dramatically help you improve your financial situation.

Strong evidence supports this idea. According to a 1998 study conducted by the Securities and Exchange Commission, investors with financial plans reported having twice as much in savings and investments as those without plans.[1] One report went so far as to say, "People who stick with written plans to govern their investments, on average, wind up with five times as much money during retirement as those who don't have a plan."[2] Like the exercise you just completed, if you have a financial game plan, you are going to do better over time than if you don't.

Figure 3 further illustrates this point. Notice that U.S. households with written financial plans have more money in savings than those who don't. This is true at every income level. Surprisingly, despite this evidence, only one of three savers has a plan to guide their financial decisions. You would do well to be part of that savvy one-third.

FIGURE 3

HOUSEHOLD INCOME	MEDIAN SAVINGS (WITHOUT A PLAN)	MEDIAN SAVINGS (WITH A PLAN)
$20,000-$39,999	$14,300	$28,500
$40,000-$99,999	$41,500	$89,650
$100,000 and up	$201,100	$325,500

Source: Consumer Federation of America and Nations Bank Survey

Many studies have been conducted to determine the impact of written goals. For example, Yale University asked their 1945 graduates how many of them had written down their goals after graduating. They found that only 3 percent of the grads had actually put their goals on paper. In 1975, it was discovered that the 3 percent with written goals were worth more financially than the other 97 percent of their Yale peers combined![3]

To develop a financial plan, begin by taking inventory of your current financial portfolio. Include the details of all of your assets and liabilities, and outline your financial goals. Then write them down! You can purchase software that will provide you with some components of a comprehensive financial plan. Be aware, however, that these programs, in most cases, fall short of completely meeting your needs. They don't provide the much-needed interpretation of the financial analysis which includes specific recommendations and help implementing the outlined strategies. These facets of a financial plan are more important than the number of pages of analysis you can generate. A software package is indeed a good starting point for a less sophisticated financial situation, but in most cases you should also seek the assistance of a financial advisor.

Once you record your goals and objectives and map out a strategy to accomplish each goal, you will immediately and dramatically increase your chances of reaching them. Like the Yale graduates who achieved tremendous success, you will do better financially with a plan than without one.

CHAPTER 3
CHOOSING A "SAFE" PORTFOLIO WITHDRAWAL RATE

Here's a critical question: After you retire, how much can you safely withdraw from your investment portfolio without incurring the risk of running out of money? A miscalculation could mean you outlive your assets and have to live on Social Security alone. This chapter is designed to help you choose a withdrawal rate that will be as safe as possible in the face of unknown life expectancies and ever-changing economic conditions.

When you **try** to calculate a safe withdrawal rate, you face two major obstacles: First, there is no **way** to know exactly how long you will live. Second, it is impossible to predict the exact rate of return your portfolio will generate during retirement. Inflation and taxes also have an effect.

Bottom line? In most cases, a 4 percent withdrawal rate is the maximum you should plan on each year, assuming you adjust your income upwards for inflation. To obtain the returns you need in order to maintain an acceptable income level, you must, in most cases, invest a portion of your assets into stocks and bonds. However, this brings with it a certain level of unpredictability because there's no way of knowing the future rate of return of stocks and bonds. Consequently, knowing how much to withdraw each year without risking the depletion of your assets is extremely difficult.

Ideally, you should have a portfolio large enough that you can rely solely on interest and dividends for the annual income you need without ever touching your investment principal. Most retirees, however, will never have that luxury. In the majority of cases, they must rely on interest, dividends, *and* a piece of their investment principal each year to generate a comfortable income.

On the surface, it doesn't seem like it should be that difficult to determine a safe withdrawal rate. If you invest 100 percent of your portfolio in stocks — which have averaged approximately an 11 percent annual rate of return since 1926 — it would make sense that keeping your withdrawal rate below 11 percent means never having to dip into your principal.

Peter Lynch, the former manager of the Fidelity Magellan fund (you've seen him on TV commercials), used this logic when he suggested that an investor who stays completely invested in stocks for the long run, could withdraw 7 percent annually without depleting any assets.[1] If you run the numbers, Mr. Lynch's advice looks pretty sound. For example, if your $500,000 portfolio provides a constant 10 percent annual return from which you withdraw just 7 percent (or $35,000) each year, the results are astonishing (Figure 1).

FIGURE 1

$500,000 portfolio growing at 10% annually. Investor withdrawing 7% ($35,000) annually.	
Year	Portfolio Value After Withdrawals
1	$515,000
5	$770,255
10	$1,261,871
15	$2,053,624
20	$3,328,750
25	$5,382,353
30	$8,689,701

In this example, we didn't even come close to touching the investment principal. There's one problem with this simple scenario, however; stocks do not provide consistent returns. While stocks may average 10-11 percent growth over the long run, they often make for a very bumpy ride along the way.

For example, the annual investment results for the portfolio in Figure 2 would also provide a 10 percent average annual return over five- and ten-year periods.

FIGURE 2

Hypothetical Portfolio Year 1 through 10.

$500,000 portfolio growing a 10% average annual return, investor withdrawing 7% ($35,000) annually			
Year	**Portfolio Return**	**7% Annual Withdrawal**	**Portfolio Value at Year End**
1	-25%	$35,000	$340,000
2	35%	$35,000	$424,000
3	-15%	$35,000	$325,400
4	25%	$35,000	$371,750
5	30%	$35,000	$448,275
6	-25%	$35,000	$301,206
7	35%	$35,000	$371,628
8	-15%	$35,000	$280,884
9	25%	$35,000	$316,105
10	30%	$35,000	$375,936

However, notice what happens to the $500,000 portfolio if the return varies from year to year and if the same 7 percent per year ($35,000) is withdrawn.

This figure shows that after only a couple of years, these modest annual withdrawals are already eroding the principal. In year eight, the nest egg that was supposed to last 30 years has been cut nearly in half. By year ten, the balance is $375,936, a far cry from the $1,262,871 balance remaining in the Figure 1 scenario.

While it seems perfectly logical to focus on average annual rates of return in the stock and bond markets when making your withdrawal decisions, these assumptions could lead to the total depletion of your investment assets. Actual returns, as opposed to average returns, vary from year to year. Taking this variance into account when deciding how much you can safely withdraw each year is crucial to your retirement planning.

Studies have been conducted to help determine a safe withdrawal rate. In what is known as the "Trinity Study," three Trinity University faculty members back-tested the effect of various withdrawal rates on five different portfolios of stocks and bonds over 15, 20, 25, and 30-year rolling time frames.[2] They used the actual returns of stocks and bonds from 1926 through 1995, rather than average returns. A success rate was calculated for each portfolio, time frame, and withdrawal rate. One hundred percent success was defined as having money remaining in the account at the conclusion of the specified withdrawal period.

For example, a retiree with a $500,000 portfolio consisting of 50 percent stocks and 50 percent bonds who plans to be in retirement for 30 years should be 100 percent successful if he withdraws less than 5 percent, or $25,000, annually. (See Figure 3, *Portfolio Composition: 50% Stocks and 50% Bonds*.) From 1926 to 1995, there were 41 thirty-year periods measured. This investment mix was successful in every thirty-year time frame, even those that included the Great Depression.

Before factoring in inflation and deflation, this same portfolio was 98 percent successful when the withdrawal rate was increased to 6 percent ($30,000/yr.), and 90 percent successful when the withdrawal rate jumped to 7 percent ($35,000/yr.). However, once inflation and deflation are added to the equation, this same retiree shouldn't plan on withdrawing any more than 4 percent, or $20,000, from the initial portfolio each year.

Most retirees will need to adjust their incomes upwards throughout retirement in order to cope with the rising costs of goods and services. At a 4 percent withdrawal rate, this portfolio was successful 95 percent of the time, when adjusted for inflation, but it had only 76 percent success when the withdrawal rate was increased to 5 percent.

What is your "safe" withdrawal rate? The tables in Figures 3, 4, and 5 on the following pages will help you answer that question. To use these tables, first determine what percentage of your portfolio will be invested in stocks and bonds during retirement. Second, estimate how many years you will be in retirement. Finally, choose a withdrawal schedule that has been successful at least 80 percent of the time. After examining the charts, you will notice that most of the portfolios could sustain a 4 percent withdrawal rate. Higher withdrawals will usually deplete the portfolio assets before your retirement period is over.

Note also, that the odds for success increase dramatically if, instead of using withdrawal tables that include the Great Depression (see Figure 3), only the markets in post-war periods are examined. The post-war results in Figure 4 are not adjusted for inflation, while the results in Figure 5 are.

FIGURE 3

Portfolio Success Rate: Percentage of all past payout periods from 1926 to 1995, supported by the corresponding portfolio. Not adjusted for inflation.

Portfolio Composition: 100% Stocks and 0% Bonds

Payout Period	Withdrawal Rate as a % of Initial Portfolio Value									
	3%	4%	5%	6%	7%	8%	9%	10%	11%	12%
15 Years	100%	100%	98%	98%	93%	91%	88%	77%	63%	55%
20 Years	100%	98%	96%	94%	92%	84%	73%	61%	47%	43%
25 Years	100%	98%	96%	91%	87%	78%	70%	50%	43%	35%
30 Years	100%	98%	95%	90%	85%	78%	68%	54%	49%	34%

Portfolio Composition: 75% Stocks and 25% Bonds

Payout Period	Withdrawal Rate as a % of Initial Portfolio Value									
	3%	4%	5%	6%	7%	8%	9%	10%	11%	12%
15 Years	100%	100%	100%	100%	96%	95%	91%	79%	63%	46%
20 Years	100%	100%	100%	96%	94%	88%	71%	51%	41%	33%
25 Years	100%	100%	98%	96%	91%	78%	57%	46%	33%	26%
30 Years	100%	100%	98%	95%	88%	73%	54%	46%	37%	24%

Portfolio Composition: 50% Stocks and 50% Bonds

Payout Period	Withdrawal Rate as a % of Initial Portfolio Value									
	3%	4%	5%	6%	7%	8%	9%	10%	11%	12%
15 Years	100%	100%	100%	100%	100%	98%	91%	71%	50%	36%
20 Years	100%	100%	100%	100%	96%	88%	61%	41%	25%	10%
25 Years	100%	100%	100%	98%	96%	70%	43%	22%	7%	0%
30 Years	100%	100%	100%	98%	90%	51%	37%	15%	0%	0%

Portfolio Composition: 25% Stocks and 75% Bonds

Payout Period	Withdrawal Rate as a % of Initial Portfolio Value									
	3%	4%	5%	6%	7%	8%	9%	10%	11%	12%
15 Years	100%	100%	100%	100%	100%	100%	91%	50%	21%	14%
20 Years	100%	100%	100%	100%	100%	71%	24%	12%	4%	2%
25 Years	100%	100%	100%	100%	78%	22%	9%	0%	0%	0%
30 Years	100%	100%	100%	100%	32%	5%	0%	0%	0%	0%

Portfolio Composition: 0% Stocks and 100% Bonds

Payout Period	Withdrawal Rate as a % of Initial Portfolio Value									
	3%	4%	5%	6%	7%	8%	9%	10%	11%	12%
15 Years	100%	100%	100%	100%	100%	79%	43%	38%	14%	7%
20 Years	100%	100%	100%	96%	47%	35%	16%	6%	0%	0%
25 Years	100%	100%	98%	52%	26%	7%	2%	0%	0%	0%
30 Years	100%	100%	51%	27%	0%	0%	0%	0%	0%	0%

Note: Numbers in the table are rounded to the nearest whole percentage. The number of overlapping 15-year payout periods from 1926 - 1995, inclusively, is 56; 20-year periods, 51; 25-year periods, 46; 30-year periods, 41. Stocks are represented by Standard and Poor's 500 index, and bonds represented by long-term, high-grade corporates. Data source: Author's calculations based on data from Ibbotson Associates.

Source: The Trinity Study

1926-1995

FIGURE 4

Portfolio Success Rate: Percentage of all past payout periods from 1946 to 1995, supported by the corresponding portfolio. Not adjusted for inflation.

Portfolio Composition: 100% Stocks and 0% Bonds

Payout Period	Withdrawal Rate as a % of Initial Portfolio Value									
	3%	4%	5%	6%	7%	8%	9%	10%	11%	12%
15 Years	100%	100%	100%	100%	100%	100%	97%	86%	69%	64%
20 Years	100%	100%	100%	100%	100%	97%	81%	61%	45%	42%
25 Years	100%	100%	100%	100%	100%	88%	77%	46%	42%	38%
30 Years	100%	100%	100%	100%	100%	90%	76%	52%	52%	38%

Portfolio Composition: 75% Stocks and 25% Bonds

Payout Period	Withdrawal Rate as a % of Initial Portfolio Value									
	3%	4%	5%	6%	7%	8%	9%	10%	11%	12%
15 Years	100%	100%	100%	100%	100%	100%	100%	86%	69%	53%
20 Years	100%	100%	100%	100%	100%	97%	77%	48%	42%	32%
25 Years	100%	100%	100%	100%	100%	85%	54%	42%	31%	27%
30 Years	100%	100%	100%	100%	100%	81%	52%	48%	38%	29%

Portfolio Composition: 50% Stocks and 50% Bonds

Payout Period	Withdrawal Rate as a % of Initial Portfolio Value									
	3%	4%	5%	6%	7%	8%	9%	10%	11%	12%
15 Years	100%	100%	100%	100%	100%	100%	94%	78%	56%	42%
20 Years	100%	100%	100%	100%	100%	94%	61%	39%	26%	13%
25 Years	100%	100%	100%	100%	100%	69%	38%	19%	4%	0%
30 Years	100%	100%	100%	100%	100%	48%	33%	10%	0%	0%

Portfolio Composition: 25% Stocks and 75% Bonds

Payout Period	Withdrawal Rate as a % of Initial Portfolio Value									
	3%	4%	5%	6%	7%	8%	9%	10%	11%	12%
15 Years	100%	100%	100%	100%	100%	100%	89%	53%	25%	17%
20 Years	100%	100%	100%	100%	100%	68%	23%	13%	6%	3%
25 Years	100%	100%	100%	100%	73%	15%	8%	0%	0%	0%
30 Years	100%	100%	100%	100%	19%	0%	0%	0%	0%	0%

Portfolio Composition: 0% Stocks and 100% Bonds

Payout Period	Withdrawal Rate as a % of Initial Portfolio Value									
	3%	4%	5%	6%	7%	8%	9%	10%	11%	12%
15 Years	100%	100%	100%	100%	100%	72%	39%	33%	19%	11%
20 Years	100%	100%	100%	94%	42%	29%	23%	10%	0%	0%
25 Years	100%	100%	96%	54%	15%	12%	4%	0%	0%	0%
30 Years	100%	100%	48%	10%	0%	0%	0%	0%	0%	0%

Note: Numbers in the table are rounded to the nearest whole percentage. The number of overlapping 15-year payout periods from 1946 - 1995, inclusively, is 36; 20-year periods, 31; 25-year periods, 26; 30-year periods, 21. Stocks are represented by Standard and Poor's 500 index, and bonds represented by long-term, high-grade corporates. Data source: Author's calculations based on data from Ibbotson Associates.

Source: The Trinity Study

"Post War" 1946-1994

FIGURE 5

Portfolio Success Rate: Percentage of all past payout periods from 1946 to 1995 supported by the corresponding portfolio after adjusting withdrawals for inflation and deflation.

Portfolio Composition: 100% Stocks and 0% Bonds

Payout Period	Withdrawal Rate as a % of Initial Portfolio Value									
	3%	4%	5%	6%	7%	8%	9%	10%	11%	12%
15 Years	100%	100%	100%	91%	79%	70%	63%	55%	43%	34%
20 Years	100%	100%	88%	75%	63%	53%	43%	33%	29%	24%
25 Years	100%	100%	87%	70%	59%	46%	35%	30%	26%	20%
30 Years	100%	95%	85%	68%	59%	41%	34%	34%	27%	15%

Portfolio Composition: 75% Stocks and 25% Bonds

Payout Period	Withdrawal Rate as a % of Initial Portfolio Value									
	3%	4%	5%	6%	7%	8%	9%	10%	11%	12%
15 Years	100%	100%	100%	95%	82%	68%	64%	46%	36%	27%
20 Years	100%	100%	90%	75%	61%	51%	37%	27%	20%	12%
25 Years	100%	100%	85%	65%	50%	37%	30%	22%	7%	2%
30 Years	100%	98%	83%	68%	49%	34%	22%	7%	2%	0%

Portfolio Composition: 50% Stocks and 50% Bonds

Payout Period	Withdrawal Rate as a % of Initial Portfolio Value									
	3%	4%	5%	6%	7%	8%	9%	10%	11%	12%
15 Years	100%	100%	100%	93%	79%	64%	50%	32%	23%	13%
20 Years	100%	100%	90%	75%	55%	33%	22%	10%	0%	0%
25 Years	100%	100%	80%	57%	37%	20%	7%	0%	0%	0%
30 Years	100%	95%	76%	51%	17%	5%	0%	0%	0%	0%

Portfolio Composition: 25% Stocks and 75% Bonds

Payout Period	Withdrawal Rate as a % of Initial Portfolio Value									
	3%	4%	5%	6%	7%	8%	9%	10%	11%	12%
15 Years	100%	100%	100%	89%	70%	50%	32%	18%	13%	7%
20 Years	100%	100%	82%	47%	31%	16%	8%	4%	0%	0%
25 Years	100%	93%	48%	24%	15%	4%	2%	0%	0%	0%
30 Years	100%	71%	27%	20%	5%	0%	0%	0%	0%	0%

Portfolio Composition: 0% Stocks and 100% Bonds

Payout Period	Withdrawal Rate as a % of Initial Portfolio Value									
	3%	4%	5%	6%	7%	8%	9%	10%	11%	12%
15 Years	100%	100%	100%	71%	39%	21%	18%	16%	14%	9%
20 Years	100%	90%	47%	20%	14%	12%	10%	2%	0%	0%
25 Years	100%	46%	17%	15%	11%	2%	0%	0%	0%	0%
30 Years	80%	20%	17%	12%	0%	0%	0%	0%	0%	0%

Note: Numbers in the table are rounded to the nearest whole percentage. The number of overlapping 15-year payout periods from 1926 - 1995, inclusively, is 56; 20-year periods, 51; 25-year periods, 46; 30-year periods, 41. Stocks are represented by Standard and Poor's 500 index, and bonds represented by long-term, high-grade corporates. Data source: Author's calculations based on data from Ibbotson Associates.

Source: The Trinity Study

"Post War" 1946-1994 adjusted for inflation

Which chart should you use? It depends on whether you choose to be conservative or aggressive. Conservative investors will make sure their portfolios survive even in worst-case scenarios like the Great Depression. If, however, you believe the market could not possibly suffer that kind of downturn in the future, use the post-war charts in setting withdrawal rates. These post-war charts do include the deep recessions of the mid-70's and early 80's, the 1987 stock market crash and other down markets like those of 1990 and 1994. The post-war charts indicate that you could withdraw up to 6-7 percent annually before inflation from most portfolios, and 4-5 percent after inflation, without the risk of running out of money.

You could use Harvard University as an example of how much to withdraw. In 1973, Harvard was interested in determining how much of its endowment portfolio could be withdrawn each year without depleting principal. University researchers determined that a portfolio made up of 50 percent stocks and 50 percent bonds could safely support a 4 percent annual withdrawal rate, adjusted for inflation.[3]

In summary, determining a safe withdrawal rate will help you avoid every retiree's worst nightmare — the premature exhaustion of portfolio assets during retirement. In this chapter we have examined a number of ways to determine that rate in light of fluctuating personal and economic conditions. To help you further in that quest, check out the resources offered by T. Rowe Price at its Web site, *www.troweprice.com*. The site offers financial planning tools, including an easy-to-use Monte Carlo retirement income calculator. This calculator can help you determine a "safe" withdrawal rate. From the "tools" section on the site, go to the retirement income calculator. It will only take a minute to enter the requested data. Indicate the success rate you would like to obtain and run the analysis. This site lets you enter different variables so you can review possible alternatives.

The following worksheet will further assist you by allowing you to record various retirement assumptions and withdrawal rates based on your analysis of the charts in this chapter:

Retirement Planning Assumptions	
a) Years in retirement	_____
b) Amount of income to sustain lifestyle	_____
c) Portfolio value at retirement	_____
d) Withdrawal rate desired (best case)	_____
e) Safe withdrawal rate (85-90% success)	_____

CHAPTER 4
EARLY RETIREMENT STRATEGIES (PRIOR TO AGE 59 ½)

If you're fortunate enough to be able to retire prior to age 59 ½, a hearty congratulations to you! Early retirement, however, can throw some challenges your way for which you need to be prepared with regard to taxes and penalties. This chapter will address those challenges and how to effectively deal with them.

Accessing the investment assets you have locked up in qualified retirement accounts (IRAs, 401(k)s, profit sharing plans, etc.) is usually the biggest issue to consider if you're planning to retire early. Each of these retirement plans carry a 10 percent penalty on withdrawals made prior to age 59 ½. This poses a dilemma: You've accumulated enough money to retire comfortably, but all, or at least a large part of that money is invested in retirement plans that limit access to your money.

There are a couple of solutions to this problem that allow you to access your retirement savings prior to age 59 ½ while avoiding early withdrawal penalties.

SECTION 72T DISTRIBUTIONS: SUBSTANTIALLY EQUAL PERIODIC PAYMENTS

Section 72T of the Internal Revenue Code (IRC) states that premature withdrawals (those occurring prior to age 59 ½) are exempt from the 10 percent early withdrawal penalty if the distributions are structured as a series of "substantially equal periodic payments."[1] To avoid the early withdrawal penalty, you must strictly adhere to the following rules as outlined in Section 72T:

1. The distributions must be a part of a "series of substantially equal payments" made on a regular basis, at least annually.

2. The amount withdrawn each year must be calculated using one of three IRS-approved distribution formulas: amortization, annuitization or life expectancy.

3. Distributions must continue for five years or until the recipient is 59 ½, whichever is longer.[2]

QUALIFYING FOR 72T DISTRIBUTIONS

Anyone who has not yet reached age 59 $^1/_2$ and who has an individual retirement account (IRA) is eligible for penalty-free distributions. Distributions can begin at any age and for any reason. The 72T distributions can even begin while you are still employed.

In fact, many people trim their work hours back to part-time as they approach full retirement. They then begin using 72T distributions to supplement their earned income. Your annual distribution amount is based largely on the size of your retirement account and your life expectancy (or if married, your joint life expectancy if you choose). Consequently, 72T distributions are typically better suited for those nearing retirement (between ages 50 and 59 $^1/_2$) with relatively large retirement balances. If you're younger or have a smaller account balance, your annual distribution amounts will be lower.

DISTRIBUTION FORMULAS

To determine how much you can withdraw annually from your IRA without penalty, you must choose one of three approved formulas: life expectancy, amortization or annuitization. Each calculation will produce a different result even though the input assumptions are the same. (A worksheet is provided in Figure 1.)

FIGURE 1   **Information Required to Perform 72T Calculations**

1. Your age _____

2. The balance in your retirement plan on Dec. 31st of the previous year _____

3. The first year of your distribution _____

4. An interest rate assumption if you are using the annuitization or amortization methods (between 4% and 12 %) _____

5. Determine if you would like to use single or joint-life expectancy? Using joint-life expectancy will lower the annual distribution amount. (Single or Joint)

6. The age of your beneficiary, if you use joint life expectancy _____ (life expectancy and amortization methods only)

The best way to determine which formula to use is to plug several combinations of variables into a 72T distribution calculator and compare the results side by side. One of the most user-friendly 72T calculators on the Web is offered by KJE Computer Solutions *(www.dinkytown.com)*. Once on the site, go to the Retirement Savings and Planning section under "more" calculators. Your tax or financial advisor also can perform these calculations for you.

Method One: Life Expectancy

This formula will produce the lowest annual payment. To calculate the life expectancy distribution amount, simply take your previous year-end retirement account balance and divide it by your life expectancy or joint life expectancy. Your life expectancy can be found in the IRS Life Expectancy Tables at *www.irs.gov* (search for Publication 590). The 72T calculators will do this number crunching for you automatically. You must recalculate your life expectancy annually and, thus, your yearly distributions will vary somewhat from year to year.

As you get older and your life expectancy decreases, your annual distribution will typically increase. This occurs, however, only if your IRA grows faster than the rate at which you are taking money out of your account.

Method Two: Amortization

This formula provides a substantially higher distribution amount than the "life expectancy" method. This method amortizes your IRA balance over your life expectancy and assumes your account will grow at a reasonable rate of return. In addition, the annual withdrawal amount is determined in the first year before the first payment is made and remains fixed for the remaining distribution years. You cannot increase the amount to combat inflation or reduce it to offset the negative impact of a down year in the stock or bond market; doing either will trigger penalties.

Method Three: Annuitization

This method will typically provide the highest annual payout. The formula computes payments using a different life expectancy table, the 1984 Up-Mortality Table, and a reasonable assumed rate of return. With this method, the retirement account balance is divided by an annuity factor to determine the penalty-free distribution amount. As in the amortization method, the withdrawal amount is fixed in year one and does not change from year to year.

REASONABLE INTEREST RATE

What is a reasonable interest rate assumption? The IRS allows flexibility in determining this. It approves using a rate under 120 percent of the Federal Mid-term rate. For example, if the 10-year U.S. Treasury Note is yielding 5 percent, any interest rate under 6 percent would be considered acceptable. An even higher rate may be considered reasonable by the IRS if the rate can be justified by the expected performance of your investment portfolio.[3] If you choose a rate greater than 120 percent of the Federal Mid-term rate you should obtain a private letter ruling from the IRS.

Private letter rulings by the IRS have allowed the use of a 10 percent or higher interest rate. It must be stressed, however, that these rulings were made for individual cases. A private letter ruling is applicable only for the person who requested the IRS opinion. It does, however, give an indication of the agency's position on the topic. If you wish to assume a higher rate than the long-term federal rate, obtain your own private letter ruling from the IRS. Your tax advisor can assist you with this.

Be cautious here. If you use an interest rate assumption that is too high and deplete your IRA prior to completing your required withdrawals, there are severe penalties. These include both an interest penalty and the 10 percent early withdrawal penalty you had tried to avoid. These penalties are retroactive on all previous 72T distributions.

AN EXAMPLE OF A 72T DISTRIBUTION

Michael Henderson's company is experiencing some corporate downsizing. At age 54 he is offered an early retirement package. The offer includes a one-time, $500,000 lump-sum distribution from the company's pension plan. With that money and the $400,000 balance he has accumulated in his 401k plan, he decides to retire now at age 54.

To obtain $60,000 per year of income, he needs to begin taking withdrawals from his $900,000 retirement portfolio. A $60,000 withdrawal represents 6.67 percent of his total investment portfolio. Because he is not yet age 59 $1/2$, distributions from his retirement plans would be subject to a 10 percent premature withdrawal penalty. However, if Michael follows the formula outlined in Section 72T, he can avoid the penalty and begin taking withdrawals.

Let's examine the three distribution methods to determine how much he can withdraw annually without penalty. Figure 2 provides an overview of his options:

FIGURE 2

Single Life Expectancy, 7% Interest Rate Assumption			
Age at Year End	Life Expectancy Payout	Amortization Payout	Annuitization Payout
54	$30,508	$72,907	$78,809
55	$30,831	$72,907	$78,809
56	$33,181	$72,907	$78,809
57	$35,706	$72,907	$78,809
58	$38,419	$72,907	$78,809
59	$41,332	$72,907	$78,809

As you can see, Michael can easily accomplish his retirement income goals using 72T distributions. By changing the interest rate assumptions in the calculation, you can change the resulting distribution amounts. For instance, if you apply a 9 percent interest assumption, instead of the 7 percent used in Figure 2, the results would change as shown in Figure 3:

FIGURE 3

Single Life Expectancy, 9% Interest Rate Assumption			
Age at Year End	Life Expectancy Payout	Amortization Payout	Annuitization Payout
54	$30,508	$87,918	$91,650
55	$30,831	$87,918	$91,650
56	$33,181	$87,918	$91,650
57	$35,706	$87,918	$91,650
58	$38,419	$87,918	$91,650
59	$41,332	$87,918	$91,650

As you manipulate the interest rate assumptions, you can dramatically vary the annual distribution amounts. This flexibility is available only when you initially perform the calculations. When using the amortization and annuitization methods, you cannot change the amount once you begin receiving distributions.

SUBSTANTIALLY EQUAL PAYMENTS

The method you choose for your distributions isn't as important as adhering to your set schedule. In order to satisfy the "substantially equal payment" rule, you must choose one of the three methods discussed above and withdraw the calculated amount at least annually.

Failure to withdraw the calculated amount will result in a 10 percent early withdrawal penalty tax, plus an interest penalty. The tax and penalty are imposed, retroactively, on all withdrawals previously received. Additionally, if you have been receiving payments and suddenly take a distribution amount that either exceeds or is below your annual distribution requirement, you will be penalized on every distribution you have received to date.

While this distribution structure is very rigid, it is also very easy to set up a systematic withdrawal program from your IRA. Most financial institutions allow you to establish automatic monthly, quarterly, or annual distributions from your IRA for a set number of years. By setting up a systematic withdrawal plan, you will not need to worry about deviating from the required distribution amounts or how frequently you receive them.

Again, once you begin taking distributions, you must continue to do so for the next five years, or until you are 59 $1/2$, whichever is longer. For example, if you begin taking distributions at age 52, you must continue for seven and a half years. However, if you begin distributions at age 57, you must continue for five years until you are 62. With this in mind, a 40-year-old man would not be wise to begin taking distributions. Many changes could occur in his financial life in the years prior to reaching age 59 $1/2$. For example, if he decides to go back to work and no longer needs the income generated from distributions, he cannot stop them without incurring the 10 percent early withdrawal penalty. Of course, this man could redirect his 72T distributions into a non-retirement investment account and earmark the funds for retirement.

Once you fulfill the five-year or age 59 $1/2$ requirement, you can withdraw any amount without incurring penalties.

TAX CONSIDERATIONS

The distributions from your IRA are penalty-free if you follow the guidelines outlined above. They are not, however, free from income tax and will be taxed as ordinary income. Each year after receiving distributions, you will receive a Form 1099R from your IRA provider indicating the amount of taxable withdrawals taken during the previous year. A distribution code "2" will be placed on the Form 1099R. This indicates that the distributions are part of premature withdrawals with a known exception — "substantially equal payments." If a code "2" does not appear on your 1099R form, the IRS will view your distributions as premature and apply penalties. In situations where this occurs, don't be alarmed. Simply file a Form 5329 along with your 1040, indicating that you are taking a series of substantially equal payments according to the rules set forth in Section 72T of the IRS code. These forms and the instructions for completing them can be found at *www.irs.gov*.

Additionally, when you begin taking distributions from your IRA, you should, in most cases, have taxes withheld. Otherwise, you'll be facing a large tax bill when you file your taxes at year-end. Withholding taxes from your distribution is similar to the taxes withheld from your payroll check while working. Your IRA provider has a tax withholding form that allows you to specify the percentage of your distributions you want to withhold to pay federal and state income taxes. When determining your distribution amount, consider up front how much money you will need for taxes and living expenses.

FUTURE FLEXIBILITY: SPLITTING YOUR IRA

Before you begin taking distributions, consider the following important questions. First, do you anticipate needing to take withdrawals from your IRA in future years larger than your calculated 72T payments? And, second, will your scheduled 72T distributions require you to continue taking withdrawals past age 59 ½ to satisfy the mandatory five-year withdrawal period? If the answer is "yes" to either of these questions, you may want to consider the following strategy.

If you have a large enough portfolio balance, split your IRA into two separate IRA accounts prior to starting 72T distributions. Both accounts will be in your name but will have different account numbers. Remember, there are no limits to the number of IRA accounts you can open.

In the first IRA account, deposit only the amount necessary to provide you with the income you will initially need, according to the 72T calculations. By manipulating the account balance and the interest rate assumptions in the distribution formulas discussed above, you can determine the minimum amount necessary to deposit into IRA #1. Be conservative in determining how much to deposit; deposit a little more than is needed so that you avoid the risk of depleting your IRA prior to completing your scheduled distributions.

Let's return to the example of Michael Henderson, who took the early-retirement package, to see how this strategy works. To accomplish his goal of a $60,000 annual income, he would be required to deposit approximately $700,000 of his $900,000 portfolio into IRA #1. If he chose an 8 percent interest rate assumption and the annuitization method, he would receive a distribution of $60,000 per year. He could then deposit the remaining $200,000 into a second IRA, deciding initially not to take any withdrawals from this account (see Figure 4). If, in the second year of his retirement, Michael decides he needs more income, he can simply repeat the same process as with his first IRA and begin taking 72T distributions from the second account.

Let's assume he needs an additional $1,000 per month. He has $200,000 in IRA #2 but would only need $150,000 to generate the desired extra income using 72T calculations. He could then direct the remaining $50,000 to a third IRA, which would be available for future needs. Splitting your IRA when taking 72T deductions gives you income flexibility in the future. If Michael had kept all his money in one IRA account and had begun taking 72T distributions, he would not be able to make any changes for five years, or until he turned 59 $^{1}/_{2}$, whichever was longer.

FIGURE 4

	Year 1	Year 2
IRA #1:	Deposit $700,000. Begin taking 72T distributions of $62,450 per year. This could be accomplished using the annuitization method and an 8% interest rate assumption.	Continue taking $62,450 annual 72T distributions
IRA #2:	Deposit $200,000. No distributions will be taken in the first year.	Transfer $50,000 from IRA #2 to IRA #3. With remaining $150,000 in IRA #2 begin 72T distributions of $12,000 per year. This could be accomplished using the amortization method and an 8% interest rate assumption.
IRA #3:		IRA #3 Now has a $50,000 balance. No distributions are being taken from this account.

Splitting your IRA also makes sense if you will turn 59 $^{1}/_{2}$ during the mandatory distribution period. Remember, normal IRA distributions (non-72T) can begin at age 59 $^{1}/_{2}$ without penalty. However, if Michael begins taking distributions at age 57, he must continue doing so until he reaches age 62 — the mandatory five-year period — to avoid the penalty. If three years after he starts taking his 72T distribution he decides to purchase a condo and needs a lump sum of money, what can he do? With only one IRA his options are limited because of the 72T rules. Until age 62, he would be unable to take any additional withdrawals beyond the 72T distributions. However, if he split his retirement money into two IRA's, the first account could provide him income through his 72T distributions and the second would be available after age 59 $^1/_2$ in any amount, without penalty. Thus, he could use the money in IRA #2 to purchase the condo. Remember, however, to do this he would have to split the IRA initially, prior to beginning any 72T distributions.

If you die during the distribution period, your beneficiary is not required to continue receiving distributions. If the IRA beneficiary is your spouse, he or she has the option to roll the money into their own IRA account.[4]

PENALTY-FREE, LUMP-SUM DISTRIBUTIONS FOR THOSE OVER AGE 55

If you are over age 55 but under age 59 $^1/_2$ and leave your company, you are eligible for a one-time, lump-sum cash distribution from your employer-sponsored retirement plan without incurring the 10 percent early withdrawal penalty. In order to avoid the penalty, you must meet the following requirements:[5]

- You must reach age 55
- You must separate from your employer
- You must request a lump-sum cash distribution

This exception to the early withdrawal penalty only applies to distributions taken directly from an employer-sponsored plan, not from an IRA. The employer must, however, withhold 20 percent of the distribution amount for taxes (see p. 233).

This distribution strategy works particularly well if you know you're going to need a large sum of money immediately upon leaving your company — to launch your own business, for example, buy resort property, or take an exotic vacation. In these instances, a penalty-free, lump-sum payment can be especially useful.

Upon separation from your company, you can request to have all or part of the lump-sum distribution sent directly to you free from penalty. Any portion not distributed directly to you can be rolled over into an IRA. This way, you avoid taxes and penalties on money you don't need immediately.

Be aware, however, that even though the early withdrawal penalty is avoided, there are still distinct disadvantages to this distribution method. First, the amount you withdraw will be taxed as ordinary income and a large distribution may launch you into a higher tax bracket. Second, your employer is required to withhold 20 percent of your distribution amount to pay taxes. If you owe more, you will be required to pay additional taxes when you file.

The biggest disadvantage, though, is the loss of tax deferral and future compound interest on both the amount you withdraw and spend, as well as the portion of the distribution that goes to pay taxes. The severe impact of this approach is discussed in the Cash Distribution section of Chapter 19. A cash distribution early in retirement that greatly reduces the size of your retirement nest egg may hamper your ability to reach your long-term retirement goals. It is highly recommended you seek professional advice before taking a cash distribution to make sure you have enough money to fund your retirement goals. Most investment advisors will recommend you take out as little as possible in the form of a lump sum so you don't undermine your ability to enjoy your golden years.

IN-SERVICE WITHDRAWALS

To maintain company benefits, especially health insurance, many people work part-time as they ease their way into retirement. This move from full- to part-time employment usually means a significant drop in income. To compensate, many employees take in-service withdrawals from their company-sponsored retirement plans to supplement their income and maintain an acceptable standard of living.

As the name suggests, this distribution method allows an employee to take a withdrawal from the company's retirement plan while still an active plan participant. This distribution can initially be rolled over into an IRA to avoid taxes and penalties. Once in the IRA account, distributions can provide additional income. Remember, the usual taxes and penalties will apply to your IRA distributions. Consequently, if you are not yet age $59^{1}/_{2}$, you should consider implementing a 72T distribution plan to avoid the 10 percent early withdrawal penalty.

This is a sound strategy if a substantial portion of your retirement savings are invested in your company-sponsored retirement plan and you need additional income. In-service withdrawals are not permitted by all company-sponsored retirement plans. If, however, the plan allows in-service withdrawals, plan provisions will specify the portions of the plan available for distribution. Typically, vested employer contributions are available for distribution. Contact your retirement benefits administrator to determine if this withdrawal method is available and to determine the portion of your plan balance that can be withdrawn.

In conclusion, if you're thinking of retiring early, don't be intimidated by the penalties associated with withdrawals from retirement plans. By applying the strategies and tactics discussed in this chapter, you can avoid pitfalls that often harm early retirees. With foresight and savvy financial planning, you can develop a strategy to minimize the impact of penalties on your hard-earned nest egg.

Opening the Door to Retirement

PART 2

SOURCES OF RETIREMENT INCOME

CHAPTER 5
SOCIAL SECURITY: HOW MUCH WILL YOU RECEIVE?

You've been paying into it all of your working life, but how much will Social Security really contribute to your income when it comes time to retire? Some people assume that because FICA taxes seem to take such a notable chunk out of their paychecks they will be able to count on Social Security as their sole source of retirement income. Others mistakenly suppose that Social Security benefits will be so insignificant that they will have almost no affect on their long-term retirement income. In truth, neither assumption is accurate.

Statistics show that 27 percent of the average retired American's income is derived from Social Security; another 27 percent comes from investments (personal savings, IRAs, 401(k)s, etc.); and 25 percent from pensions. The other 21 percent is obtained through part-time work, home equity, and other sources, as illustrated in Figure 1.

While Social Security was never intended to be a reliable single source of retirement income, in most cases it will make up more than one-fourth of your retirement income pie and is therefore certainly worth taking the time to understand.[1]

FIGURE 1

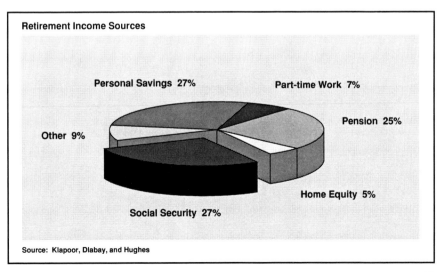

Retirement Income Sources

Personal Savings 27%　　Part-time Work 7%

Pension 25%

Other 9%

Home Equity 5%

Social Security 27%

Source: Klapoor, Dlabay, and Hughes

ELIGIBILITY TO RECEIVE BENEFITS

If you think that simply being a U.S. citizen qualifies you for Social Security benefits, think again. As you work and pay FICA taxes, you earn Social Security credits. You must earn a minimum of 40 credits to be eligible for benefits. In 2002, you had to earn $870 in income during the year to obtain one credit. You can earn a maximum of four credits per year, earning them all in the first month or over the entire 12 months. You must work at least 10 years to be eligible for retirement benefits.

Before 1978, you could earn only one credit per quarter, but this has changed. Now your credits are calculated based on your total earnings on an annual basis. Therefore, if you earn $3,480 per year (according to 2002 rules), you will receive four Social Security credits. These credits simply qualify you to receive benefits. Most people will earn more credits than the minimum 40 they need to be eligible for benefits. Extra credits will not increase the amount of benefits you receive; however, you won't receive any benefits if you don't have the minimum 40 credits.

SOCIAL SECURITY TAX

You contribute 6.2 percent of your income annually into the Social Security trust fund with your employer paying an additional 6.2 percent of your salary into the fund. However, you only contribute 6.2 percent of the first $84,900 you earn (in 2002). Once you hit this level of earning, no more Social Security tax is required for the year.

DETERMINING YOUR BENEFIT AMOUNT

The average earnings over your working life determine how much your monthly Social Security benefits will be in retirement. The following calculation will be used to determine your benefit:

- Your actual earnings are adjusted to account for inflation. For example, if a 3 percent inflation rate is used, the $10,000 you earned in 1982 would be equivalent to a little over $18,000 in 2002.

- Your total earnings during the 35 years in which you earned the most income are averaged to determine your average monthly "indexed" earnings. The maximum earnings used per year is $84,900 (in 2002).

- A formula is applied to these earnings to arrive at your basic benefit or "primary insurance amount" (PIA). This is the amount you receive at your full retirement age. For most people, full retirement age is 65. (See upcoming section on age requirements for more details.)

The benefit computation is complex, and there are no simple tables published by the Social Security Administration (SSA) to show exactly how much you will receive. However the SSA does provide the following resources:

- The SSA is now sending a Social Security estimate statement to all participants over age 25. You should receive this statement each year approximately three months prior to your birthday.
- Participants can request a Social Security estimate via the Web by logging onto *http://www.ssa.gov/online/ssa-7004.html.* A detailed report of your lifetime earnings and an estimate of your retirement, disability and dependent benefits will be mailed to you. You also can request an estimate via mail by completing a Request for Social Security Statement (Figure 2).

FIGURE 2

Form Approved
OMB No. 0960-0466 ☐ SP

Request for Social Security Statement

☐ Please check this box if you want to get your statement in Spanish instead of English.

Please print or type your answers. When you have completed the form, fold it and mail it to us. (If you prefer to send your request using the Internet, contact us at *www.ssa.gov*)

1. Name shown on your Social Security card:

First Name ______ Middle Initial ______

Last Name Only ______

2. Your Social Security number as shown on your card:

☐☐☐-☐☐-☐☐☐☐

3. Your date of birth (Mo.-Day-Yr.)

☐☐-☐☐-☐☐☐☐

4. Other Social Security numbers you have used:

☐☐☐-☐☐-☐☐☐☐

☐☐☐-☐☐-☐☐☐☐

5. Your Sex: ☐ Male ☐ Female

For items 6 and 8 show only earnings covered by Social Security. Do NOT include wages from State, local or Federal Government employment that are NOT covered for Social Security or that are covered ONLY by Medicare.

6. Show your actual earnings (wages and/or net self-employment income) for last year and your estimated earnings for this year.

A. Last year's actual earnings: *(Dollars Only)*

$☐☐☐,☐☐☐.00

B. This year's estimated earnings: *(Dollars Only)*

$☐☐☐,☐☐☐.00

7. Show the age at which you plan to stop working.

☐☐ *(Show only one age)*

8. Below, show the average yearly amount (not your total future lifetime earnings) that you think you will earn between now and when you plan to stop working. Include performance or scheduled pay increases or bonuses, but not cost-of-living increases.

If you expect to earn significantly more or less in the future due to promotions, job changes, part-time work, or an absence from the work force, enter the amount that most closely reflects your future average yearly earnings.

If you don't expect any significant changes, show the same amount you are earning now (the amount in 6B).

Future average yearly earnings: *(Dollars Only)*

$☐☐☐,☐☐☐.00

9. Do you want us to send the statement:
   - To you? Enter your name and mailing address.
   - To someone else (your accountant, pension plan, etc.)? Enter your name with "c/o" and the name and address of that person or organization.

"C/O" or Street Address (Include Apt. No., P.O. Box, Rural Route)

Street Address

Street Address (If Foreign Address, enter City, Province, Postal Code)

U.S. City, State, Zip code (If Foreign Address, enter Name of Country

NOTICE:
I am asking for information about my own Social Security record or the record of a person I am authorized to represent. I understand that if I deliberately request information under false pretenses, I may be guilty of a Federal crime and could be fined and/or imprisoned. I authorize you to use a contractor to send the Social Security Statement to the person and address in item 9.

▶

Please sign your name (Do Not Print)

Date ______ (Area Code) Daytime Telephone No. ______

Form **SSA-7004-SM** (6-2002) EF (08-2002)
Destroy prior editions

AVERAGE AND MAXIMUM BENEFITS

The Social Security Administration publishes average and maximum benefits. Figure 3 outlines the *maximum* monthly benefit, while Figure 4 details the *average* monthly benefit for a worker retiring at age 65.

FIGURE 3

Maximum Social Security Benefit		
	2001	2002
Worker Retiring at Age 65 in January:	$1,433/mo	$1,536/mo
Worker Retiring at Age 62:	$1,314/mo	$1,382/mo

Source: Social Security Administration

FIGURE 4

Average Social Security Benefit	
Type of Benefit	Average Monthly Benefit
All retired workers	$874
Aged couple	$1,454
Widowed mother & 2 children	$1,764
Aged widow(er) alone	$841
Disabled worker, spouse, & one or more children	$1,360
All disable workers	$815

Source: Social Security Administration

FULL RETIREMENT AGE

Full retirement benefits are available when you reach full retirement age, which for many years was age 65. In the past few decades, however, that age has been gradually raised to reduce the strain on the Social Security system caused by increased life expectancy in the U.S. As Americans continue living longer, it's reasonable to expect that the retirement age will continue to increase. The table in Figure 5 displays the Social Security Administration's definition of full retirement age.

FIGURE 5

Full Retirement Age	
Year of Birth	**Full Retirement Age**
1937 or earlier	65
1938	65 and 2 months
1939	65 and 4 months
1940	65 and 6 months
1941	65 and 8 months
1942	65 and 10 months
1943-1954	66
1955	66 and 2 months
1956	66 and 4 months
1957	66 and 6 months
1958	66 and 8 months
1959	66 and 10 months
1960 and later	67

Source: Social Security Administration

EARLY OR DELAYED RETIREMENT

Not everyone chooses to start receiving benefits at their full retirement age. Some begin earlier, while others postpone receiving benefits until after reaching full retirement age.

You can begin receiving benefits as early as age 62 and get a reduced benefit or delay receiving benefits until age 70, and receive an enhanced benefit. As previously mentioned, your "primary insurance amount" (PIA) is the benefit you are eligible to receive at your full retirement age.

RECEIVING BENEFITS PRIOR TO YOUR FULL RETIREMENT AGE

If you choose to receive benefits early, prior to reaching your full retirement age, your benefits will be reduced (Figure 6); waiting beyond your full retirement age will increase benefits (Figure 7).

Let's consider the dilemma facing Edwin, age 62, who would like to retire now before he is eligible for full retirement benefits. Edwin has determined that he will need at least $700 monthly in Social Security benefits to supplement his other retirement income to maintain his desired standard of living. Will his Social Security benefits amount to $700 if he retires at age 62, 36 months prior to full retirement? At full retirement age, 65, his Social Security monthly benefit is $1,000.

Using the information in Figure 6, we can determine how much his full benefit ($1000) will be reduced if he

FIGURE 6

Social Security Reduction for Early Retirement				
Year of Birth	Full Retirement Age	Age 62 Reduction Months	Monthly % Reduction	Total % Reduction
1937 or earlier	65	36	.555	20.00
1938	65 and 2 months	38	.548	20.83
1939	65 and 4 months	40	.541	21.67
1940	65 and 6 months	42	.535	22.50
1941	65 and 8 months	44	.530	23.33
1942	65 and 10 months	46	.525	24.17
1943-1954	66	48	.520	25.00
1955	66 and 2 months	50	.516	25.84
1956	66 and 4 months	52	.512	26.66
1957	66 and 6 months	54	.509	27.50
1958	66 and 8 months	56	.505	28.33
1959	66 and 10 months	58	.502	29.17
1960 and later	67	60	.500	30.00

Note: Persons born on January 1 of any year should refer to the previous year.

Source: Social Security Administration website, www.ssa.gov

retires now (top row). In this case, his full retirement benefit (PIA) would be reduced by 20 percent (.555 multiplied by 36 months equals 20 percent). Consequently, his benefit would drop from $1000 to $800 per month. If he decided to wait and receive benefits at age 64, his benefits would be reduced by only 7 percent (.555 multiplied by 12 months equals 7 percent). In this case, his monthly benefits would be reduced by only $70 to $930 per month.

The SSA Web site, *www.ssa.gov*, offers the following guideline: "If your full retirement age is 67, the reduction for starting your benefits at 62 is about 30 percent; at age 63, it's about 25 percent; at age 64, about 20 percent; at age 65, about 13 $1/3$ percent; and at age 66, about 6 $2/3$ percent."

Early retirement will give you about the same total Social Security benefits over your lifetime. However, the monthly payments are smaller in order to take into account the extra years you will be receiving them.

Every person approaching retirement age should keep in mind one very important point: If you choose to receive Social Security prior to your full retirement age, your benefit is PERMANENTLY reduced.

DELAYING SOCIAL SECURITY BENEFITS

Depending on your circumstances, it may be beneficial to delay receiving Social Security until after age 65. The longer you wait to begin receiving benefits, up to age 70, the larger your benefit will be. Figure 7 outlines the rate of increase for delaying your retirement benefits.

FIGURE 7

Social Security Increase for Delayed Retirement		
Year of Birth	Yearly rate of increase for each year you delay benefits	Monthly rate of increase for each month you delay receiving benefits
1930	4.5%	3/8 of 1%
1931-1932	5.0%	5/12 of 1%
1933-1934	5.5%	11/24 of 1%
1935-1936	6.0%	1/2 of 1%
1937-1938	6.5%	13/24 of 1%
1939-1940	7.0%	7/12 of 1%
1941-1942	7.5%	5/8 of 1%
1943 or later	8.0%	2/3 of 1%

Source: Social Security Administration

Let's take the example of Allen, a 65-year-old who enjoys his job as a sales manager for a pharmaceutical company. Because he likes working and has a comfortable income from his employer, he has decided to delay Social Security benefits until age 67. What will his benefit amount be at 67 if his PIA at age 65 is $1,000 per month (Figure 7)?

In Allen's case, the benefit increase is 6 percent per year. Delaying benefits two years will increase the amount Allen receives by a total of 12 percent. As a result, his benefit at age 67 will be permanently increased by $120, to $1,120 per month.

The SSA issues the following advice to those who delay retirement. "If you decide to delay your retirement, be sure to sign up for Medicare at age 65. In some circumstances, medical insurance costs more if you delay applying for it."

APPLYING FOR BENEFITS

The year before you plan to retire, meet with a Social Security representative or professional financial advisor. The rules governing Social Security are complicated and, according to the SSA, "it may be to your advantage to start your retirement benefits before you actually stop working."

You can apply for your benefits in three ways:

- Apply online at *http://www.ssa.gov/applytoretire/*
- Call toll-free: 1-800-772-1213. Hearing impaired: TTY at 1-800-325-0778.
- Apply in person or by phone at your local Social Security office. Locate the nearest office at *http://s3abaca.ssa.gov/pro/fol/fol-home.html*.

SPOUSAL BENEFITS

Your spouse's Social Security benefits will be calculated in the same manner as your own — by using the number of years he or she has worked and the amount he or she has earned. Your spouse will receive his or her earned benefit or one-half the amount of your benefit, whichever is greater (this rule also applies to non-working spouses who haven't qualified for their own benefit). The same rules apply for early or delayed retirement. Additionally, your spouse can qualify for Medicare on your record at age 65, if he or she has not qualified on their own.

DIVORCED SPOUSE

Your divorced spouse (even if you have remarried) may qualify for benefits based on your record, if you are 62 or older, even if you are not receiving benefits yet. There are three main requirements for your ex-spouse to qualify for benefits based on your record:

- The marriage must have lasted at least 10 years
- Your ex-spouse must be at least 62 years old
- Your ex-spouse must currently be unmarried

The amount of benefits your divorced spouse will receive does not affect your benefits nor those of your current spouse.

WORKING AND RECEIVING BENEFITS

Many people simply enjoy working and choose to continue doing so well past conventional retirement age. Others continue to work because they need or want extra income. The good news is that you can work and receive Social Security at the same time. However, there are limits on the amount you can earn while receiving Social Security. Exceeding those limits will reduce your benefit. The annual earning limitations are posted on the SSA Web site.

If you are working and collecting benefits between ages 62 and your full retirement age (65 in 2002), your benefit will be reduced if you earn more than $11,280 (in 2002). Your benefits will be reduced one dollar for every two dollars you earn over $11,280 between the ages of 62 and 65. If you plan to continue working after age 62, this reduction will dictate whether or not you should begin taking your benefits.

In 2002, for example, if you began receiving the maximum Social Security benefit ($15,936 per year) and earn over $43,152 in salary, your benefits would be reduced to nothing. Obviously, if you planned on earning $43,152, you would not want to begin taking your benefits at age 62. In the year you reach full retirement age, you will lose one dollar of benefits for every three dollars you earn over $11,280. In the month you reach full retirement age you can work and earn any amount without having your benefits reduced.

Let's look at an example: Diane qualified for the maximum benefit available at age 62 ($1,328 per month, or $15,936 per year) and decided to begin receiving Social Security. She wants to know how much her benefits will be reduced if she continues to work in 2002 and earns $25,000 for the year. The $25,000 is $13,720 over the $11,280 earnings limit. Her benefit will be reduced by one dollar for every two dollars she earns over $11,280. Consequently, in this scenario Diane's benefit will be reduced by $6,860, to $9,076 per year. By earning $25,000, her $15,936 benefit will be cut by almost half.

TAXATION OF YOUR SOCIAL SECURITY

Your Social Security benefits may or may not be taxed. It depends on the level of your "provisional income" during retirement.

Your provisional income level will not affect the actual amount you are paid in Social Security benefits, however it may affect whether or not you have to pay income taxes on the benefits you receive. If your provisional income is between $25,000 and $34,000 for individual filers, or between $32,000 and $44,000 for joint filers, 50 percent of your Social Security benefit is subject to income tax. If your provisional income is greater than $34,000 for single filers and $44,000 for joint filers, up to 85 percent of your Social Security benefits are subject to income tax.

Provisional income is calculated by combining all of your wages, earned interest, taxable dividends, tax-free interest, and retirement plan distributions, and then adding half of your Social Security benefit.

FIGURE 8

Taxation of Social Security Benefits		
Filing Status	**% of benefit taxable** **50%**	**% of benefit taxable** **85%**
If you file a federal tax return as an "individual"	Provisional Income Between $25,000 and $34,000	Provisional Income Above $34,000
If you file a joint return	Provisional Income Between $32,000 and $44,000	Provisional Income Above $44,000

Source: Social Security Administration website, www.ssa.gov

At the beginning of each year, the SSA issues a Social Security Benefit Statement (Form SSA-1099), which shows the total amount of benefits you received during the previous year. Use this statement when you complete your federal income tax return.

STRATEGIES FOR REDUCING TAXES ON SOCIAL SECURITY BENEFITS

One item that may be pushing your provisional income above the threshold listed in Figure 8 is interest and dividends derived from stocks, bonds, mutual funds, bank accounts, Money Market accounts, municipal bonds, and other interest-bearing investments. If you are not spending the interest or principal from these investment vehicles and are just reinvesting all of your earnings, you may want to consider repositioning the money into a fixed or variable annuity.

Annuities provide tax-deferred growth. Therefore, your investment earnings are not reported each year for tax purposes and aren't added to your provisional income. If you are not using the money right now, it does not make sense to have the earnings increase your provisional income and thus, the amount of tax you pay on your Social Security benefits.

THE STATUS OF THE SOCIAL SECURITY TRUST FUND

Many people are wondering these days, and understandably so, whether Social Security benefits will be there when they are eligible to receive them. Even the Social Security Administration acknowledges that the program is on dangerous ground. The SSA has made the following statement on its Web site:

"Social Security now takes in more in taxes than it pays out in benefits. The excess funds are credited to Social Security's trust funds, which are expected to grow to over $4 trillion before we need to use them to pay benefits. In 2015, we will begin to pay out more in benefits than we collect in taxes. By 2037, the trust funds will be exhausted and the payroll taxes collected will be enough to pay only 72 percent of benefits owed. We're working to resolve these issues."

The main thing that contributes to the depletion of Social Security is Americans' increased life expectancy. We're healthier today than ever before, and life expectancies continue climbing. When the Social Security program first began paying benefits in 1940, the average life expectancy for men and women reaching age 65 was 77 and 78, respectively. Today life expectancy has increased four years for men, to age 81, and six years for women, to age 84.

In addition, we face a shift in demographics as the baby boomer generation moves toward retirement. In the future, there will be fewer workers to support each retiree. The ratio of workers-to-retirees has plummeted and will continue to fall (Figure 9).

FIGURE 9

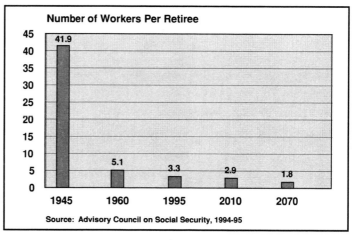

Number of Workers Per Retiree

Source: Advisory Council on Social Security, 1994-95

There is considerable debate today over what the government should do to ensure that Social Security is around for future generations. Several options are currently being discussed. Now more than ever, with the program's future less certain, you should devote significant attention to other sources of retirement income, such as pensions and personal savings.

Despite Social Security's uncertainty, it currently comprises more than one-fourth of most retirees' income and therefore requires that you understand how the program works and how to incorporate Social Security into your retirement plan. Using the information presented in this chapter, you should now be better informed about the issues surrounding Social Security and how you can best take advantage of it.

CHAPTER 6
COMPANY PENSIONS AND PENSION MAXIMIZATION STRATEGIES

There was a time not long ago, when most full-time employees could count on their companies to provide a generous pension plan at retirement. But today, the traditional company pension plan is fast becoming an endangered species. More and more U.S. corporations are discontinuing their pension plans to cut costs and are shifting the responsibility of retirement saving to their employees through employee savings programs such as 401(k)s and other types of qualified plans. While more companies are doing away with traditional pension plans, if you are fortunate enough to work for a company that can still afford to offer one and you qualify for benefits at retirement, you will receive a monthly pension check for the rest of your life. This benefit can be an important piece of your retirement income pie as statistics show that company pensions currently account for 25 percent of the average retiree's income (Figure 1).

Understanding the advantages and disadvantages of pensions and their payment options will be important to the overall success of your retirement planning. This chapter is intended to help you better understand these options and to help you learn simple, but effective strategies to maximize your pension and put more money in your pocket during retirement.

FIGURE 1

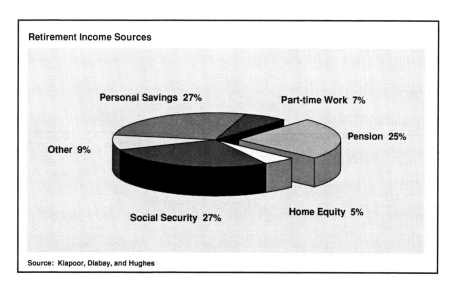

Retirement Income Sources

Personal Savings 27%

Part-time Work 7%

Other 9%

Pension 25%

Social Security 27%

Home Equity 5%

Source: Klapoor, Dlabay, and Hughes

HOW BIG WILL YOUR PENSION PAYMENT BE?

The formula that determines the size of your pension payments is usually based on your level of income and the length of service with your employer. When you retire, you will be given a pension statement outlining several pension payout options. Some employers will even provide you with the option of taking a one-time, lump-sum distribution rather than monthly payments. It's important to realize that the decision you make at this time is irrevocable. Thus, you should fully understand your options and make a choice that will help you accomplish your retirement goals.

In addition, make sure you don't retire just before your pension benefit is going to be bumped up. All it takes is a quick call to your human resources benefits coordinator to find out when benefits are scheduled to increase and, also, at what point your benefits level out. This will help you set your exact retirement date.

COMMON PENSION PAYMENT OPTIONS

Figure 2 outlines the most common pension payout options and an example of what each may pay in relation to the other options:

FIGURE 2

Pension Payout Options (Sample)		
	Monthly Benefit During Your Life	Monthly Benefit To Your Spouse Upon Death
Immediate Life Annuity	$500	$0
Single Life Annuity	$1,000	$0
Joint and 100% Survivor Annuity	$850	$850
Joint and 75% Survivor Annuity	$880	$660
Joint and 50% survivor Annuity	$920	$460
Life and 10 Year Period Certain	$950	*$950

One Time Lump-Sum Distribution (not offered by all plans) $150,000.

* Note: This option provides a $950 monthly benefit for your lifetime. However, if you die within the period certain (10-years), payments will continue to your beneficiary for the remainder of the ten-year period.

Definitions for each of the options in Figure 2 are outlined on the following page. Which should you choose? This is an important decision you will be required to make at retirement. *Study your options carefully because once you make your choice, you can't change it.*

Immediate Life Annuity: This annuity will pay a monthly lifetime benefit beginning immediately. Benefits cease at your death.

Single Life Annuity: This option provides you with the most money each year during retirement. However, benefits cease upon your death so your surviving spouse and heirs will not continue receiving any income. Additionally, if you pass away only weeks after signing the final pension paperwork, all payments will immediately cease.

Joint & 100% Survivor Option: At retirement, this annuity pays a pension for your lifetime and continues to pay your surviving spouse the same amount after you die. Benefits will not be paid to your heirs upon your spouse's death. Defined benefit plans are required to provide this annuity as an option. If you decide to choose an option other than this one, you must obtain your spouse's consent.

Joint & 75% Survivor Option: This option allows you to receive a higher benefit than the aforementioned Joint and 100% Survivor Option. However, your surviving spouse receives only 75 percent of the benefit amount upon your death.

Joint & 50% Survivor Option: This option provides you with an even higher benefit than the Joint and 100% and 75% Survivor Options. As the name suggests however, your surviving spouse receives only 50 percent of the monthly benefit amount upon your death.

Life Only With Ten-Year Period Certain: This annuity provides benefits to you for your lifetime. However, if you die within the period certain (10 years from the time payments commence), payments will continue to your beneficiary (spouse or others) for the remainder of the 10-year period. (Some plans will provide 15- and 20-year period certain payment options, but the longer the period certain, the lower your annuity benefits will be.) If you die after the period certain time frame, benefits will be discontinued.

Lump Sum Distribution (not offered by all plans): At retirement, the pension will make a one-time distribution. This money can be rolled into an IRA, avoiding taxes and penalties. If you choose this payout option, you must be ready to make decisions that the plan would have otherwise made for you. These include where to invest the money and how much you can take out each year without completely depleting your assets during retirement.

Other Annuity Options: Although not as common, some plans offer additional options such as the Refund option and the Joint with Period Certain option.

PENSION PLAN ADVANTAGES

Pension plans have some distinct advantages, the biggest being the peace of mind that comes with receiving a consistent paycheck for the rest of your life, regardless of how the market or economy perform. Your employer hires a team of professional money managers to handle the portfolio of investments in the pension plan for you, lifting the management burden from your shoulders. In addition, the Pension Benefit Guaranty Corporation (PBGC) guarantees most defined benefit pension plans. If your plan does not have sufficient money to pay all of your promised benefits, the PBGC will step in and keep your benefits flowing. Your benefits, however, could be reduced if this occurs.

PENSION PLAN DISADVANTAGES

Even though pension plans have many perks, there are some disadvantages of which you need to be aware. First, many pensions do not have a cost-of-living adjustment (COLA). This means inflation will take its toll on your pension. You will receive the same amount of money every year, even though the prices of goods and services will increase dramatically during your retirement. Prices will most likely double every 20-22 years. For example, the $35,000 annual pension payment you receive today may be more than adequate to meet your income needs right now. However, in 20 years you will likely need $70,000 to buy the same amount of goods and services you're purchasing today. This is a definite disadvantage, but one that you can overcome if you have sufficient investment assets to provide you with the additional income you may require.

Also, the fact that your choice of an annuity option is irrevocable can be problematic. Let's assume, for example, you choose the Joint and 100% Survivor annuity option (see Figure 2), allowing you to receive an $850 monthly pension. You would be choosing a lower monthly check than the $1000 you could have received with the single life annuity option. By accepting the reduced amount, you are ensuring that upon your death, your spouse will continue to receive $850 per month during his or her lifetime. But what if your spouse passes away first? You will continue to receive this reduced $850 amount for your lifetime and can't change it to reflect your new circumstances. Additionally, if you choose this option and both of you die during the first year, no further benefits will be paid to your heirs.

A chart summarizing each of the pension plan options outlined in this chapter appears in Figure 3.

FIGURE 3

Pension Payout Summary			
Payout Method	**Description**	**Advantages**	**Disadvantages**
Life	Benefit lasts for participant's lifetime.	Highest income level	May not take full advantage of life savings if die early
Certain	Benefits lasts for participants lifetime or at minimum the term specified if you die sooner (usually 10, 15, or 20 years)	Beneficiary gets income for remaining term if a participant dies	Income less than "life" option If spouse predeceases participant the benefit will continue at the reduce amount and will not adjust to the higher life only payout
Refund Payout	Benefit lasts for participants death Upon participants death the remaining benefits are paid to a beneficiary until exhausted	Beneficiary gets income up to value of remaining contract if participant dies.	Income less than "life" and "certain" (depending on length of certain term)
Joint and Survivor	Benefit lasts for lifetime of the participant and joint participant (usually spouse or partner)	Flexibility in setting joint annuitant's income	Payments less than all single life options - No payment to beneficiary If spouse predeceases participant the benefit will continue at the reduce amount and will not adjust to the higher life only payout
Joint and Survivor with Certain	Benefit lasts for lifetime of participant and joint participant, or at minimum the term specified if both die sooner	Beneficiary gets income up to value of remaining contract if both holders die	Income even less than "joint and survivor" If spouse predeceases participant the benefit will continue at the reduce amount and will not adjust to the higher life only payout

PENSION MAXIMIZATION STRATEGIES

Selecting the best pension pay-out option can be difficult. Should you choose the option with the highest monthly payment that will provide a benefit for your lifetime only? Or do you select the option with the largest pay-out to your surviving spouse?

Believe it or not, there is a way to have your proverbial cake and eat it, too. You can obtain the highest annuity payment and still provide for your spouse upon your death. Before pursuing this strategy, there are a couple of points you need to consider. The younger you are, the better this strategy will work. Most advisors will suggest you implement this strategy prior to retirement; although, if you're in good health, it may be worth considering even after you've retired.

Here's how it works: Let's assume you have decided to take a Joint and 100% Survivor Annuity to ensure that your spouse is provided for upon your death. In the example shown in Figure 4, you will receive $35,000 per year and, upon your death, your spouse will continue to receive $35,000 annually.

FIGURE 4

Comparison		
Option	**Income During Your Lifetime**	**Income To Your Survivor**
Single Life Annuity	$45,000 year	$0
Joint and 100% Survivor Annuity	$35,000 year	$35,000

To make sure your spouse is financially protected, you are essentially forfeiting $10,000 per year — the difference between the highest-paying Single Life Annuity and the Joint and 100% Survivor Annuity. Wouldn't it be nice to have the best of both options — the higher annual pay-out, $45,000 in our example above, plus an income stream to your surviving spouse of at least $35,000 per year? Such an option is possible. Read on.

Ask yourself this question, "How much money would I need in a separate interest-bearing account to produce $35,000 of income per year for my spouse for 20-30 years of retirement?" If you had an investment portfolio earning just 6 percent per year, you would need a little under $500,000 to produce $35,000 of annual income for 30 years. A portfolio growing at 8 percent would require a total of about $400,000 to produce the required income.

So, if you had a separate portfolio from which your spouse could draw $35,000 of income per year at your death, you could then opt for the Single Life Annuity and obtain $10,000 more in income per year[1] and enjoy the best of both worlds.

It may also be possible to choose the higher-paying Life Only Annuity option. However, this strategy requires the use of life insurance. Like most people who are preparing to retire, the idea of purchasing more life insurance isn't that appealing. Realize, however, that choosing the Joint and Survivor Annuity is, in fact, just like buying an expensive life insurance policy. In the above example, you are buying insurance that will pay your spouse $35,000 per year for his or her lifetime upon your death. How much is this insurance costing you? In the above example, it's costing you $10,000 each and every year. Is that a good deal? Perhaps not.

If you can purchase a life insurance policy with a death benefit of $400,000 for less than $10,000 per year, then this pension maximization strategy makes sense for you. If, for example, a $400,000 insurance policy costs only $5,000 per year, you could choose the Single Life Annuity option. Your pension will now be paying you $10,000 more than you would have received otherwise. You can use half of that $10,000 to pay your life insurance premium and still be ahead of the Joint and 100% Survivor Annuity Option by $5,000 per year. When you die, your Single Life pension benefit will cease, but your spouse will receive $400,000 tax-free from the life insurance policy. Your spouse can use that money to buy a portfolio of investments that will provide him or her with needed retirement income. In addition, while you are alive, you can access the cash value of the policy as needed.

The critical question in making this strategy work is how much will $400,000 of life insurance actually cost? This depends on your age and your health. Figure 5 illustrates actual annual life insurance price ranges at different ages. Based on these premium levels, the pension maximization strategy would work if you are younger than age 60 and purchase a universal life insurance policy for less than $10,000 in annual premium costs. Ask your insurance agent for a quote to see if you can get an acceptable price to make this strategy work.

FIGURE 5

Whole Life vs. Universal Life		
Age	**Whole Life**	**Universal Life**
50	$9,000 - $11,000	$3,000 - $6,000
55	$12,000 - $14,000	$5,000 - $8,000
60	$16,000 - $18,000	$6,000 - $10,000
65	$22,000 - $24,000	$9,000 - $13,000

HOW MUCH INSURANCE DO YOU NEED TO MAKE THIS STRATEGY WORK?

The amount of insurance you need depends on three factors: 1) The amount of annual income needed; 2) the length of time for which the income will be needed; and 3) an interest rate assumption. Figures 6, 7, and 8 contain tables to help you determine how much insurance you would need in order to make this strategy work for you. The interest rate assumption you choose will determine which chart you should use. For example, Figure 6 assumes when the proceeds of your insurance policy are paid out to your surviving spouse, he or she will invest the money in a portfolio earning 4 percent annually. Figure 7 uses 6 percent, while Figure 8 uses an 8 percent assumption.

Here's how to use the charts: Assume you would like to provide your spouse with $30,000 of annual income for 30 years following your death. At a 4 percent rate of return (Figure 6), he or she would need a $518,761 investment portfolio to generate $30,000 of annual income for 30 years.[2] Invested at 6 percent, your spouse would need $412,945 (Figure 7). At 8 percent, the portfolio would have to contain $337,734 (Figure 8).

First, choose the chart that most closely reflects the rate of return (4 percent, 6 percent, 8 percent) you believe your surviving spouse could achieve if required to invest your insurance proceeds upon your death. After making this assumption, determine the amount of annual income required and the number of years the income will be needed. Then, follow the row across the chart and the respective column down the chart until they meet. The resulting dollar amount represents the amount of insurance you should consider purchasing to make this strategy work.

FIGURE 6

Pension Maximization
How much insurance do you need?

Interest Rate Assumption 4%

Amount of Income Needed Annually	Number of years income is needed					
	10	15	20	25	30	35
$ 10,000	$81,109	$111,184	$135,903	$156,221	$172,920	$186,646
$ 15,000	$121,663	$166,776	$203,855	$234,331	$259,380	$279,969
$ 20,000	$162,218	$222,368	$271,807	$312,442	$345,841	$373,292
$ 25,000	$202,772	$277,960	$339,758	$390,552	$432,301	$466,615
$ 30,000	$243,327	$333,552	$407,710	$468,662	$518,761	$559,938
$ 35,000	$283,881	$389,144	$475,661	$546,773	$605,221	$653,261
$ 40,000	$324,436	$444,735	$543,613	$624,883	$691,681	$746,585
$ 45,000	$364,990	$500,327	$611,565	$702,994	$778,141	$839,908
$ 50,000	$405,545	$555,919	$679,516	$781,104	$864,602	$933,231
$ 55,000	$446,099	$611,511	$747,468	$859,214	$951,062	$1,026,554
$ 60,000	$486,654	$667,103	$815,420	$937,325	$1,037,522	$1,119,877
$ 65,000	$527,208	$722,695	$883,371	$1,015,435	$1,123,982	$1,213,200
$ 70,000	$567,763	$778,287	$951,323	$1,093,546	$1,210,442	$1,306,523
$ 75,000	$608,317	$833,879	$1,019,274	$1,171,656	$1,296,902	$1,399,846
$ 80,000	$648,872	$889,471	$1,087,226	$1,249,766	$1,383,363	$1,493,169
$ 85,000	$689,426	$945,063	$1,155,178	$1,327,877	$1,469,823	$1,586,492
$ 90,000	$729,981	$1,000,655	$1,223,129	$1,405,987	$1,556,283	$1,679,815
$ 95,000	$770,535	$1,056,247	$1,291,081	$1,484,098	$1,642,743	$1,773,138
$ 100,000	$811,090	$1,111,839	$1,359,033	$1,562,208	$1,729,203	$1,866,461

FIGURE 7

Pension Maximization
How much insurance do you need?

Interest Rate Assumption 6%

Amount of Income Needed Annually	Number of years income is needed					
	10	15	20	25	30	35
$ 10,000	$73,601	$97,122	$114,699	$127,834	$137,648	$144,982
$ 15,000	$110,401	$145,684	$172,049	$191,750	$206,472	$217,474
$ 20,000	$147,202	$194,245	$229,398	$255,667	$275,297	$289,965
$ 25,000	$184,002	$242,806	$286,748	$319,584	$344,121	$362,456
$ 30,000	$220,803	$291,367	$344,098	$383,501	$412,945	$434,947
$ 35,000	$257,603	$339,929	$401,447	$447,417	$481,769	$507,439
$ 40,000	$294,403	$388,490	$458,797	$511,334	$550,593	$579,930
$ 45,000	$331,204	$437,051	$516,146	$575,251	$619,417	$652,421
$ 50,000	$368,004	$485,612	$573,496	$639,168	$688,242	$724,912
$ 55,000	$404,805	$534,174	$630,846	$703,085	$757,066	$797,404
$ 60,000	$441,605	$582,735	$688,195	$767,001	$825,890	$869,895
$ 65,000	$478,406	$631,296	$745,545	$830,918	$894,714	$942,386
$ 70,000	$515,206	$679,857	$802,894	$894,835	$963,538	$1,014,877
$ 75,000	$552,007	$728,419	$860,244	$958,752	$1,032,362	$1,087,368
$ 80,000	$588,807	$776,980	$917,594	$1,022,668	$1,101,186	$1,159,860
$ 85,000	$625,607	$825,541	$974,943	$1,086,585	$1,170,011	$1,232,351
$ 90,000	$662,408	$874,102	$1,032,293	$1,150,502	$1,238,835	$1,304,842
$ 95,000	$699,208	$922,664	$1,089,643	$1,214,419	$1,307,659	$1,377,333
$ 100,000	$736,009	$971,225	$1,146,992	$1,278,336	$1,376,483	$1,449,825

FIGURE 8

Pension Maximization
How much insurance do you need?

Interest Rate Assumption 8%

Amount of Income Needed Annually	Number of years income is needed					
	10	15	20	25	30	35
$ 10,000	$67,101	$85,595	$98,181	$106,748	$112,578	$116,546
$ 15,000	$100,651	$128,392	$147,272	$160,122	$168,867	$174,819
$ 20,000	$134,202	$171,190	$196,363	$213,496	$225,156	$233,091
$ 25,000	$167,752	$213,987	$245,454	$266,869	$281,445	$291,364
$ 30,000	$201,302	$256,784	$294,544	$320,243	$337,734	$349,637
$ 35,000	$234,853	$299,582	$343,635	$373,617	$394,022	$407,910
$ 40,000	$268,403	$342,379	$392,726	$426,991	$450,311	$466,183
$ 45,000	$301,954	$385,177	$441,817	$480,365	$506,600	$524,456
$ 50,000	$335,504	$427,974	$490,907	$533,739	$562,889	$582,728
$ 55,000	$369,054	$470,771	$539,998	$587,113	$619,178	$641,001
$ 60,000	$402,605	$513,569	$589,089	$640,487	$675,467	$699,274
$ 65,000	$436,155	$556,366	$638,180	$693,860	$731,756	$757,547
$ 70,000	$469,706	$599,164	$687,270	$747,234	$788,045	$815,820
$ 75,000	$503,256	$641,961	$736,361	$800,608	$844,334	$874,093
$ 80,000	$536,807	$684,758	$785,452	$853,982	$900,623	$932,365
$ 85,000	$570,357	$727,556	$834,543	$907,356	$956,912	$990,638
$ 90,000	$603,907	$770,353	$883,633	$960,730	$1,013,201	$1,048,911
$ 95,000	$637,458	$813,150	$932,724	$1,014,104	$1,069,489	$1,107,184
$ 100,000	$671,008	$855,948	$981,815	$1,067,478	$1,125,778	$1,165,457

If your situation is such that the insurance premiums are less than the difference between the Life Only annuity option and the Joint and 100% Survivor Annuity Option you are planning to take, then the pension maximization strategy will work well for you. It is definitely worth obtaining an insurance quote prior to locking yourself into a pension payment. It may mean thousands of extra dollars each year during retirement.

TAKING A ONE-TIME LUMP-SUM DISTRIBUTION

Assume your company gives you the following choices: (1) An annual pension payment of $35,000 per year for the rest of your life and the life of your spouse, or (2) a one-time lump-sum distribution of $500,000? Is it better to take the lump sum or receive a lifetime of annuity payments? The answer depends on your personal objectives. We've already considered the advantages and disadvantages of pension annuity payments. Let's do the same with the lump-sum distribution. Of course, we will assume at the outset that you will want to roll the lump-sum money over into an IRA to avoid taxes and penalties. Doing this requires the same steps discussed in the IRA Rollover section outlined in Chapter 19.

Lump-sum Advantages

Once the lump-sum money has been transferred into an IRA, you gain tremendous flexibility with those dollars. For example, you can choose to give yourself a "raise" each year to compensate for inflation — a benefit you usually don't get with a regular pension. This is done by simply withdrawing a little more from your IRA than you did during the previous year.

You can also withdraw principal at any point in time if you ever need a large cash infusion, if you're buying real estate for example, or paying for your daughter's wedding. Because the money is in your IRA, you are able to manage your own account (or hire a professional manager to do it for you) instead of relying on your former employer to do it for you. In your IRA, you can develop and manage an investment strategy on your own or with the aid of an advisor.

Any assets left in your IRA at your death can be transferred into your spouse's IRA without taxes or penalties. Your spouse can continue managing the money and take out income as needed. Upon your spouse's death, the remaining balance in the portfolio will pass on to your heirs.

Lump-sum Disadvantages

When you invest in an IRA and buy stocks or bonds (or stock or bond funds) as part of your investment mix, there are no guarantees that you will obtain a certain rate of return. If you are unable to successfully manage your portfolio, you could be in danger of depleting your IRA assets prematurely. This risk doesn't exist if you choose the pension option with the guaranteed monthly payments.

FIGURE 9

Pension	Lump-Sum
Choice of annuity payout option is irrevocable	Flexible and changeable payout schedule
Income is guaranteed	Income is not guaranteed
Recipient does not have to manage an investment portfolio	Investor must manage an investment portfolio
N/A	Investment returns are not guaranteed
Access to investment principal is not available	Investment principal is available at any time
Once annuity has been paid based on terms of option chosen no money is left to heirs	Any money not spent during retirement passes on to heirs

Let's return to our example: Assume you and your spouse retired in 1975. At that time, you had the option of receiving a $35,000 Joint and 100% Survivor annual pension (without a cost-of-living adjustment) or taking a lump-sum distribution of $500,000. Which would you choose? Let's break it down.

In 1975, $35,000 would have seemed like a substantial income. (In fact, it would be equivalent to $73,000 in 2000 dollars, assuming a 3 percent inflation rate.) If you opted for the lump-sum distribution, you would need growth of at least 7 percent per year to outperform the pension ($35,000 is 7 percent of $500,000). Can you construct a portfolio to perform better than that? To answer that question, let's further assume that you invested 50 percent of your lump-sum money into blue-chip U.S. stocks[3] and 50 percent into government and corporate bonds[4] — essentially meaning that half of your money is in more conservative investments (bonds), while the other half is at risk in the stock market.

To make this a fair comparison, let's also assume you withdrew only $35,000 annually — the same amount you would have received from your pension — from your IRA every year since 1975, with no cost-of-living adjustment. How much would be left in your IRA account 35 years later?

Brace yourself. The answer is a whopping $4,489,963. You'd have that much money even after withdrawing $35,000 per year, or $875,000 in total withdrawals. Your balanced portfolio would have enjoyed an average annual return of 12.98 percent. Even if you had given yourself a 3 percent raise every year to keep up with rising prices, increasing your annual income from $35,000 per year in 1975 to $71,148 in 2000, your portfolio would still contain a very substantial $3,019,865 at the end of 2000.[5]

Although these numbers look very convincing, it should be noted that your portfolio would have followed the natural ups and downs of the stock and bond markets. During six of the 25 years, you would have taken withdrawals from your portfolio when it produced negative returns. Your success, then, would depend on your ability to tolerate the rough economic circumstances of the mid 70s, early 80s, the 1987 stock market crash and negative markets in 1990, 1994, and 2000, without deviating from your balanced investment strategy. Some people simply do not have the ability to weather this kind of volatility.

If you have the choice between a lump sum and a pension, it's not a choice you should make lightly. Look at both options very carefully, work through the different scenarios you could pursue, and then make the decision that will best help you reach your retirement objectives.

After reading this chapter you should be more familiar with the various pension payment options and the risks and benefits associated with each. With a more firm understanding of the way your pension will be paid out, you can now use the maximization strategies outlined in this chapter to help you make the most of those payments at retirement.

CHAPTER 7
SAVINGS AND INVESTMENTS:
AVOIDING THE 10 MOST COMMON INVESTOR MISTAKES

With pressure increasing on the Social Security system and the continued reduction of traditional pension plans, more people are going to need solid returns from their investment portfolios in order to produce a livable retirement income. In fact, it's not overstating the matter to say that your investment success may well dictate whether or not you reach your retirement goals.

Today, the average retiree relies upon personal savings for about one-third of his or her retirement income (see Figure 1). In the future, savings and investments will take on an even greater importance.

For many, this increased reliance on personal savings and investments presents a bit of a problem. That's because many people simply don't invest very well.

FIGURE 1

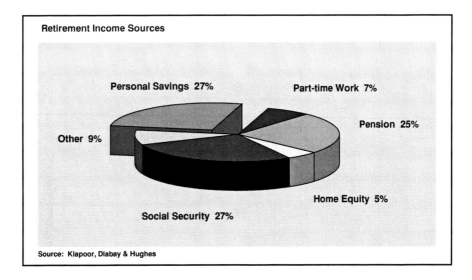

Retirement Income Sources

Personal Savings 27% Part-time Work 7%

Other 9% Pension 25%

Home Equity 5%

Social Security 27%

Source: Klapoor, Dlabay & Hughes

Over the long-term, most investors struggle to obtain performance better than low-yielding investments like Money Markets and certificates of deposit. You should be aware of several basic reasons why investors don't obtain good long-term returns and understand how you can avoid the obstacles that plague so many investors. By avoiding common investor mistakes, you will be in a better position to reach your retirement goals.

A 16-year investor study dramatically illustrates the grim lack of success many investors have experienced. According to the study, the average stock fund investor achieved only a 5.3 percent average annual rate of return from 1984 through 2000. Had these same investors simply invested their money in the Standard and Poor 500 index (large U.S. company stocks) and forgotten all about it, they would have achieved a 16.3 percent annual gain.[1] The market provided results almost three times better than those experienced by millions of stock mutual fund investors!

We've just concluded one of the strongest raging bull markets in stock market history. It should have been easy for even the average investor to make substantial sums of money, but many didn't capitalize on this strong market.

Consider for a moment the difference between an investor earning an average annual return of 5.3 percent as opposed to an investor earning a 16.3 percent return as outlined in the study above. The impact is also dramatic when compared to the lower 11 percent average annual return achieved by the stock market since 1925 instead of the 16.3 percent achieved by the market from 1984 to 2000 as mentioned in the previous study. Compare the results in Figure 2:

FIGURE 2

$100,000 Invested at Different Growth Rates for 10, 20 and 30 years		
5.3%	**11%**	**16.3%**
10-Years $167,604	$283,942	$452,686
20-Years $280,910	$806,231	$2,049,247
30-Years $470,816	$2,289,230	$9,276,656

How is it that investors do so poorly at times when investments are doing so well? No single mistake explains this poor performance. Rather, there are a combination of errors repeated over and over — mistakes that can be overcome by simply implementing and adhering to a disciplined investment strategy (developing a strategy is discussed in Chapters 8 through 13).

Understanding the investment pitfalls others have made in the past will help you avoid these same errors in the future. Here are some of the most common investor mistakes:

Mistake #1: Excessive Buying and Selling

Like the amateur chef that continually seasons food until it's inedible, investors who are overactive in their trading undermine their own returns.

In a study of over 66,000 households with investment accounts at a well-known brokerage firm, it was found that investors who traded most frequently under-performed those who traded the least. For the study, the investors were split into five groups based on their trading activity. The returns achieved by the 20 percent of investors who traded the most lagged behind the least active group of investors by 5.5 percent annually. The study also showed that men trade 45 percent more actively than women investors and, consequently, women outperformed men.[2]

Many investors make the mistake of thinking that the more often they trade, the better their returns will be. The advertisements aired by many discount brokerage firms promoting active trading want you to believe this is true. However, the evidence suggests exactly the opposite.

Mistake #2: Information Overload

Too much information can be dangerous to your wealth.

Not long ago at the beginning of an investment seminar, a financial advisor asked the audience how many knew the previous day's closing level of the Dow Jones Industrial Average. Many hands went up, and these "smart" investors had no difficulty citing the index's closing value.

The advisor then asked who in the audience didn't have a clue where the market had closed. Reluctantly, a lady with very little investment experience timidly raised her hand. The advisor surprised the crowd by handing her a $20 bill, and then asked the audience why she should get the money when she was the only one who hadn't known the Dow Jones value. He explained that investors who rarely check the market and the value of their investments tend to keep more of their money invested in stocks, thus obtaining better long-term returns. Those who monitor the market too closely have a tendency to blow up their portfolios with self-destructive behavior.

What role should information play in your investment decisions? Recently,

Professor Richard Thaler and three other professors specializing in investment behavior studied the decisions investors made over a 25-year period, focusing on the amounts they invested in stocks.

Three groups of investors were studied. The first group was bombarded every six weeks with reports on market gyrations and investment performance. The second group received performance information about their investments just once each year, while the third group received investment updates only once every five years.

The investors who received the most performance information allocated the smallest amount of their portfolios — about 40 percent — to stocks. They not only maintained the lowest equity exposure but tended also to reduce their equity exposure immediately following a loss.[3] The group that received updates only every fifth year devoted 66 percent of their portfolios to stocks. And, as we all know, based on the history of the market, investors with greater exposure to the equity markets enjoyed far better long-term performance.

The bottom line: The more closely investors follow the market, the more tentative they become about investing in stocks, which ultimately hurts their returns.

FIGURE 3

Information Overload		
	Group A	**Group B**
# of Reports:	100's	5
Time Span:	6 weeks	5 years
Stock Allocation Next 40 Years:	40%	66%

Investment Performance Reported over a 25-Year Period

Source: Richard Thaler, University of Chicago, 1996

The solution: Develop a fundamentally sound investment strategy and maintain your stock allocation through up and down markets. Stay away from financial sites on the Internet, turn off CNBC, consider cancelling your subscription to the *Wall Street Journal,* and quit worrying *daily* about your investments. Professor Thaler, author of the aforementioned research said it best, "My advise to you is to invest in equities, and then don't open the mail."[4]

Mistake #3: Market Timing

History has shown that the stock market rises about 70 percent of the time. The danger, when investing, is in finding yourself out of the market during the 70 percent of the time it is going up, all because you're trying to avoid the 30 percent of the time the market is falling.

Trying to choose the right times to jump in and out of the market is an impossible task. Too many investors make the mistake of thinking they can do it.

Investors attempting to time the ebbs and flows of the market tend to jump in too late, missing major upswings, and jump out after the market has fallen. Consequently, many investors end up buying high and selling low, yielding poor results that often lead to the kind of frustration that keeps investors out of the market altogether.

If you had invested in the stock market (S&P 500) from 1989 to 2001 (3,028 trading days) you would have enjoyed a 10.3 percent average annual total return. If you spent just 40 days out of the market, the days the market went up by the greatest amounts, your average annual return during this 12-year period would be a negative one percent. That's a dramatic difference in return between one investor who spent 2,988 days in the market and another who stayed invested in equities all 3,028 days of this 12-year period (Figure 4).[5]

FIGURE 4

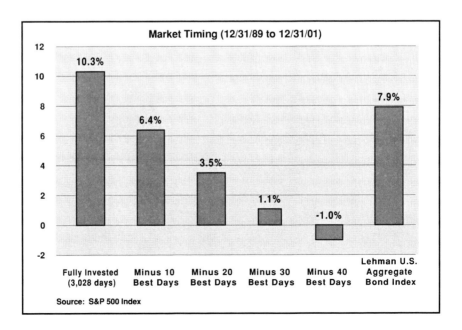

Market Timing (12/31/89 to 12/31/01)

Source: S&P 500 Index

Mistake #4: Chasing Returns

Investors are famous for buying last year's winners. For example, studies show that money tends to flow into mutual funds that have just enjoyed the greatest performance. Throughout 2000, for example, investors poured over $60 billion into the ten funds that had the greatest performance during the previous year. These ten funds, on average, had triple the performance of the stock market as a whole in 1999. In 2000, however, these same funds reported returns less than half that of the stock market overall.[6] In other words, investors who bought these funds were caught chasing returns. It's a very common investor mistake. Investments that post strong returns in the previous year often receive a great deal of media attention. For many, the lure of phenomenal past returns is just too tempting to pass up; this allure can lead to critical mistakes.

For example, in 1999, the Nicholas-Applegate Global Tech I Fund posted an unbelievable 493.74 percent return — investors saw instant riches parading before their eyes. An individual investing $100,000 into this fund at the start of 2000, experienced the following returns: -36.37 percent in 2000, -49.26 percent in 2001, and -44.96 percent in 2002 (Figure 5).[7] At the end of three years, that $100,000 investment was only worth $17,770.

FIGURE 5

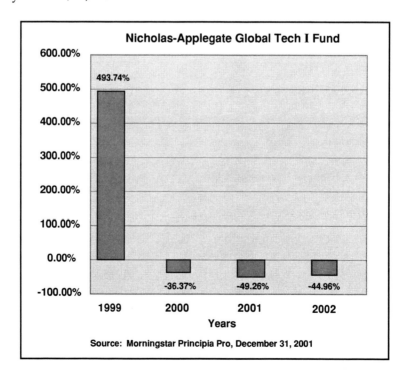

Source: Morningstar Principia Pro, December 31, 2001

When the fine print says "Past performance is no guarantee of future returns," believe it!

Mistake #5: Believing Persuasive Advertising Messages

Many brokerage firms advertise in order to convince you how easy, fun and inexpensive it is to delve into the stock market and make big money. In fact, the entire brokerage industry spends hundreds of millions of dollars each year on TV commercials convincing us that there's nothing to being a success in the market.

Remember Stuart? He was that red-headed, punk-rocker made famous in the late 90's through a series of commercials for a large discount brokerage firm, teaching us and his boss how easy it is to make money in the stock market. Stuart advised that all you had to do was open an online account, start trading and watch the money roll in. As Stuart said in the commercial, "I don't want to beat the market. I wanna grab it, sock it in the gut a couple of times, turn it upside down, hold it by the pants and shake it 'til all those pockets empty out the spare change."

While the "Stuart" commercials, like many ads for the investment houses, are hilarious they tend to do more damage than good. We don't see Stuart talking about investing anymore because he probably learned that there is more to developing a solid investment strategy than merely opening an online brokerage account and trading.

No question about it, buying and selling stocks can be exhilarating. Many investors roll up their sleeves and play with their money, checking stock prices and market values multiple times throughout each day. While this may be a great form of entertainment, most discover it's also a successful formula for losing money.

Rarely a day passes when a brokerage firm isn't telling Americans that they can trade stocks for as little as $5 to $8 per transaction. Think about it. If these firms are offering such cheap deals, they want to make up for it by dealing in quantity. Their goal is to have you trade as often as you want, without concern for cost. This, of course, often leads to hyperactive trading and poor performance.

Mistake #6: Poor Diversification

Investors tend to be over-concentrated in one or two companies or sectors of the market. This can hurt a portfolio whether the market is good or bad. Poor diversification leads to excessive volatility, and excessive volatility causes investors to make hasty, poor decisions.

Suppose you had placed the bulk of your portfolio in companies like Lucent Technologies, Enron, WorldCom, Qwest, and Adelphia Communications. In 2001 and 2002, you would have watched your portfolio head into an unrecoverable tail-spin. Those investors who had concentrated the bulk of their portfolios in these companies saw values drop to almost zero. They were left with no other option but to start from scratch, and begin rebuilding an entirely new portfolio.

Likewise, many investors got caught up in the technology craze of the late 1990's, pouring money into technology mutual funds. They had some major regrouping to do when the average tech fund fell 31.98 percent in 2000, and another 38.16 percent in 2001.[8] A well-diversified portfolio, even invested aggressively in the stock market alone, would have fallen just 8 percent in 2000, and 12 percent in 2001. A more moderate growth portfolio consisting of 80 percent stocks, 10 percent bonds, and 10 percent cash would have dropped 4.5 percent in 2000, and 8.7 percent in 2001.[9] When volatility is controlled, it's easier for investors to maintain a long-term outlook.

Poor diversification even takes its toll during good times in the market. In 1999, the S&P 500 index recorded a positive 21 percent return. However, just eight of the 500 stocks in the index accounted for half of the 21 percent gain. The odds were stacked against the investor who bought just a few S&P stocks during 1999. The chances of an investor successfully choosing those eight big winners out of 500 would be a little better than the lottery but not by much.[10] Most would be far more successful by simply buying an S&P 500 index fund and owning stakes in all 500 companies.

Mistake #7: Lack of Patience

Most investors hold their mutual funds for only two or three years before impatience gets the best of them. Individual stock investors are even less patient, turning over about 75 percent of their portfolios each year.[11] You simply can't realize good returns from the stock market if you only invest for weeks, months, or even a couple of years. When investing in stocks or stock funds, investors must learn to set their investment sights on five- and ten-year periods.

Investors would do well to study the example of the Calamos Growth-A mutual fund, the best performing diversified domestic equity fund for the 10-year period ending December 31, 2001. During that decade-long period, this mid-sized company stock fund provided investors with a stunning average annual return of 19.27 percent. Most of us, it's safe to say, would be very happy with this performance. However, it didn't deliver this solid performance every single year. In fact, during that 10-year period, four of the years were rough ones with a -1.71 percent return in 1992, 4.35 percent in 1993, -5.7 percent in 1994, and –7.68 percent in 2001.[12] An investor would have had to endure these four difficult years to gain the 19.27 percent long-term average annual return. Patient investors were rewarded.

Anne Scheiber is a model of patience that all investors should emulate. She retired from her $3,150-per-year, IRS auditor job in 1943. At that time, she invested $5,000 — a little over one year's salary — into a portfolio of stocks. Over the years, she bought mostly blue-chip U.S. stocks and municipal bonds. She didn't worry about daily market fluctuations and rode out the difficult market periods. When Anne died in 1995, at age 101, her $5,000 had grown to over $22 million, which she donated to a Jewish university. Patience was vital to Anne's stunning investment success.[13]

Mistake #8: Unrealistic Expectations

Many investors are convinced that their investments should always go up. When returns don't meet expectations, these investors tend to give up and throw in the towel. This is a mistake.

During market boom times like those in 1998 and 1999, if portfolios weren't posting returns of 20 percent or better, investors felt they were being ripped off. The fact is, huge investment returns should be viewed as an unexpected blessing, not an entitlement. Over the long-term, the stock market has averaged 10-12 percent returns, the bond market 5-7 percent, and the cash markets 3-5 percent. If you own stocks, bonds, or cash investments, it is reasonable to expect that these long-term returns will repeat themselves.

The old adage, "If it seems too good to be true, it probably is," has a lot of truth to it, especially when it comes to investing in the stock market. When investors are promised big returns, greed can lead them to throw caution to the wind. For instance, in 1998 and 1999, investors poured money into technology companies. Many of these companies were trading at extremely high prices even though they had yet to post a profit. The allure of windfall profits drove investors to continue bidding prices up to astronomical levels. Investors unwisely believed that stock prices would continue to climb indefinitely, even though the companies themselves weren't making money. When the market began to show signs of slowing, these companies were the first to come crashing down. Many technology companies began a stock free-fall in March of 2000 that quickly ate up much, if not all, of the gains of the previous few years.

Should investors have seen this coming? Absolutely! The "must own" tech stocks of 1999, were very similar to "must own" tech stocks of 1968 (Figures 6 and 7). In both cases, as these charts show, companies without strong corporate earn-

FIGURE 6

The "Must Own" Techs of 1968

Stock	1968 High	1970 Low	% Drop
Fairchild Camera	$102	$18	-82%
Teledyne	$721	$13	-82%
Control Data	$163	$28	-83%
Mohawk Data	$111	$18	-84%
Electronic Data	$162	$24	-85%
Optical Scanning	$146	$16	-89%
Itek	$172	$17	-90%
University Computing	$186	$13	-93%

Source: Los Angeles Times, 1/10/99

FIGURE 7

The "Must Own" Techs of 1999

Stock	1999 High	2001 Low	% Drop
Qualcomm	$179.31	$38.46	-78.55%
Dell Computer	$58.13	$16.63	-71.39%
Cisco Systems	$79.38	$11.24	-82.84%
Sun Micro Systems	$64.31	$7.91	-87.70%
AOL Timewarner	$93.82	$29.85	-68.18%
Amazon.com	$106.63	$6.01	-91.62%
Yahoo	$237.50	$8.68	-96.35%
JDS Uniphase	$153.40	$5.10	-96.34%
Juniper Networks	$244.50	$8.90	-96.00%
Palm, Inc.	$165.00	$1.30	-98.47%

Source: Big Charts.com 1999-2001

ings could not sustain unrealistic stock prices.

When you invest in a portfolio of stocks and bonds (or stock and bond funds), be aware of the potential upside and downside associated with your individual investments and your overall portfolio. If you don't understand your risks at the outset, you are more likely to make poor investment decisions during periodic market setbacks. Invest with your eyes wide open and you won't get scared out of the market when things get rough.

Whenever you purchase an investment, it's a good idea to note the investment's worst performing years during the past decade. Then ask yourself honestly how you would have reacted if you had invested during one of those down years. It's important to do this because the worst-case scenario can always repeat itself.

You should plan on worst-case scenarios occurring when you invest. If this downside will keep you from sleeping at night, you'd be wise to invest elsewhere.

Mistake 9: Focusing on Individual Investment Holdings Rather Than Your Portfolio as a Whole

What are the various components of your investment portfolio?

You may have some money in a 401(k) plan, IRA's, a trust account, bank accounts, a fixed annuity, and insurance cash value. If you are like many investors, you have accounts scattered among various financial institutions. Among all of these accounts, you may have one or two that are invested more aggressively than others. In down markets, these accounts typically get hit harder than accounts containing more conservative investments. If you focus too closely on the falling accounts, you may be tempted to get rid of the investments in those accounts when they're low in value and replace them with investments experiencing success.

This leads to a strategy of buying high and selling low. It's a mistake made by investors who gauge their entire portfolio by the performance of just one account or one investment.

FIGURE 8

Balanced Portfolio: 50% Stocks, 50% Bonds, and 0% Cash	
Large-Cap Growth Stocks	12.5%
Large-Cap Value Stocks	12.5%
Mid-Cap Growth Stocks	5.0%
Mid-Cap Value Stocks	5.0%
Small-Cap Growth Stocks	2.5%
Small-Cap Value Stocks	2.5%
Large-Cap International Growth Stocks	5.0%
Large-Cap International Value Stocks	5.0%
Corporate Bonds	25.0%
U.S. Government Bonds	25.0%
International Bonds	0%
Cash	0%
Other	0%

In 2000, let's assume you owned a diversified portfolio of 50 percent stocks and 50 percent bonds, shown in Figure 8. Let's also assume that each investment was owned in a separate account, giving you ten accounts in all.

How would you respond if the account containing your large company growth fund reported a substantial loss as many did in 2000 and 2001. Would you sell it? If you do, you might well be hurting your overall, long-term performance. Although this fund had a couple of bad years, it does fill an important

89

role in your portfolio, and you should maintain your position, assuming it is an above-average, large company growth fund.

Evaluate your portfolio as a whole rather than its individual pieces. The diversified portfolio in the previous example actually did very well as a whole, providing a positive 3.4 percent return in 2000, a year in which the Standard and Poors 500 was down 9.1 percent and the NASDAQ lost a whopping 39.29 percent.

Mistake 10: Lack of a Clearly Defined Investment Strategy

Let's imagine for a moment that you are in charge of investing the $100 million in your state's retirement pension plan. The money will be used to provide pension incomes and other benefits to thousands of employees who have diligently worked for the state. These employees are counting on you to make good investment decisions to help secure their financial futures. What steps would you take to make sure this money was managed properly?

Most likely you would utilize the services of institutional money managers to handle the day-to-day buying and selling of stocks and bonds. You would likely interview many financial professionals, hire the best ones, then monitor their performance very closely.

Picture yourself in one of these interviews. You would no doubt ask lots of specific questions about each manager's investment strategy and how successfully they have managed money. How much confidence would you have in a candidate who answered your question with this statement?

> *"Well, our investment management company doesn't really have a strategy. We usually read* Money *magazine and look for hot ideas. We always watch* CNBC *and often get good investment ideas there. Sometimes we even look on the Internet for investment ideas. On occasion, I talk to my doctor or father-in-law to get some real hot stock tips. We buy a little here and a little there and hope the investments work well and compliment each other. Once we own a portfolio of investments, we go to the Internet to obtain stock quotes several times each day. When it FEELS right, we sell. It's kind of a gut feeling we get. I think you will be happy with our investment management services."*

How much of your state's $100 million are you going to invest with this money manager candidate? It's safe to say you would usher him out of your office as quickly as possible.

CHAPTER 7 – SAVINGS AND INVESTMENTS: AVOIDING THE 10 MOST COMMON INVESTOR MISTAKES

Now, put yourself in that hot seat. You are the person in charge of your own portfolio. How would you respond if asked, "What strategy do you follow in managing your own portfolio?" All too often, investors respond the same way the money manager did in our previous example. If your investment strategy consists of hot tips from television, the Internet and the guy next door, would you trust yourself to manage your own portfolio?

Just as you wouldn't hire a money manager to oversee your state's pension plan unless they had a clearly-defined investment strategy, you shouldn't manage your own money without developing a disciplined strategy. A strategy doesn't work unless it has structure and is carried out with discipline. An investment policy statement will help accomplish this.

Investors who do not follow a disciplined investment strategy continue to repeat the same costly mistakes. By following the steps for developing a successful investment strategy that will be outlined in the subsequent chapters, your chances of securing sound returns will be greatly increased.

Opening the Door to Retirement

PART 3

DEVELOPING A SUCCESSFUL INVESTMENT STRATEGY

CHAPTER 8
STEP 1: ASSET ALLOCATION

Here's a quick quiz:

What is the most important variable in determining your investment success?

(A) Accurate market timing — the ability to be in or out of the market at the right time.
(B) Asset allocation — establishing an appropriate mix of stocks, bonds and cash.
(C) Selection of securities — the ability to uncover the next Microsoft.

The correct answer is (B), and it's not even a close race. A recent study of accounts managed by institutional money managers (those who invest money for state pension accounts, large retirement plans, and endowment money) discovered that 91.5 percent of their total account performance was attributed to the money manager's asset allocation policies. Only 8.5 percent of their return was a result of security selection and market timing combined.[1] Accordingly, if a money manager produced a 10 percent rate of return, that return was almost entirely a result of how assets were allocated.

Thus, the most important variable in determining investment success is how you divide your money between stocks, bonds and cash.

Most people don't realize what Figure 1 proves, and conse-

FIGURE 1

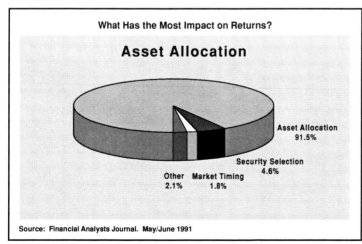

What Has the Most Impact on Returns?

Asset Allocation

Asset Allocation 91.5%

Security Selection 4.6%

Other 2.1%   Market Timing 1.8%

Source: Financial Analysts Journal. May/June 1991

quently, approach the investment process backwards. Rarely do investors call their brokers or financial advisors and initially discuss what percentage of their money should be invested in stocks, bonds, or cash. In most cases, the first question an investor asks is "What stock is hot?" The second is "When should I buy?" Most investors are concentrating on security selection and market timing, the two variables that matter least in investment success.

If over 90 percent of your investment return is determined by how well you allocate your money, it makes sense that your asset allocation policy should be your primary focus.

ASSET ALLOCATION METHODS

Figure 2 outlines the investment performance of stocks, bonds, and U.S. Treasury Bills from 1925 to 2001. Stocks provide the highest returns but, of course, also carry the greatest risks. What percentage of your portfolio should be invested in each of these asset classes? There is no one answer to this question for all investors across the board. You must factor in your own time frames, ages, income requirements, levels of risk tolerance, and desired rates of return. Let's examine several asset allocation methods based on each of these variables, and then depending on your priorities, determine your personal asset allocation policy.

FIGURE 2

Stocks, Bonds, and Bills 1925-2000	
Stocks	11.0%
Bonds	5.3%
Cash	3.8%

Compound annual returns from 12/31/25 to 12/31/00. All income is reinvested. Stocks are represented by the Standard and Poors 500 index, Bonds are represented by the 20-year U.S. Government Bond and cash is represented by U.S. Treasury Bills.

Source: 2000 Ibbotson Associates. Inc.

ASSET ALLOCATION METHOD: AGE-BASED

An age-based approach is a conservative one, and the way it works is simple. Take the number 110 and subtract your age. The result is the percentage of your investment portfolio you should invest in stocks or stock mutual funds. For example, if you're 60, subtracting your age from 110, tells you that 50 percent of your money should be invested in stocks and the rest in bonds or cash. An 80-year-old, by this formula, should invest less money — 30 percent of the portfolio — in stocks.

Why at that age would you continue to invest money in securities with a higher risk factor? Is there a chance an 80-year-old could live another 20 years? Yes, there is, and due to this possibility a portion of the portfolio needs to be growing at a higher rate to provide a hedge against inflation. If you follow this formula and adjust your portfolio each year, your investment strategy will slowly become more conservative as you get older. Although this formula is a good general guideline, it may be too conservative for some people.

The chart in Figure 3, using the age-based formula, outlines asset allocation mixes at different ages with their corresponding historical returns.

FIGURE 3

Stock and Bond Allocations at Various Ages			
Age	Stock %	Bond %	Average Return
20	90%	10%	14.1%
30	80%	20%	13.2%
40	70%	30%	12.4%
50	60%	40%	11.5%
60	50%	50%	10.7%
70	40%	60%	9.8%
80	30%	70%	9.0%
90	20%	80%	8.1%

Source: Rittenhouse: Asset Allocation Return Calculator 1949-1999

ASSET ALLOCATION METHOD: INCOME NEEDS

This formula can be more aggressive than the age-based formula. With this method, you simply allocate your money based on when you are planning to spend it.

Picture three buckets in front of you (Figure 4). The first bucket contains money you plan on spending during the next year or two. The second bucket contains money you will need for income from year three to year seven, and in the third bucket, you place money you don't plan on spending for more than seven years.

The money in Bucket 1 is invested in cash-type investments that protect your principal (CD's, Money Markets, Treasury Bills, bank accounts, etc.). This is your short-term money and is not put at risk by being invested in the stock or bond markets.

In Bucket 2 intermediate term money is invested in bonds (corporate, government, municipal, etc.). You can structure your bond portfolio by purchasing bonds that mature each year from "Year Three through Year Seven." This is

FIGURE 4

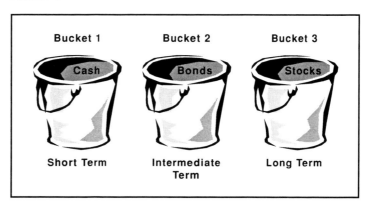

Bucket 1 — Cash — Short Term

Bucket 2 — Bonds — Intermediate Term

Bucket 3 — Stocks — Long Term

known as a "bond ladder." As each bond matures, money is available to provide income during the upcoming year. Bonds are guaranteed by the bond issuer and typically pay a higher rate of interest than cash-type investments. Although bonds will fluctuate in value, the volatility is usually far less than that of stocks.

Your long-term money in Bucket 3 is invested in stocks (individual stocks or stock mutual funds). This money won't be spent for at least seven years. This is the growth portion of your portfolio and will naturally increase or decrease with the fluctuations in the stock market.

When handled properly, the pieces of this strategy fit together perfectly to assure a steady flow of retirement income. As you spend and deplete the money in your cash accounts, a bond will mature to replenish your cash reserves and provide the income needed during the upcoming year. To maintain your allocation, you will occasionally need to sell some stock positions to replenish your bond portfolio as bonds mature. If the stock market has a poor year, you can wait to transfer money from stocks to bonds so you're not selling stocks in a down market.

At any point, you are assured to have income for seven years (two years via cash and five years via bonds). Consequently, you don't need to worry excessively about a down year in the stock market because you're not going to be spending any of your stock investments for at least seven years. In that lengthy time-span, your stock portfolio has plenty of opportunity to regain any losses from a down year or two.

Let's consider Catherine, a 60-year-old retiree who has accumulated $500,000 and has an income need of $25,000 per year. Following the Income Based Allocation Method, she has decided to invest $50,000 in secure cash investments to provide her income during the first two years of retirement, $125,000 in bonds to provide income in years 3-7, and the remaining $325,000 in stocks to help her meet her long-term retirement goals (see Figure 5):

Investing $325,000, or 65 percent, of

FIGURE 5

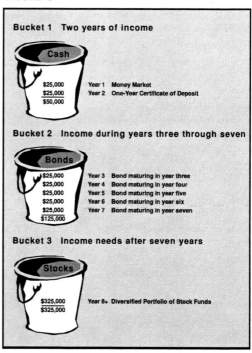

Bucket 1   Two years of income

Cash

$25,000   Year 1   Money Market
$25,000   Year 2   One-Year Certificate of Deposit
$50,000

Bucket 2   Income during years three through seven

Bonds

$25,000   Year 3   Bond maturing in year three
$25,000   Year 4   Bond maturing in year four
$25,000   Year 5   Bond maturing in year five
$25,000   Year 6   Bond maturing in year six
$25,000   Year 7   Bond maturing in year seven
$125,000

Bucket 3   Income needs after seven years

Stocks

$325,000   Year 8+   Diversified Portfolio of Stock Funds
$325,000

her money in stocks may be too aggressive for Catherine. If this is the case, she can adjust her portfolio very easily, making it more conservative by simply reducing her stock exposure and adding a little more money to bonds.

FIGURE 6

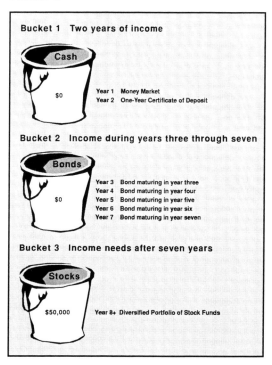

Bucket 1   Two years of income

Cash

$0   Year 1   Money Market
     Year 2   One-Year Certificate of Deposit

Bucket 2   Income during years three through seven

Bonds

$0   Year 3   Bond maturing in year three
     Year 4   Bond maturing in year four
     Year 5   Bond maturing in year five
     Year 6   Bond maturing in year six
     Year 7   Bond maturing in year seven

Bucket 3   Income needs after seven years

Stocks

$50,000   Year 8+ Diversified Portfolio of Stock Funds

Now, let's look at the case of Darin, age 30, who plans to retire at age 60. So far, he has accumulated $50,000 in his company's 401(k) plan. Because retirement is far into the future, his primary goal is to see his money grow. He has a regular paycheck and doesn't require income from his investment portfolio. Choosing to use the income-needs allocation approach, he allocates his portfolio as shown in Figure 6.

As you can see, Darin has allocated 100 percent of his portfolio to stocks. This approach is much more aggressive than the age-based strategy, which would have allocated just 80 percent of Darin's money to the stock market (110-30 = 80%). Darin eschews the age-based approach because his priority is growth rather than income.

ASSET ALLOCATION METHOD: RISK TOLERANCE

How much volatility can you endure? That's the central question in the risk tolerance allocation method.

Many investors over-confidently choose an investment mix because they like the high potential rate of return, but they often fail to consider the potential downside. When the markets go south, these investors frequently run for the hills, selling their most volatile investments at the worst possible time and losing sight of their long-term objectives. Obviously, selling is not a wise option when investments are down in value. By simply examining the potential downside of your asset allocation mix, prior to initiating your investment strategy, you can avoid unfortunate decisions down the line.

The average rate of return for different mixes of stocks, bonds, and cash from

1926 through 2001, is illustrated in Figure 7. The chart also outlines how often each portfolio lost money and the magnitude of the average loss. Most importantly, it shows the worst-case scenario for each mix.

FIGURE 7   **Asset Allocation - Risk & Reward**
Annual Returns (1926 - 2001)

Portfolio	Average Return	Largest Gain	Largest Loss	Average Gain	Average Loss	Percentage Positive Years	Percentage Negative Years
90% Stocks 0% Bonds 10% Cash	11.77%	48.62%	-38.90%	20.88%	-10.58%	71.1%	28.9%
80% Stocks 10% Bonds 10% Cash	11.06%	43.40%	-34.79%	18.83%	-9.29%	72.4%	27.6%
70% Stocks 20% Bonds 10% Cash	10.34%	38.19%	-30.69%	16.30%	-8.84%	76.3%	23.7%
60% Stocks 30% Bonds 10% Cash	9.63%	32.97%	-26.59%	14.79%	-7.02%	76.3%	23.7%
50% Stocks 40% Bonds 10% Cash	8.91%	27.76%	-22.49%	13.09%	-5.58%	77.6%	22.4%
40% Stocks 50% Bonds 10% Cash	8.19%	24.17%	-18.39%	11.29%	-4.40%	80.3%	19.7%
30% Stocks 60% Bonds 10% Cash	7.48%	24.94%	-14.29%	9.41%	-3.58%	85.5%	14.5%
20% Stocks 70% Bonds 10% Cash	6.76%	25.70%	-10.18%	7.91%	-3.00%	89.5%	10.5%
10% Stocks 80% Bonds 10% Cash	6.04%	26.47%	-6.08%	6.66%	-2.69%	93.4%	6.6%
0% Stocks 90% Bonds 10% Cash	5.04%	27.24%	-4.24%	6.09%	-1.12%	89.5%	10.5%

Ibbotson Associates. Stocks-S&P Index, Bonds-U.S. Intermediate Term Government Bonds, Cash- U.S. 30 Day Treasury Bill

Determining your asset allocation using this method is simple and involves a question only you can answer: "What is my breaking point?" Determine how far your portfolio can drop before you decide you want out. If your portfolio starts at $100,000, and market losses take it down to $90,000, $80,000, or even $70,000, at what point do you begin losing sleep at night?

Locate the "largest loss" column in Figure 7, and review the worst-case scenarios for the different asset allocation models. How much downside can you tolerate? For example, if you could handle a 25 percent loss in the worst-case scenario — without modifying your investment strategy — then a mix of 50-60 percent stocks would be suitable for you. Although you may never see the worst-case scenario occur, this method of asset allocation prepares you in advance for the downturns that may occur in the markets.

ASSET ALLOCATION METHOD: TARGET RATE OF RETURN

What rate of return is required for you to reach your retirement goals? Once you've determined that rate by developing a retirement plan, you can also use Figure 7 to determine an appropriate asset allocation mix. This will help you create a portfolio that has historically produced the rate of return you've targeted. If, for example, you've determined that you need an 8 percent return on your investments, then your portfolio should consist of at least 40 percent stocks, 50 percent bonds, and 10 percent cash according to historical market returns from 1926 to 2001 (see column 2 in Figure 7).

COMBINING ALL FOUR ALLOCATION METHODS

Each of these asset allocation methodologies — age, income needs, risk tolerance and target rate of return — are useful. To obtain the most accurate asset allocation model, you should blend each method together. The best way to accomplish this is to complete an investment questionnaire like the one that follows. These questions are a sampling of those most financial advisors ask before making any specific recommendations. Your answers to these questions will help you select the most appropriate asset allocation model for your individual goals and circumstances.

Asset Allocation Questionnaire

Investment Objective
1. What is your primary purpose for investing?
    A. Preserve investment capital (2)
    B. Emphasis on current income (4)
    C. Emphasis on income with some growth (6)
    D. Emphasis on growth with some income (8)
    E. Maximum growth (10)

Time Horizon

2. When do you plan on spending the money you are investing?
    A. 0-2 Years (2)
    B. 3-7 Years (4)
    C. 8-15 Years (6)
    D. 16+ Years (10)

Risk Tolerance

3. Which statement best describes your feelings about risk?
    A. I am willing to take a lot of risk to obtain maximum growth. (8)
    B. I am willing to take some risk to obtain moderate growth. (6)
    C. I am willing to take a little risk realizing that my potential for growth will be less. (4)
    D. I am not willing to risk my investment principal. (2)

4. I can endure periods of principal erosion and volatility if my portfolio has potential for high returns.
    A. Strongly Agree (10)
    B. Agree (8)
    C. Somewhat Agree (6)
    D. Somewhat Disagree (4)
    E. Disagree (2)

5. Review the risk and returns of the following hypothetical investment portfolios. Choose the portfolio that most accurately reflects your long-term *return* requirements and *risk* tolerance.

		Average Year	Worst Year	Best Year	
A.	Portfolio A	12%	-27%	53%	(10)
B.	Portfolio B	10%	-17%	36%	(8)
C.	Portfolio C	9%	-11%	26%	(6)
D.	Portfolio D	7%	-3%	25%	(4)
E.	Portfolio E	6%	-2%	12%	(2)

6. What would your reaction be to a 15 percent drop in the value of your investment portfolio?

    A. I would consider this an opportunity to buy more investments at lower prices. (8)

    B. I am investing for the long-term. I would not alter my strategy if the market fell 15 percent. (6)

    C. This would make me very anxious. I would consider repositioning my portfolio more conservatively in attempts to cut any further losses. (4)

    D. I would sell my volatile investments. (2)

SCORING

After answering each of these six questions, total your score. Simply add up the numbers found at the end of each of your answers, then find the portfolio below that corresponds with your score.

Scoring Point Range	Portfolio	Percent of Portfolio to Invest in Stocks
12 to 21	Conservative	0-25%
22 to 30	Conservative to Moderate	25-50%
31 to 40	Moderate	50-70%
41 to 50	Moderate to Aggressive	70-85%
51 to 56	Aggressive	85-100%

Review Figure 7 again, and locate the portfolio that consists of stock exposure that most closely fits your score. Figure 7 will help set your expectations for your target portfolio.

EMERGENCY CASH RESERVES

The investment recommendations in this chapter assume you have already set aside emergency cash reserves. As a general guideline, you should have three to six months worth of living expenses in a reserve fund.

Let's be clear on this point. Three to six months of living expenses should not be confused with three to six months of income. Living expenses equal your gross income minus taxes and savings. For example, if you earn $5,000 each month, pay $1,500, in taxes and save $500, your monthly living expenses come to $3,000. So, in this scenario, your reserve fund should contain between $9,000 and $18,000.

The purpose of this money is to provide you with instant cash in an emergency. For example, if you were to lose your job, you would not need 100 percent of your current income to sustain yourself. Without a job, you're not paying income taxes and you wouldn't be saving, but you would need to cover living expenses for several months while you look for a new job.

Some of your reserves should be invested in liquid cash investments so the money can be withdrawn immediately without risk of principal loss due to adverse market conditions. Depending on how comfortable you are with risk, a portion could also be invested in stocks and bonds in a non-retirement investment account. Stocks and bonds can be sold and turned into cash within three business days. As a general guideline, the older you are, the more money you want to have in cash and bonds and the less in stocks.

Step 1 of the investment process, as outlined in this chapter, was designed to help you see the importance of having a wise asset allocation policy; the different methods of asset allocation discussed herein can help you determine how much of your money should be allocated to stocks, bonds, and cash. Allocating your portfolio properly can help you develop a successful investment strategy that will aid in the overall strength of your retirement plan. Step 2 of the investment process, which is covered over the next three chapters, will help you understand the reasons for diversifying your portfolio within each asset class, the various components of a diversified portfolio and examples of how various portfolios have performed in the past.

CHAPTER 9
STEP TWO: REASONS FOR DIVERSIFYING

Even the most casual baseball fan knows that a winning team doesn't put all nine of its players in the same position. How good would the New York Yankees be if most of the players stood in left field?

FIGURE 1

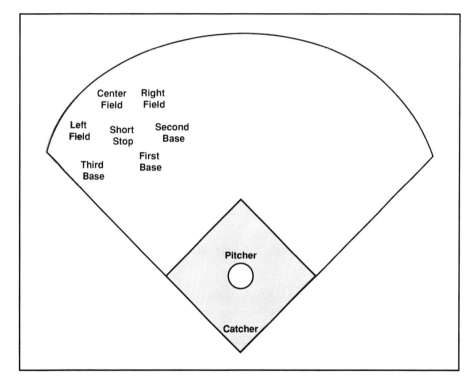

There's an obvious reason why coaches distribute their players all over the field: they have no way of knowing where the batter will hit the ball. With some players in the infield and some in the outfield, there is a good chance, as shown in Figure 2, of having someone in the right place to field the ball.

FIGURE 2

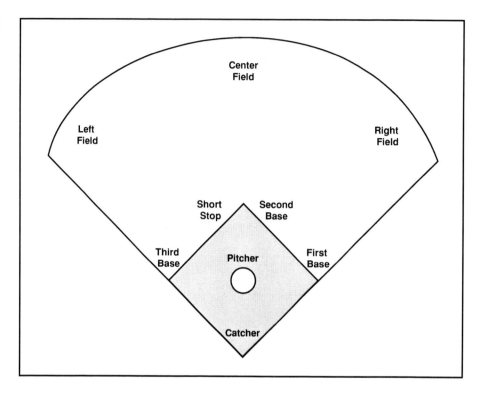

The stock and bond markets are much like a batter in a baseball game. When the batter steps up to the plate, nobody knows exactly where the ball is going to fly. Will the markets go up or down? Will interest rates rise or fall? Will the economy see expansion or recession? Will there be tax reforms? Will the nation experience a change in leadership? Will there be inflation? What will foreign economies do?

There is no way of knowing the answers to these questions with absolute certainty. In other words, you can't know exactly where the market is going to "hit the ball." You can try to project the future, but you can't guarantee an accurate prediction. However, if you have properly covered the field with your investments, you will be able to take advantage of market conditions, whatever they may be. It is crucial that you are properly diversified so that no matter what occurs in the market, some of your investments do well.

Did this hold true even during the bleak markets of 2000 and 2001? If your portfolio was properly diversified, then yes, you would have seen growth in some of your investments even during some of the worst stock market conditions in decades.

During 2000 and 2001, large company U.S. stocks, as measured by the Standard and Poors 500 Index, were down 9.10 percent and 11.88 percent, respectively. More aggressive U.S. companies, as measured by NASDAQ Index, fell -39.29 percent in 2000, and -21.05 percent in 2001. If you were diversified and owned bonds and value stocks in your portfolio during these two difficult years, you may have actually done very well. For example, mid-cap value stocks rose 24.91 percent in 2000, and 7.10 percent in 2001;[1] small cap value stocks increased by 23.21 percent and 10.06 percent;[2] long-term U.S. government bonds climbed 20.28 percent and 4.34 percent;[3] and municipal bonds grew 11.69 percent and 5.08 percent.[4]

Although baseball coaches would never consider the thought of positioning all their players in left field, many investors make this very mistake, often failing to properly diversify their portfolios, leaving many bases uncovered and portions of the investment field entirely vacant. Too often, investment portfolios are positioned like the team in Figure 1. This was certainly the case in 2000 and 2001. Many investors accumulated a long list of investments in 1998 and 1999, only to find out that every investment they owned was concentrated in one or two asset classes, typically large and mid-sized company growth stocks. Many technology stocks fell into these categories. This strategy worked fine in 1998 and 1999, when the market routinely enjoyed good performance, whacking the ball to these two areas of the growth market. However, in 2000 and 2001, the market changed directions and hit the ball the other way, to value stocks and bonds. Investors who didn't own value stocks and bonds experienced dramatic losses.

Many investors get confused about what it means to be properly diversified, falsely believing that diversification can be achieved by owning ten different stocks or mutual funds. This, however, doesn't guarantee true diversification. For example, it is possible to own ten or more mutual funds and still end up with a portfolio that looks like the baseball team in Figure 1, if each fund buys the same types of stocks or bonds.

For example, how diversified is a portfolio that holds ten funds, each of which invests the majority of their assets in high-tech growth stocks? If this particular part of the market does well, the investor feels like he hit a home run; if it does poorly, the portfolio suffers dramatically. Many technology fund investors felt this way in 1999 when the average technology fund rose over 134 percent. A $100,000 investment made on January 1, 1999, grew to $234,680 by year-end; that would definitely be considered a grand slam. However, in 2000 and 2001, this sector of the market came plummeting back to earth, losing 32 percent and 38 percent, respectively[5]. The portfolio that grew so quickly to $234,680, nose-dived below the original amount invested, finishing at $98,714. This inconsistency and unusually high volatility often leads to frequent portfolio changes and ultimately poor returns.

Why is diversification so important to successful long-term investing? Here are three major reasons why it is so vital:

1) Lowers portfolio risk by reducing volatility.
2) Protects the overall portfolio from one or two poor performing investments.
3) Provides investors with more consistent returns and helps them stay invested for the long-term.

Diversification allows you to purchase investments that alone may be very volatile, but when combined with other investments, reduces the volatility of the portfolio as a whole.

> *In essence, diversification is a way of covering the entire field to make sure all of those hits get caught.*

Lowering Portfolio Risk By Reducing Volatility

Compare the two hypothetical investments in Figures 3 and 4. Assuming the two investments experience the ups and downs depicted in the charts and over time both provide an average annual return of 10 percent, which would you choose? As you can see, regardless of the investment you select, an investment of $100,000 would grow to $259,274. Notice, however, that although the average return for each investment is identical over the long run, Investment A and Investment B experienced ups and downs at different times.

FIGURE 3

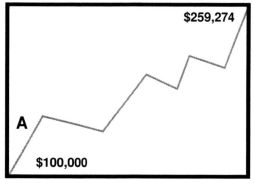

$259,274

A

$100,000

FIGURE 4

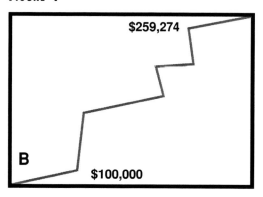

$259,274

B

$100,000

Let's say, however, that you split your investment — moving $50,000 from Investment A over to B, or vice versa (see Figure 5). Your $100,000 would still grow to $259,274 in ten years. However, from year to year, your performance would be much more consistent. In fact, in this example the overall portfolio would never encounter a down year. In years when one investment does poorly, the other picks up the slack. They have what is called a "lead-and-lag" relationship. The key to developing a portfolio that reduces volatility is to buy investments that complement each other as Investment A and B do in Figure 5. Diversification reduces portfolio volatility.

FIGURE 5

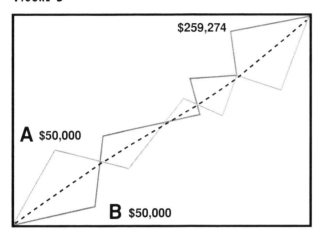

$259,274

A $50,000

B $50,000

PROTECTING YOUR PORTFOLIO FROM THE RISK OF A BAD INVESTMENT CHOICE

One or two bad investment decisions could dramatically reduce the returns of your overall portfolio. Diversification will protect you from this possibility.

Edward, a 45-year-old pre-retiree, recently decided to invest $100,000. He is not going to retire for 20 years. At that time, he plans to start withdrawing money from his portfolio. He decides to diversify the $100,000 into five investments equally. Unfortunately, Edward made a couple of poor investment decisions. Figure 6 shows his results.

Although Edward didn't hit a home run, his portfolio still produced a respectable 8.74 percent return even though three of the five investments performed very poorly. Edward could have taken a big swing, invested

FIGURE 6

5 Equal Investments	Value After 20 Years
Investment #1: $20,000 loses 100%	$0
Investment #2: $20,000 breaks even	$20,000
Investment #3: $20,000 gains 5% per year	$53,066
Investment #4: $20,000 10% per year	$134,550
Investment #5: $20,000 15% per year	$327,330
Total Initial Investment	$100,000
Total After 10 Years	$534,946
Compounded Annual Rate of Return	8.74%

all of his money in one or two investments and hoped for much better returns. He could have guessed right and ended up with an average annual return of 10-15 percent; if he guessed wrong however, he would have been stuck with growth of 5 percent or even less.

Diversification protected Edward from the risk that comes with having a majority of his assets in losing investments. If he had placed all his money in poor-performing investments, his portfolio at retirement, instead of being valued at $534,946, could have been worthless. Poor diversification often occurs with recently retired investors who have the bulk of their money invested in their former company's stock. This is not a good risk to take with money you are relying upon for retirement. Handling company stock will be discussed in Chapter 16.

Let's take a look at another example. Linda retired from her company in June 1999. At retirement, she had over $1 million invested in her former employer's stock. In the past, the company had generated good results, helping Linda accumulate a substantial sum for retirement. At retirement she had to choose between leaving the shares alone in hopes of similar returns in the future, or selling some or all of the shares in order to diversify her portfolio. She made the decision to diversify, realizing that a drop in her employer's stock could keep her from accomplishing her retirement goals.

Linda's decision was a good one. Shortly after retirement, the market went south and her company's stock dropped from a high of $53 in June 1999, to $11 in February 2002, a price drop of 79 percent. Although the diversified portfolio she chose did suffer a 15 percent drop during this same period, this loss won't stop her from accomplishing her retirement goals. In fact, a 15 percent loss is very likely to be quickly recovered in the next bull market. A 79 percent loss, however, would require growth of an almost impossible 385 percent for her to break even.

If your portfolio loses 20 percent of its value, how much does it need to earn to get back to even? It seems logical that 20 percent of growth would offset a 20 percent loss; this is not the case, however. For example, if a $100,000 portfolio dropped 20 percent to $80,000, it would require a 25 percent gain to get back to $100,000 ($20,000 is 25 percent of $80,000). If the same portfolio dropped 50 percent to $50,000, it would require a 100 percent return to climb back up to $100,000.

IMPORTANCE OF PERFORMANCE CONSISTENCY

How important is performance consistency? We can best determine that by studying the following examples of Grant and Ann, two people who each have

FIGURE 7

Performance Results For Grant

Year 1	20%
Year 2	40%
Year 3	20%
Year 4	-50%
Year 5	40%
Five-Year Average Annual Return	14%

$100,000 to invest. After reviewing the returns each achieved in Figures 7 and 8, who do you believe will accumulate the most money over the five-year period?

Profile of Investor One: Grant

Grant is an aggressive investor whose goal is to take advantage of the big moves in the market. All of Grant's money is concentrated in one sector of the stock market. Consequently, he experiences very high "highs" and very low "lows." Figure 7 illustrates his results over the past five years.

Profile of Investor Two: Ann

Ann is a moderate investor whose goal is to obtain good, consistent returns. She has split her money into two different investments. Each investment moves in a typical cycle of ups and downs. The two investments, however, have a "zig-zag" relationship. When one is zigging, the other is zagging. The net result is consistent performance. Her diversified portfolio does not produce returns as high as Grant's, but it doesn't drop as low as his does either. Figure 8 illustrates Ann's results.

Who experienced better performance, Grant or Ann? Whose results would you rather have? Not only did Ann's portfolio perform much better (see the results in Figure 9), but her portfolio was also far less volatile than Grant's. One also can't help but wonder how many bad decisions Grant made due to the additional volatil-

FIGURE 8

Performance Results For Ann

Year 1	9%
Year 2	9%
Year 3	9%
Year 4	9%
Year 5	9%
Five-Year Average Annual Return	9%

ity in his quest to capture the big moves. Higher returns coupled with lower risk is the magic combination that every investor should seek. This can often be accomplished with proper diversification. It is interesting that Grant's average annual return was 14 percent, compared to Ann's 9 percent (add up the returns for each year and divide by five). Ann's actual compounded annual rate of return was 2 percent higher than Grant's. Don't be misled by average annual rates of return; *consistency is the key*.

FIGURE 9

Initial Investment of $100,000				
Investor: Ann			Investor: Grant	
Year	%change	Dollar Value	% Change	Dollar Value
1	9%	$109,000	20%	$120,000
2	9%	$118,810	40%	$168,000
3	9%	$129,502	20%	$201,600
4	9%	$141,158	-50%	$100,800
5	9%	$153,863	40%	$141,120

In this chapter, we have discussed the vital importance of having a properly diversified portfolio so that no matter what occurs in the market, some of your investments will perform well. As we continue our discussion on Step 2 in the following chapter, the various components of a well diversified portfolio will be outlined.

CHAPTER 10
STEP TWO (CONTINUED): COMPONENTS OF DIVERSIFICATION

In order to properly diversify, it is important to understand each asset class and how each has performed historically in relation to the others. Once you understand each investment's playing abilities, you will be better equipped to position them to your portfolio's advantage.

Figure 1 illustrates the components of a well-diversified investment portfolio. Remember that like the fielders on a baseball team, each asset class covers a different part of the market field. Some of your money should be invested in each asset class.

FIGURE 1

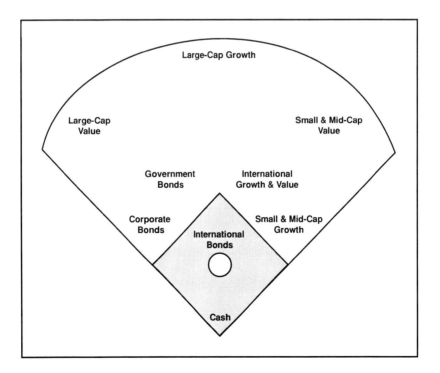

STOCK SIZE

Stocks can be sub-categorized as large-cap, mid-cap, or small-cap. A stock's size is determined by its market capitalization. Capitalization is the price of a stock multiplied by the number of outstanding shares. For example, a stock that is priced at $50 per share with 100 million shares outstanding would have a market capitalization of $5 billion.

WHICH ASSETS HAVE PROVIDED THE BEST RETURNS: LARGE-, MID-, OR SMALL-CAP STOCKS?

Over the long run, small- and mid-cap stocks have outperformed large-cap stocks. From 1926 through 2000, small company stocks had an average annual return of 12.6 percent, while large company stocks returned 11 percent.[6] Large companies tend to hold up better in market downturns due to their financial strength and stability. Although small- and mid-sized company stocks offer more potential growth, they also possess more potential for loss — to obtain higher returns, you must be willing to endure more risk.

While smaller stocks have provided higher returns than larger stocks over the long term, don't be fooled into thinking this is a consistent rule. During some periods, large-caps have outperformed their small- and mid-cap counterparts. Because there are no hard and fast rules to indicate which size will perform best in the future, it is important to diversify your portfolio and own an array of large-, mid- and small-cap stocks.

Figure 2 shows the performance associated with large-, mid- and small-cap stocks for the last five-, ten- and fifteen-year periods (ending December 2001). Mid-cap stocks were the best performing asset for the last five and fifteen years while large-cap stocks led the way during the last ten years.

FIGURE 2

Category	5-Year Average Return	10-Year Average Return	15-Year Average Return
Large-Cap Growth	8.75%	16.61%	12.74%
Large-Cap Value	9.01%	13.07%	13.12%
Mid-Cap Growth	8.97%	11.14%	12.45%
Mid-Cap Value	12.49%	15.01%	14.06%
Small-Cap Growth	3.76%	8.19%	9.25%
Small-Cap Value	10.73%	15.13%	12.94%

Wilshire market indexes were used to measure each asset class.
Source: Morningstar Principia Pro, December 31, 2001

LARGE U.S STOCKS

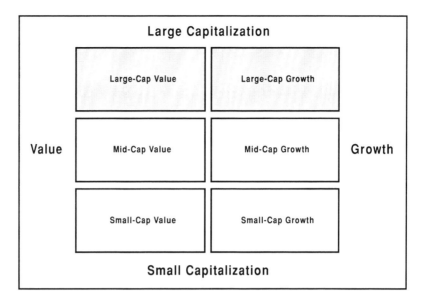

Large capitalization U.S. stocks are usually defined as companies with market capitalizations of over $10 billion. The market capitalization for the average large-cap U.S. stock mutual fund is $40.24 billion. The largest U.S. company stocks with their respective market capitalizations are listed in Figure 3.

FIGURE 3

Company	Symbol	Industry	Market Capitalization
General Electric	GE	Electric Equipment	$371 billion
Microsoft	MSFT	Software	$326 billion
ExxonMobil	XOM	Oil/Gas	$299 billion
Wal-Mart Stores	WMT	Department Stores	$273 billion
Citigroup	C	Banks	$254 billion
Pfizer	PFE	Pharmaceuticals	$250 billion
Intel	INTC	Semiconductors	$203 billion
Johnson & Johnson	JNJ	Household Products	$197 billion
International Business Mac.	IBM	Computer Equipment	$179 billion

Source: Morningstar Principia Pro, December 31, 2001

MID-CAP U.S. STOCKS

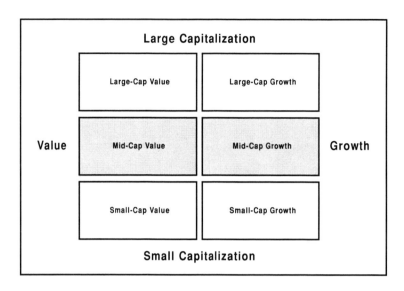

Mid-cap U.S. stocks are defined as companies with market capitalizations usually between $1.5 billion and $10 billion. The market capitalization for the average mid-cap U.S. stock fund is $6.075 billion. Examples of mid-cap U.S. stocks with their respective market caps are listed in Figure 4.

FIGURE 4

Company	Symbol	Industry	Market Capitalization
Bed Bath & Beyond	BBBY	Furniture Retail	$9.8 billion
Staples	SPLS	Stores	$9.2 billion
Principal Financial Group	PFG	Insurance	$9.1 billion
Mattel	MAT	Toys	$8.9 billion
Apple Computer	AAPL	Computer Equipment	$8.3 billion
H&R Block	HRB	Business Services	$8.1 billion
Washington Post	WPO	Publishing	$5.7 billion
T.Rowe Price	TROW	Money Management	$4.7 billion
Goodyear Tire & Rubber	GT	Rubber Products	$4.1 billion
Blockbuster	BBI	Rental	$4.1 billion

Source: Morningstar Principia Pro, December 31, 2001

SMALL U.S. STOCKS

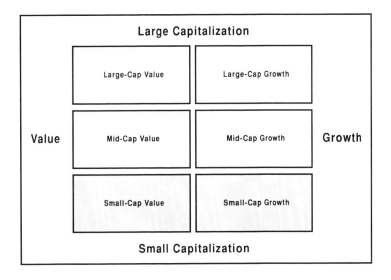

Small-cap U.S. stocks are defined as companies with market capitalizations below $1.5 billion. The market capitalization for the average small-cap U.S. stock fund is $986 million. Examples of small-cap U.S. company stocks with their respective market caps are shown in Figure 5.

FIGURE 5

Company	Symbol	Industry	Market Capitalization
Circuit City Group	CC	Furniture Retail	$3.7 billion
Callaway Golf	ELY	Stores	$1.4 billion
Ameritrade Holding A	AMTD	Insurance	$1.4 billion
Payless Shoe Source	PSS	Toys	$1.3 billion
Applebee's International	APPB	Computer Equipment	$1.3 billion
Land's End	LE	Business Services	$1.3 billion
Priceline.com	PCLN	Publishing	$1.1 billion
7-Eleven	SE	Money Management	$1.1 billion
Sylvan Learning Systems	SLVN	Rubber Products	$1.0 billion
Red Hat	RHAT	Rental	$965 million

Source: Morningstar Principa Pro, December 31, 2001

INVESTMENT STYLES — GROWTH AND VALUE

Individual stocks or stock mutual funds, whether large-, mid-, or small-cap can be further classified as either growth stocks or value stocks. This is an important distinction because growth and value stocks have proven to have a lead and lag relationship over time (see Figure 6). If your portfolio contains both types of stocks, you can reduce your overall portfolio risk and volatility.

FIGURE 6

Year	Growth	Value	Winning Style
1979	15.72%	23.16%	Value
1980	39.40%	23.59%	Growth
1981	-9.81%	.02%	Value
1982	22.03%	21.04%	Growth
1983	16.24%	28.89%	Value
1984	2.33%	10.52%	Value
1985	33.31%	29.68%	Growth
1986	14.50%	21.67%	Value
1987	6.50%	3.68%	Growth
1988	11.95%	21.67%	Value
1989	36.40%	26.13%	Growth
1990	.20%	-6.85%	Growth
1991	38.37%	22.56%	Growth
1992	5.07%	10.53%	Value
1993	1.68%	18.60%	Value
1994	3.13%	-.63%	Growth
1995	38.13%	37.00%	Growth
1996	23.98%	21.99%	Growth
1997	36.38%	29.99%	Growth
1998	42.15%	14.68%	Growth
1999	28.25%	12.72%	Growth
2000	-22.08%	6.08%	Value
2001	-12.72%	-11.71%	Value
2002	23.59%	-20.85%	Value

Source: S&P 500/ Barra Growth Index and S&P 500 Barra Value Index

GROWTH STOCKS

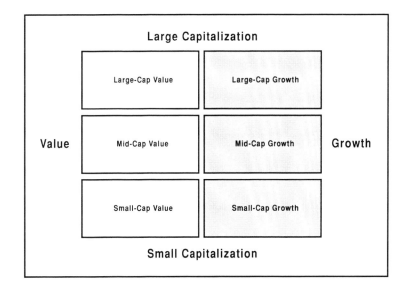

Buying a growth stock is similar to shopping at a trendy store and purchasing fashions that are currently in vogue. Because these items are in such high demand, you will be required to pay "up" for them — maybe even more than they are worth.

Growth stocks are typically in high demand due to their high earnings growth rates and their tendency to outperform the market when the economy is strong and robust. Because of investor demand, prices are often bid up to astronomical levels, as occurred in 1998 and 1999. Growth investors buy high in hopes that the company's earnings momentum will carry the price even higher. However, when the stock market falters, growth stocks tend to fall harder than their value stock equivalents because of their high prices. Conversely, in strong bull markets growth stocks usually outperform value stocks. For example, the American Century Ultra fund, one of the largest large-cap, U.S. growth funds, posted a 32.09 percent return during its best 3-month period and a dismal –22.86 percent during its worst 3-month stretch of the past ten years. By comparison, the Vanguard Windsor II fund, one of the largest U.S. large-cap value funds finished its best 3-month period up 18.57 percent, and its worst down at only –15.64 percent.

There are many technical measurements to help investors identify growth stocks, the most common being high P/E ratios (stock price divided by the previous 12 month's earnings per share) and higher projected earnings growth rates. The P/E ratio measures how much investors are willing to pay for each dollar of profit (earnings). Other characteristics to look for are high price-to-sales ratios and high price-to-book ratios. Growth companies typically pay no or low dividends. For example, in December of 2001, the average large company growth mutual fund had the following technical measurements:

FIGURE 7

Technical Measure of the Average Large Company Growth Mutual Fund	
Price-to-Earnings Ratio (P/E): stock price divided by earnings per share:	35.5
Price-to-Cash Flow Ration: stock price divided by the amount of cash generated per share by a company's operations:	22.7
Price-to-Book Ratio: Stock's price divided by the company's per share book value:	6.4
Three-year earnings growth rate:	21.3
Beta is a measurement of volatility. The beta of the overall market equals 1:	1.2
Ten-year standard deviation:	21.3

Source: Morningstar Principia Pro, December 31, 2001

Following are some examples of individual, large company growth stocks and their P/E's and yields:

FIGURE 8

Company	P/E	Yield
Microsoft	55.3	0%
Johnson & Johnson	35.3	1.4%
Intel	160.1	.4%
Pfizer	32.6	1.4%
Home Depot	37.7	.5%
Cisco Systems	93.0	0%

June 30, 2002

VALUE STOCKS

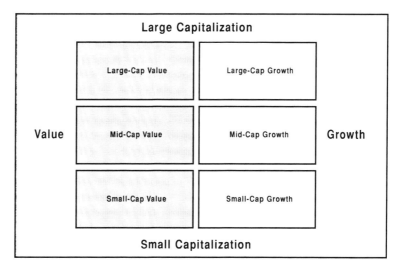

Like growth stocks, buying value stocks is similar to shopping at your favorite store. In this case, though, instead of buying the high-priced, trendy items, you're sifting through the discount racks and purchasing only items that are marked down. Value companies are considered "on-sale" in the stock market because they have temporarily fallen out of favor and sell for less than their true value. Their prices are low because of their relative standing in categories like earnings, book values, and sales. These companies are often located in industries that have fallen out of favor or have profitability or management problems. Investors who buy value stocks buy low, patiently wait, and hope the company rebounds.

Because value stocks are already trading at lower prices, there is less room to fall if the stock market turns sour. Value companies usually pay dividends. In December of 2001, the average large company value mutual fund had the following technical measurements:

FIGURE 9

Technical Measure of the Average Large Company Value Mutual Fund	
Price-to-Earnings Ratio (P/E): stock price divided by earnings per share:	25
Price-to-Cash Flow Ration: stock price divided by the amount of cash generated per share by a company's operations:	13.8
Price-to-Book Ratio: Stock's price divided by the company's per share book value:	4.1
Three-year earnings growth rate:	14.8
Beta is a measurement of volatility. The beta of overall market equals 1:	.7
Ten-year standard deviation:	14.4

Source: Morningstar Principia Pro, December 31, 2001

Figure 10 offers examples of individual large company value stocks and their respective P/E's and yields:

FIGURE 10

Company	P/E	Yield %
Washington Mutual	9.2	2.6
Bank One	18.7	2.0
Phillip Morris	13.6	4.3
Union Pacific	16.5	1.3
MBIA	14.3	1.1
Bank of America	13.7	3.4

June 30, 2002

WHICH STYLE IS BETTER?

Although the performance for growth and value stocks has been dramatically different from year to year, over the long-term they have both provided approximately the same returns. Statistics bear this out.

A $10,000 investment in large U.S. company growth stocks made on December 31, 1978, grew to $265,936 by the end of 2000.[8] Similarly, a $10,000 investment made into large U.S. company value stocks[9] over the same period grew to $287,167. The average compounded rate of return of growth stocks was 16.08 percent, while value stocks grew at 16.48 percent. Although the investment performance was about the same, growth stocks experienced more volatility than value stocks.

There is no crystal ball to predict exactly when growth stocks will be in favor and value stocks out of favor. Rather than making futile attempts at guessing, it is better to have a portfolio balanced between both styles (this is referred to as "style neutral"). A well-diversified stock portfolio will be balanced between growth and value stocks in each asset class: large-, mid-, and small-cap U.S. stocks, as well as international stocks.

Let's compare two hypothetical investors to examine how growth and value stocks can compliment each other and reduce volatility. On January 1, 1990, Gene invested $100,000 into large U.S. company growth stocks. By the end of 2001, 12 years later, the $100,000 had grown in value to $401,482 (see Figure 11). That doesn't sound too bad, does it? However, notice the extreme volatility Gene experienced when the markets fell in 2000 and 2001. He watched his portfolio drop from a high mark of $671,981, the value at the end of 1999, to $401,482. That represents a loss of $270,499 or 40.25 percent. Although large U.S. company growth stocks were the single best performing asset class for this 12-year period, not many investors could sustain a loss of this magnitude and continue to adhere to a long-term investment strategy. Many investors shaken by market downturns sell when the market is near bottom levels and don't regain enough confidence to return until it is reaching new highs again. Sound familiar? It's called buying high and selling low.

FIGURE 11

Gene Howard's Portfolio: 100% Large-Cap Growth

Year	Weighted Average Return	Growth of $100,000
1990	.34%	$100,340
1991	46.62%	$147,119
1992	5.93%	$155,843
1993	-.54%	$155,001
1994	2.97%	$159,605
1995	37.88%	$220,063
1996	19.08%	$262,051
1997	31.38%	$344,282
1998	42.21%	$489,604
1999	37.25%	$671,981
2000	-24.98%	$504,121
2001	-20.36%	$401,482

Average Annual Return	14.82%
Average Compounded Rate of Return	12.28%
Number of negative years	3
Percent of years negative	25%
Worst Year	-24.98%
Number of positive years	9
Percent of years positive	75%
Best Year	46.62%

Source: Wilshire Large Growth Index

Now let's look at our second hypothetical investor, Renee, who followed a different strategy during the same time frame.

Renee invested 50 percent of her money into large U.S. company growth stocks and 50 percent into large U.S. company value stocks. She experienced about the same amount of growth but did so with much less volatility (see Figure 12). Her balanced growth and value portfolio also dropped from its high water mark of $530,644 at the end of 1999, to an ending value of $400,604, at the end of 2001. This

FIGURE 12

Renee William's Blended Portfolio:		
Large-Cap U.S. Growth Stocks	50%	
Large-Cap U.S. Value Stocks	50%	

Year	Weighted Average Return	Growth of $100,000
1990	-3.63%	$100,000
1991	36.13%	$96.375
1992	10.16%	$131,195
1993	6.46%	$144,525
1994	.69%	$153,854
1995	40.68%	$152,800
1996	23.02%	$214,951
1997	32.54%	$264,422
1998	26.73%	$350,452
1999	19.48%	$444,128
2000	-11.95%	$530,259
2001	-14.27%	$400,604

Performance from 1/1/1990 - 12/31/2001 (12 Years)

Average Annual Return	13.72%
Average Compounded Rate of Return	12.26%
Number of negative years	4
Percent of years negative	33%
Worst Year	-14.27%
Number of positive years	8
Percent of years positive	67%
Best Year	40.68%

Note: Assumes portfolio is rebalanced annually
Source: Wilshire Large Growth Index and Wilshire Large Value Index

represents a $130,040 loss or 24.51 percent, compared to the 40.25 percent drop in Gene's growth portfolio. Who is more likely to adhere to their investment strategy? Chances are it will be Renee, who had comparably more stability.

INTERNATIONAL INVESTING

International stocks are also a key ingredient of a well-diversified portfolio, but investors too often overlook their benefits. Most portfolios should contain international exposure of between 5-20 percent. There are several important reasons not to overlook the international component of your portfolio:

- Investing in foreign stocks can provide an extra layer of diversification, reducing volatility while increasing your overall portfolio returns.

- Many foreign economies are growing much faster than the U.S. economy. By investing in these markets, you can often enhance your returns. Historically, international markets have provided better returns than the U.S. market.

- As a consumer, each day you purchase products and services manufactured by international companies. Perhaps without even realizing it, you are boosting the profitability of many international companies.

- Foreign market opportunities are growing as capitalism spreads throughout the world.

International Investing Adds More Diversification

An extra layer of diversification can reduce your portfolio volatility and increase your returns. International stocks, like the different styles of U.S. stocks discussed earlier in this chapter, go through cycles of ups and downs. If international stocks are doing well and the U.S. market is struggling, the international portion of your portfolio will help offset the U.S. downturn and lower your portfolio's volatility. In other words, international stocks provide another potential "zigging" investment when other parts of your portfolio may be "zagging."

We've seen this principle played out over the past 30 years. In the 1970s and 1980s, the foreign stock markets outperformed the U.S. market. By owning international stocks during those two decades, you would have increased your portfolio returns. However, in the 1990s, the investment winds changed, as they often do, and the U.S. market dominated the global equities marketplace (see Figure 13).

Again, because there is no way of knowing exactly when one market will take off and another will falter, it is simply best to buy and hold both U.S. and foreign-based assets. You will enjoy more consistent long-term performance by diversifying rather than trying to supercharge your performance through attempts to be in the hottest market at just the right time.

FIGURE 13

U.S. Stocks Versus International Stocks	
1970-1979 (10 years)	**Cumulative Return**
U.S. Market (S&P 500)	77%
Major International Markets (EAFE)	162%
1980-1989 (10 years)	**Cumulative Return**
U.S. Market (S&P 500)	400%
Major International Markets (EAFE)	678%
1/1/1990-12/21/2000 (11 years)	**Cumulative Return**
U.S. Market (S&P 500)	424%
Major International Market (EAFE)	89%

Better Performance

Virtually every year, the U.S. stock market is surpassed in performance by a foreign market. In fact, take a guess at how many times during the last 18 years the U.S. stock market was the best performing market in the world. The answer, surprisingly, is zero. The United States finished in second place twice during the past 18 years (1995 and 1997).

Figure 14 shows the top performing markets each year from 1983 through 2000. The lesson is clear: By participating in international markets, you can potentially boost your portfolio returns.

Our Consumer Purchases

Another reason to own international stocks is because Americans — all of us — are making foreign companies more profitable each day through our consumer purchasing habits. If you examine your daily purchases, you will find that you buy many products produced by overseas companies. Your daily spending is making foreign companies more profitable. It makes sense

FIGURE 14

The Best Performing Markets in the World 1983-2000			
Year	Market	Return	U.S. Market Return
1983	Australia	56%	23%
1984	Hong Kong	47%	3%
1985	Germany	137%	32%
1986	Japan	100%	17%
1987	Japan	43%	2%
1988	France	39%	18%
1989	Germany	47%	29%
1990	United Kingdom	10%	-5%
1991	Hong Kong	50%	34%
1992	Hong Kong	32%	10%
1993	Hong Kong	117%	11%
1994	Finland	52%	.2%
1995	Switzerland	44%	37%
1996	Spain	40%	22%
1997	Portugal	47%	32%
1998	Finland	122%	24%
1999	Finland	153%	21%
2000	Switzerland	6%	-8%

Source: Return Represented by MSCI Country Index

to participate in that profitability by owning some shares of foreign companies.

For instance, this may be a typical day for you if you are an average American soccer mom:

> *It's Saturday and you have a big day ahead. While drinking some* Quik *chocolate milk for breakfast, you feed the baby some* Gerber *baby food. After throwing on a* Benetton *outfit and your favorite* Fila *tennis shoes, you quickly grab the* Aquafresh *toothpaste and brush your teeth. Even though it's Saturday, you opt for a little* Maybelline *make-up. Finally before leaving the house, you struggle to pull the kids away from the* Nintendo *game they are playing on your* Pioneer *projection TV. Everyone piles into the* Jeep Cherokee *and off you go. Before you can pick your husband up at the airport, you've got to get some gas at the nearby* Shell *station. While in route the kids play on their* Game Boy *and you call your sister on your* Vodafone *cell phone and make plans for an upcoming family party. An hour later you find your husband, a stockbroker for* PaineWebber, *waiting at the airport thumbing through some* Alliance *mutual fund reports and crunching a few numbers on his* Sharp *calculator. After spending the week in business meetings and creating reports on his* Packard Bell *laptop, he's ready for a break.*
>
> *With the family reunited, there's just enough time for a quick bite. The kids want a burger at* Burger King *but are quickly talked out of it when you mention there is a* Hard Rock Café *on the way to the* Los Angeles Dodger *game. After the game you make a stop at* 7-Eleven *for a Slurpee and pick up a video. With the kids in bed, you and your husband are ready to wind down while watching a* Columbia TriStar *movie on your* Magnavox *VCR.*

Taking advantage of a number of tried and true American companies, right? Wrong. If you have used any of the products or services listed above, you have actually helped the profitability of a foreign company (Figure 15). Why not own some of these companies (outright or through a mutual fund) and participate in that profitability?

Expansion of Foreign Equity Markets

In the past, the majority of all global stock market opportunities, as measured by total market capitalization, existed in the United States. For example, in 1970,

FIGURE 15

Product	Parent Company	Country
Quik Chocolate Milk	Nestle	Switzerland
Gerber	Novartis	Switzerland
Benetton	Benetton Group	Italy
Fila	Fila Holding Sp.	Italy
Aquafresh	GlaxoSmithKline	United Kingdom
Maybelline	L'Oreal	France
Nintendo	Nintendo	Japan
Pioneer	Pioneer Electronic	Japan
Jeep Cherokee	Daimler Chrysler	Germany
Shell	Royal Dutch Petroleum	Netherlands
Game Boy	Nintendo	Japan
Vodafone	Vodafone	United Kingdom
Paine Webber	UBS	Switzerland
Alliance Funds	AXA	France
Sharp	Sharp	Japan
Packard Bell	NEC	Japan
Burger King	Diageo PLC	United Kingdom
Hard Rock Cafe	Rank Group	United Kingdom
Los Angeles Dodgers	News Corporation*	Australia
7-Eleven	Ito-Yokado	Japan
Columbia TriStar	Sony	Japan
Magnovox	Philips Electronics	Netherlands

* part owner of the Los Angeles Dodgers

66 percent of the global equity opportunities were found in the U.S., while only 34 percent were in foreign markets. The total market cap in 1970 was $850 billion. This has dramatically changed. In 2000, only 52 percent of the global opportunities were found in the U.S. with 48 percent being located overseas. The total market cap of the world equity markets in 2000 increased to over $20 trillion.

Developed or Emerging Markets

International stocks are further categorized by size (large and small) and style (growth and value) similar to domestic stocks as previously discussed. In addition, foreign stocks can be sub-categorized by the maturity of the international market. Overseas stocks are either located in mature stable markets or in developing emerging markets. Our discussion about the international markets up to this point has revolved around the developed markets of the world. Some consideration, however, also must be given to the worlds emerging markets.

There are many markets located in countries such as Asia, Latin America and Eastern Europe that are considered "emerging" because their economies are in the beginning stages of development. There is, of course, more risk when investing in these countries, but there is also more upside potential when the emerging markets take off. The room for growth in these economies is the attractive feature about investing in these markets. It may be hard to believe, but the United States was once considered an emerging country. There well may be future economic powers that have not yet popped up on the radar screen.

Less-developed countries have tremendous potential for growth. As the global standard of living improves, millions of people will have more money to spend. As spending increases, financial markets are driven upward. As more people in these emerging countries buy basic items like telephones, televisions and computers, the companies providing these services will likely do very well. Consider the statistics in Figure 16 outlining the number of telephone lines, televisions and computers per 100 people in various countries and how much room there is for future growth.

FIGURE 16

Country	Telephone Lines	Televisions	Computers
United States	59.5	79	29.7
Hungary	17.0	42	3.4
Greece	47.8	22	2.9
Argentina	14.1	38	1.7
Russia	16.2	38	1.0
Brazil	7.4	29	.92
South Africa	9.5	10	.2
China	2.3	23	.2
India	1.1	5	.1

Source: World Telecommunications Development Report, 1994

BONDS

Most investors, with the possible exception of young people in their 20's and early 30's, should own some bonds. Bonds provide diversification and a cushion to soften the blow of a falling stock market. This is important particularly if you are a retiree, since you will not have as much time to make up for sharp market losses.

While stocks represent a piece of ownership in a company, bonds simply represent the outstanding debt of a company. If you purchase a bond, you are loaning money to the issuer, which could be a corporation, a municipality or a government entity. In return, the bond's issuer promises to pay you interest and to repay your principal at a stated maturity date. For example, if you bought a 10-year bond yielding 8 percent, you would loan the issuer $1,000 and the issuer would promise to repay you the $1,000 at maturity and pay you $80 of interest each year along the way (see Figure 17). The promise to repay your principal with interest is as sound as the institution that issued the bond.

Like stocks, there are several types of bonds, each with differences in categories such as credit ratings, maturities and yields. However, most bonds share some

 FIGURE 17

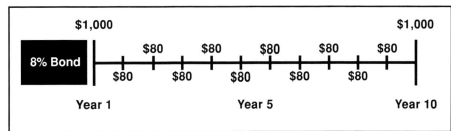

common characteristics. First of all, when interest rates go up, bond prices fall. Conversely, when rates fall, bond prices increase (see Figure 18). Secondly, longer-term bonds are more volatile than shorter-term bonds. Thirdly, bonds issued by lower-quality companies pay higher yields than those issued by high-quality companies.

FIGURE 18

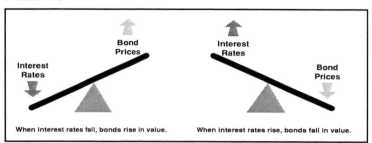

INTEREST RATES & BOND PRICES

The easiest way to understand the relationship between movements in interest rates and bond prices is to consider an individual bond. Let's assume on January 1, 1990, you invested $1,000 in a 10-year corporate bond maturing on December 31, 1999 with a yield of 8 percent. In this case, you would receive $80 per year for ten-years. At the end of ten years, you would receive your original investment of $1,000 back. The $80 of interest you receive each year and your return of principal ($1,000), if you hold the bond to maturity, are guaranteed by the underlying bond issuer, in this example a corporation.

Although the underlying bond issuer guarantees the interest (coupon) and principal, the value or price of your bond will fluctuate between now and when it matures. Price movements in bonds are largely due to changes in interest rates.

Let's continue with our example above and assume after owning the bond for five years that interest rates increase and newly issued bonds similar to yours are now paying much more interest.

If the rate increased by 2 percent an investor could buy a new bond

FIGURE 19

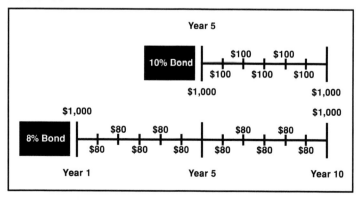

yielding 10 percent ($100/year interest). If the newly issued 10 percent bond matures at the same time as yours and has similar features, why would investors want to buy your 8 percent bond when they can buy a newly issued bond paying 10 percent (see Figure 19)? Obviously, investors wouldn't be interested in your 8 percent bond.

If you decided to go ahead and sell your bond in this higher interest rate environment, you would have to discount your bond (lower the price) to make it attractive to bond investors. Someone may buy your bond if you are willing to discount it by $76 and sell it for $924. A bond purchased for $924 paying $80 of interest per year and maturing in five years at $1,000 would be equivalent to a new five year bond paying $100 of interest each year (this assumes the bond type, maturity, and credit ratings are similar). Of course the opposite is true also. When interest rates fall, the value of outstanding bonds will go up for the same reasons. So remember, when buying bonds, if interest rates are climbing, bond prices will fall and if rates are falling bond prices will climb.

FIGURE 20

Value of a 10-Year bond being sold in year five (8% coupon)	
Interest Rate Change	Approximate Value of The Bond
Up 1%	$961
Up 2%	$924
Up 3%	$889
Up 4%	$855
Up 5%	$824
Down 1%	$1,041
Down 2%	$1,084
Down 3%	$1,130
Down 4%	$1,178
Down 5%	$1,228

Let's take our example one step further and examine the price movement of your bond as interest rates change. What would the value of your 8 percent bond be if rates are rising or falling? Figure 20 illustrates how rising and falling interest rates would impact the price of your 8 percent bond maturing in five years. The first column indicates how much rates have either increased or decreased since you purchased your bond. The second column outlines the change in the value of your bond as rates fluctuate. You will notice that the more interest rates either increase or decrease the more impact these rate fluctuations will have on the value of your bond.

Within each bond category, each type of bond can again be further classified as short-term (0-5 years), intermediate-term (5-10 years) or long-term (10 years plus). Bonds of different maturities react differently when rates go up and down. For example, if interest rates fall, the prices of long-term bonds will go up to a greater degree than short-term bonds. If rates rise, the opposite is true. Thus, there is more risk in owning longer-term bonds.

If you are planning to hold your bonds to maturity, the bond's issuer guarantees that you will receive your principal, the face value of the bond, back. If you are not planning to sell, the price fluctuations between now and maturity are irrelevant even though they will be reported on your brokerage statement. The price movements only become important if you are going to sell your bond prior to maturity.

Bond Ratings

Most bonds are rated. Bond ratings help investors determine the credit worthiness of the issuing company. Just as credit bureaus give you a credit score as an individual, bond-rating agencies give scores to companies. Those with little outstanding debt, a solid balance sheet and the ability to repay their debt obligations are given the highest credit ratings. To attract investors and to offset the additional risk, bonds issued by lower-quality companies must offer higher yields than those issued by high-quality companies. Changes in credit ratings will also cause the value of bonds to fluctuate. If a corporation's bond rating is downgraded, the value of the bond will generally fall. A rating upgrade will, of course, increase the bond's value. Bonds are rated as shown in Figures 21 and 22. There are two main bond-rating services: Moody's and Standard & Poors.

FIGURE 21

Moody's Bond Ratings	
Rating	**Description**
Aaa	Bonds of the highest quality.
Aa	Bonds of high quality.
A	Bonds whose security of principal and interest is considered adequate but may be impaired in the future.
Baa	Bonds of medium grade that are neither highly protected nor poorly secured.
Ba	Bonds of speculative quality whose future cannot be considered well assured.
B	Bond that lack characteristics of a desirable investment.
Caa	Bonds in poor standing that may be defaulted.
Ca	Speculative bonds that are often in default.
C	Bonds with poor prospects of any investment value (lowest rating).

Source: Moody's Bond Record, June 1995

Taxable and Tax-Free Bonds

Bonds are of two basic types: taxable and tax-free. Taxable bonds can be further separated into corporate, government (with the exception of Treasury Bonds) and international bonds. Tax-free bonds are issued by municipalities and offer interest that is not subject to federal income taxes. In some states, if you purchase a bond issued by the state, the interest is free from both state and federal taxes (double tax-free). Treasury bonds are exempt from state taxes.

To determine whether to buy taxable or tax-free bonds, compare the yields of each. In order to make an apples-to-apples comparison, yields must be compared after taxes are applied. Of course, tax-free bonds are not needed in a retirement account where all interest is already tax-deferred.

James, a bond investor in a 35 percent tax bracket, is considering buying one of the following: a taxable bond yielding 7.50 percent or a tax-free bond yielding only 5.50 percent. Of course, there are more factors to consider than just yield, but we'll keep this example simple and stick strictly to yields.

Before applying taxes, it looks as if the taxable bond provides the greatest yield. However, the interest on the taxable bond will be taxed while the tax-free bond will not. James must factor in his tax-bracket and determine how much a taxable bond would have to yield to be equivalent to the 5.50 percent tax-free bond. In James's tax bracket, which bond offers the best after-tax yield? The formula in Figure 23 will provide the answer:

FIGURE 22

Standard and Poor's Bond Ratings	
Rating	**Description**
AAA	Bonds of the highest quality.
AA	High-quality debt obligations.
A	Bonds that have a strong capacity to pay interest and principal but may be susceptible to adverse effects.
BBB	Bonds that have an adequate capacity to pay interest and principal but are more vulnerable to adverse economic conditions of changing circumstances.
BB	Bonds of lower medium grade with few desirable investment characteristics.
B	Primarily speculative bonds with great uncertainties and major risk if exposed to adverse conditions.
CCC	Primarily speculative bonds with great uncertainties and major risk if exposed to adverse conditions.
C	Income bonds on which no interest is being paid.
D	Bonds in default.

Source: Standard & Poor's Bond Guide, June 1995

FIGURE 23

Tax Equivalent Yield
Tax-Free Yield/(1-Investors Tax Bracket) = Equivalent Taxable Bond Yield .055/(1-.35) = 8.46%

By inputting the tax-free yield and his tax bracket, James can easily see that the tax-free bond would be the better investment. A taxable bond would have to yield over 8.46 percent to be superior to the tax-free yield of 5.50 percent in James' high tax bracket. Based on yield alone, James would be better off owning the tax-free bond.

Bond Diversification

The many types of bonds, with their varying issuers, credit ratings, maturities and yields all provide different rates of return from year to year. Like stocks, it is impossible to know exactly which types of bonds will be the best performing during the next 12 months. Because of this uncertainty, it is equally important to diversify your bond portfolio. Figures 24 and 25 highlight the performance of different types of bonds between 1991 and 2001.

FIGURE 24

Bond Performance				
Year	High Yield Bonds	Investment Grade Bonds	U.S. Government Bonds	Municipal Bonds	Money Markets
1991	40.22%	16.18%	14.63%	12.04%	5.82%
1992	18.36%	7.22%	6.10%	8.90%	3.45%
1993	19.84%	10.00%	8.32%	12.43%	2.72%
1994	-3.68%	-3.21%	-4.74%	-6.04%	3.74%
1995	17.38%	17.12%	16.94%	17.31%	5.53%
1996	12.98%	3.43%	2.16%	3.58%	5.01%
1997	13.17%	8.79%	9.12%	9.39%	5.14%
1998	-.07%	7.87%	7.84%	5.64%	5.10%
1999	4.78%	-.98%	-2.66%	-4.07%	4.74%
2000	-9.71%	10.58%	11.89%	11.10%	5.94%
2001	-1.04%	8.22%	6.67%	4.15%	3.80%

The returns of each asset class are represented by the flowing index: High yield bonds: Lipper High Yield Bond Funds Index, Investment Grape Bonds: Lipper Intermediate Investment Grade Funds Index, U.S. Government Bonds: Lipper General U.S. Government Funds Index, Muni Bonds: Lipper General Municipal Funds Index, Money Markets: Lipper Money Market Funds Index.

CASH

Cash equivalents are investments easily turned into cash without the risk of principal loss. This is called liquidity. Examples of cash equivalents include money market accounts, checking, savings, certificates of deposit, U.S. Treasury Bills and life insurance cash values. Cash investments can be an important component in a diversified portfolio due to their stability and consistent positive returns even during deep stock and bond market downturns. To locate the highest yielding cash investments from around the country or to compare cash investments at financial institutions in your area, visit *www.bankrate.com*.

Retirees and Cash

Some cash investments make sense for retirees. If you are a retiree and living off of your investments, consider maintaining one to three years of needed annual income in cash-type investments. This is your short-term money — money that you can use immediately to supplement your income. Because your time frame is shorter and you will be spending this money over the next one to three years, you should not put this money at risk in the stock or bond markets. If you keep a one- to three-year cash cushion in your portfolio, you can avoid having to liquidate stock and bond investments during market downturns. This added stability will help you maintain a disciplined investment strategy and keep your intermediate- and long-term money invested in the stock and bond markets. Too much cash in a portfolio, however, can hamper long-term performance and may ultimately keep you from reaching retirement goals.

FIGURE 25

Bond Rank From Best to Worst Performance Each Year from 1991 to 2001				
Year	High Yield Bonds	Investment Grade Bonds	U.S. Government Bonds	Municipal Bonds	Money Markets
1991	1	2	3	4	5
1992	1	3	4	2	5
1993	1	3	4	2	5
1994	3	2	4	5	1
1995	1	3	4	2	5
1996	1	4	5	3	2
1997	1	4	3	2	5
1998	5	1	2	3	4
1999	1	3	4	5	2
2000	5	3	1	2	4
2001	5	1	2	3	4

Young Investors and Cash

One of the biggest mistakes younger investors make is investing long-term money (i.e. retirement money) into low yielding investments (i.e. cash equivalents). In fact, investors in their 20's and 30's invest 14 percent[10] of their retirement savings into money market funds and guaranteed interest contracts. This can cost them substantial money over the long run.

Money in retirement accounts should be invested to provide the returns required to reach retirement goals. The returns on cash instruments will not accomplish this.

MARKET TIMING

Figure 26 lets you see at a glance how each asset class has performed annually for the past 12 years. As you review the chart, notice that each year there are several asset classes with a "zig-zag" relationship. Trying to choose the asset class that you think will perform the strongest during the upcoming year is a natural temptation. Don't trap yourself. Moving in and out of asset classes trying to find the "hot" investment is a mistake. This usually ends up hurting your overall performance. Decide on an appropriate asset allocation and diversification model and then adhere to it for the long-term.

FIGURE 26

Asset Class Performance 1990-2001

Year	Large Cap Growth	Large Cap Value	Mid Cap Growth	Mid Cap Value	Small Cap Growth	Small Cap Value	Int'l Stock	Corporate Bonds	U.S. Gov't Bonds	Municipal Bonds	Int'l Bonds	Cash
1990	.34%	-7.59%	-7.90%	-15.97%	-19.02%	-19.39%	-23.45%	6.48%	6.29%	7.30%	15.29%	7.52%
1991	46.62%	25.64%	44.07%	39.68%	56.80%	49.00%	12.12%	20.98%	18.68%	12.15%	16.24%	5.68%
1992	4.48%	11.14%	7.26%	21.05%	8.50%	29.95%	-12.17%	9.34%	8.09%	8.82%	4.77%	3.59%
1993	3.26%	16.95%	15.11%	15.93%	15.91%	22.10%	32.57%	13.64%	17.18%	12.28%	15.12%	3.12%
1994	1.69%	-0.80%	-1.87%	-1.65%	-3.11%	.38%	7.78%	-5.76%	-7.59%	-5.14%	5.99%	4.45%
1995	34.10%	41.19%	34.35%	34.67%	32.99%	27.33%	11.22%	27.94%	30.90%	17.46%	19.55%	5.79%
1996	22.46%	21.92%	14.96%	20.95%	12.76%	21.16%	6.05%	2.20%	-.83%	4.44%	4.08%	5.26%
1997	32.78%	33.26%	17.55%	32.88%	14.34%	33.90%	1.78%	13.46%	15.12%	9.20%	-4.26%	5.31%
1998	42.32%	14.94%	9.04%	-2.26%	6.92%	20.00%	20.00%	9.16%	13.32%	6.48%	17.79%	5.02%
1999	34.73%	8.27%	62.35%	3.69%	52.56%	-1.41%	26.96%	-5.76%	-8.26%	-2.07%	-5.07%	4.87%
2000	-24.99%	1.09%	-15.38%	24.91%	-24.74%	23.21%	-14.17%	9.18%	20.28%	11.69%	-2.63%	6.32%
2001	-20.36%	-8.17%	-12.72%	7.10%	-14.31%	10.06%	-21.44%	12.16%	4.34%	5.08%	-3.54%	3.67%

Returns are measured from 1990-2001, by the following indexes: Large-Cap Growth: Wilshire Large Growth Index, Large-Cap Value: Wilshire Large Value Index, Mid-Cap Growth: Wilshire Mid-Cap Growth Index, Mid-Cap Value: Wilshire Mid-Cap Value Index, Small-Cap Growth: Wilshire Small-Cap Growth Index, Small-Cap Value Stocks: Small-Cap Value Index, International Stocks: Morgan Stanley EAFE Index ND, Corporate Bonds: Lehman Brothers Long-Term Corporate Bond Index, Term Government Bond Index, International Bonds: Salommon Brothers Non-$ World Government Bond Index, Cash: 3 Month Treasury Bill.

As we continue our discussion on Step 2 in the next chapter, we will examine various case studies of portfolio diversification. These examples illustrate the various components of diversification and how diversification can affect overall portfolio performance.

CHAPTER 11
STEP TWO (CONTINUED): DIVERSIFICATION AT WORK

In Chapters 10 and 11 we discussed the importance of diversification and the components of a diversified portfolio. Our discussion on Step 2 will conclude with this chapter wherein various examples of diversification will be showcased.

Let's consider the investment approaches employed by the following three investors: John Chase, Sam Rebound, and Mike Balance. Each chose a distinctly different method in utilizing six investment choices (bonds, small/mid cap stocks, large cap value stocks, large cap growth stocks, large cap blend stocks and international stocks).

JOHN CHASE

Like many investors, John chases investment performance by paying premium prices to buy last year's winners. From December 1981 through December 2001, John makes a $10,000 investment into the best performing investment of the previous year. Mutual funds from these "winning" market sectors are often in the press and on the covers of *Money* and *Smart Money*, and attract record levels of new money. John's approach could be called: "Invest With the Crowd." After following this strategy for 20 years and investing a total of $200,000, John has amassed a portfolio valued at $620,460 and averaged a 10.7 percent compounded annual rate of return.

SAM REBOUND

Sam Rebound decides to be an investment contrarian and purchases the worst performing investment from the previous 12 months, betting that it will rebound into profitability. On the last day of each year from December 1981 through December 2001, Sam invests $10,000 into the worst performing investment of the previous year. Investing in these "losers" is a difficult task — after all, you don't find such investments on magazine covers — and it requires Sam to invest against the crowd. However, Sam was rewarded for his tenacity and, after 20 years, his $200,000 total investment ($10,000 per year for 20 years) grew to $738,804 compounding at an average rate of 12.21 percent. Sam ended up with $118,344 more than John.

MIKE BALANCE

Mike Balance didn't attempt to guess which part of the market was going to provide the best performance in the upcoming year based on last year's results. Nor did he try to buy last year's losers. Instead, Mike followed a simple strategy spreading his annual $10,000 investment into all six different investments. He continued to do this each year over the same period as John and Sam. After investing a total of $200,000 over 20 years like his counterparts, Mike's portfolio had grown to $864,868, compounding at an annual rate of 13.56 percent (see Figure 1).

FIGURE 1

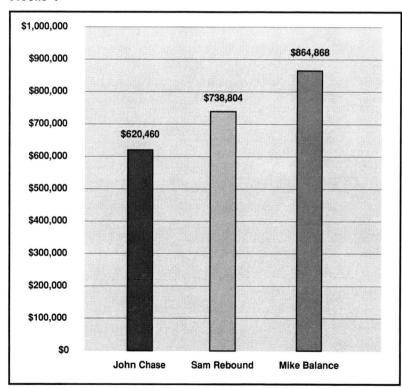

Not only did Mike's portfolio outperform John's by $244,408 and Sam's by $126,064, but Mike was able to achieve this performance with less risk and volatility.

DIVERSIFICATION IN ACTION: HOW DO ALL THESE INVESTMENTS WORK TOGETHER?

Now that we have thoroughly examined each asset class comprising a diversified portfolio, let's see what happens when we put the asset classes together in an actual portfolio. Remember as we look at the portfolios to follow, our goal is to increase long-term returns and reduce risk. Notice the performance of each portfolio during both good and bad markets. To determine which portfolio is right for you, refer to the portfolio you identified in Chapter 8, based on your asset allocation score.

Each of the portfolios in Figures 2 through 7 are diversified as shown in the following chart. In addition, each portfolio was rebalanced annually (this will be discussed in detail in Chapter 13).

Stocks	
Large-Cap Growth	25%
Large-Cap Value	25%
Mid-Cap Growth	10%
Mid-Cap Value	10%
Small-Cap Growth	5%
Small-Cap Value	5%
International	20%
Total Stocks	100%
Bonds	
Long-Term Government	40%
Long-Term Corporate	45%
International	15%
Total	100%
Cash	
Cash Equivalents	100%

FIGURE 2

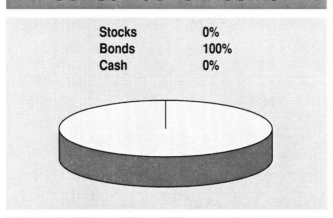

Conservative Income

Stocks	0%
Bonds	100%
Cash	0%

Portfolio Performance (1990-2001)

Average Annual Rate of Return	9.20%
Number of years positive	10
Best Year	27.87%
Number of years negative	2
Worst Year	-6.66%

Annual Portfolio Performance

Year	Weighted Return	Growth of $100,000
1990	7.73%	$ 107,726
1991	19.35%	$ 128,569
1992	8.15%	$ 139,053
1993	15.28%	$ 160,298
1994	-4.73%	$ 152,717
1995	27.87%	$ 195,272
1996	1.27%	$ 197,752
1997	11.47%	$ 220,426
1998	12.12%	$ 247,139
1999	-6.66%	$ 230,688
2000	11.85%	$ 258,021
2001	6.68%	$ 275,249

Stocks are allocated as follows: 25% Large-Cap Growth, 25% Large-Cap Value, 10% Mid-Cap Growth, 10% Mid-Cap Value, 5% Small Cap Growth, 5% Small-Cap Value, 20% International Stocks. Bonds are allocated as follows: 40% Long-Term Governments, 45% Long-Term Corporates, and 15% International Bonds. Cash is allocated as follows: 100% Cash Equivalents.

Returns are measured from 1990-2001, by the following indexes: Large-Cap Growth: Wilshire Large Growth Index, Large-Cap Value: Wilshire Large Value Index, Mid-Cap Growth: Wilshire Mid-cap Growth Index, Mid-Cap Value: Wilshire Mid-cap Value Index, Small-Cap Growth: Wilshire Small Cap Growth Index, Small-Cap Value Stocks: Small-Cap Value Index, International Stocks: Morgan Stanley EAFE Index ND, Corporate Bonds: Lehman Brothers Long-Term Corporate Bond Index, Term Government Bond Index, International Bonds: Salomon Brothers Non-$ World Government Bond Index, Cash: 3 Month Treasure Bill.

Portfolio's rebalanced annually.

FIGURE 3

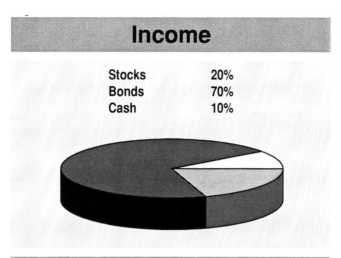

Income

Stocks	20%
Bonds	70%
Cash	10%

Portfolio Performance (1990-2001)

Average Annual Rate of Return	9.35%
Number of years positive	11
Best Year	26.28%
Number of years negative	1
Worst Year	-2.61%

Annual Portfolio Performance

Year	Weighted Return	Growth of $100,000
1990	4.00%	$ 103,998
1991	20.94%	$ 125,778
1992	7.31%	$ 134,975
1993	14.32%	$ 154,305
1994	-2.61%	$ 150,281
1995	26.28%	$ 189,777
1996	4.93%	$ 199,140
1997	13.42%	$ 225,867
1998	12.78%	$ 254,740
1999	.89%	$ 257,002
2000	7.34%	$ 275,865
2001	2.60%	$ 283,042

Stocks are allocated as follows: 25% Large-Cap Growth, 25% Large-Cap Value, 10% Mid-Cap Growth, 10% Mid-Cap Value, 5% Small Cap Growth, 5% Small-Cap Value, 20% International Stocks. Bonds are allocated as follows: 40% Long-Term Governments, 45% Long-Term Corporates, and 15% International Bonds. Cash is allocated as follows: 100% Cash Equivalents.

Returns are measured from 1990-2001, by the following indexes: Large-Cap Growth: Wilshire Large Growth Index, Large-Cap Value: Wilshire Large Value Index, Mid-Cap Growth: Wilshire Mid-cap Growth Index, Mid-Cap Value: Wilshire Mid-cap Value Index, Small-Cap Growth: Wilshire Small Cap Growth Index, Small-Cap Value Stocks: Small-Cap Value Index, International Stocks: Morgan Stanley EAFE Index ND, Corporate Bonds: Lehman Brothers Long-Term Corporate Bond Index, Term Government Bond Index, International Bonds: Salomon Brothers Non-$ World Government Bond Index, Cash: 3 Month Treasury Bill.

Portfolio's rebalanced annually.

FIGURE 4

Income & Growth

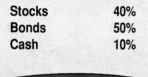

Stocks	40%
Bonds	50%
Cash	10%

Portfolio Performance (1990-2001)

Average Annual Rate of Return	9.92%
Number of years positive	10
Best Year	26.91%
Number of years negative	2
Worst Year	-1.40%

Annual Portfolio Performance

Year	Weighted Return	Growth of $100,000
1990	.29%	$ 100,291
1991	23.90%	$ 124,264
1992	6.93%	$ 132,871
1993	14.58%	$ 152,243
1994	-1.40%	$ 150,106
1995	26.91%	$ 190,492
1996	8.20%	$ 206,109
1997	15.99%	$ 239,070
1998	14.16%	$ 272,916
1999	7.28%	$ 292,784
2000	3.38%	$ 302,690
2001	-1.17%	$ 299,141

Stocks are allocated as follows: 25% Large-Cap Growth, 25% Large-Cap Value, 10% Mid-Cap Growth, 10% Mid-Cap Value, 5% Small Cap Growth, 5% Small-Cap Value, 20% International Stocks. Bonds are allocated as follows: 40% Long-Term Governments, 45% Long-Term Corporates, and 15% International Bonds. Cash is allocated as follows: 100% Cash Equivalents.

Returns are measured from 1990-2001, by the following indexes: Large-Cap Growth: Wilshire Large Growth Index, Large-Cap Value: Wilshire Large Value Index, Mid-Cap Growth: Wilshire Mid-cap Growth Index, Mid-Cap Value: Wilshire Mid-Cap Value Index, Small-Cap Growth: Wilshire Small Cap Growth Index, Small-Cap Value Stocks: Small-Cap Value Index, International Stocks: Morgan Stanley EAFE Index ND, Corporate Bonds: Lehman Brothers Long-Term Corporate Bond Index, Term Government Bond Index, International Bonds: Salommon Brothers Non-$ World Government Bond Index, Cash: 3 Month Treasure Bill.

Portfolio's rebalanced annually.

FIGURE 5

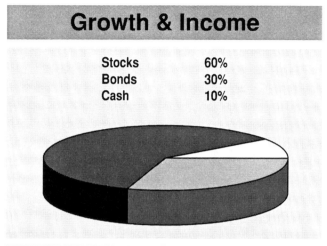

Growth & Income

Stocks	60%
Bonds	30%
Cash	10%

Portfolio Performance (1990-2001)

Average Annual Rate of Return	10.49%
Number of years positive	8
Best Year	27.53%
Number of years negative	4
Worst Year	-4.95%

Annual Portfolio Performance

Year	Weighted Return	Growth of $100,000
1990	-3.42%	$ 96,584
1991	26.87%	$ 122,531
1992	6.54%	$ 130,545
1993	14.84%	$ 149,915
1994	-.20%	$ 149,615
1995	27.53%	$ 190,803
1996	11.46%	$ 212,673
1997	18.56%	$ 252,153
1998	15.53%	$ 291,315
1999	13.67%	$ 331,144
2000	-.57%	$ 329,247
2001	-4.95%	$ 312,960

Stocks are allocated as follows: 25% Large-Cap Growth, 25% Large-Cap Value, 10% Mid-Cap Growth, 10% Mid-Cap Value, 5% Small Cap Growth, 5% Small-Cap Value, 20% International Stocks. Bonds are allocated as follows: 40% Long-Term Governments, 45% Long-Term Corporates, and 15% International Bonds. Cash is allocated as follows: 100% Cash Equivalents.

Returns are measured from 1990-2001, by the following indexes: Large-Cap Growth: Wilshire Large Growth Index, Large-Cap Value: Wilshire Large Value Index, Mid-Cap Growth: Wilshire Mid-cap Growth Index, Mid-Cap Value: Wilshire Mid-cap Value Index, Small-Cap Growth: Wilshire Small Cap Growth Index, Small-Cap Value Stocks: Small-Cap Value Index, International Stocks: Morgan Stanley EAFE Index ND, Corporate Bonds: Lehman Brothers Long-Term Corporate Bond Index, Term Government Bond Index, International Bonds: Salomon Brothers Non-$ World Government Bond Index, Cash: 3 Month Treasure Bill.

Portfolio's rebalanced annually.

FIGURE 6

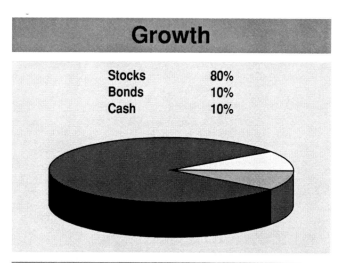

Growth

Stocks	80%
Bonds	10%
Cash	10%

Portfolio Performance (1990-2001)

Average Annual Rate of Return	11.06%
Number of years positive	9
Best Year	29.83%
Number of years negative	3
Worst Year	-8.72%

Annual Portfolio Performance

Year	Weighted Return	Growth of $100,000
1990	-7.12%	$ 92,877
1991	29.83%	$ 120,578
1992	6.15%	$ 127,998
1993	15.10%	$ 147,322
1994	1.00%	$ 148,801
1995	28.15%	$ 190,693
1996	14.73%	$ 218,776
1997	21.13%	$ 265,013
1998	16.91%	$ 309,814
1999	20.06%	$ 371,976
2000	-4.53%	$ 355,129
2001	-8.72%	$ 324,157

Stocks are allocated as follows: 25% Large-Cap Growth, 25% Large-Cap Value, 10% Mid-Cap Growth, 10% Mid-Cap Value, 5% Small Cap Growth, 5% Small-Cap Value, 20% International Stocks. Bonds are allocated as follows: 40% Long-Term Governments, 45% Long-Term Corporates, and 15% International Bonds. Cash is allocated as follows: 100% Cash Equivalents.

Returns are measured from 1990-2001, by the following indexes: Large-Cap Growth: Wilshire Large Growth Index, Large-Cap Value: Wilshire Large Value Index, Mid-Cap Growth: Wilshire Mid-cap Growth Index, Mid-Cap Value: Wilshire Mid-cap Value Index, Small-Cap Growth: Wilshire Small Cap Growth Index, Small-Cap Value Stocks: Small-Cap Value Index, International Stocks: Morgan Stanley EAFE Index ND, Corporate Bonds: Lehman Brothers Long-Term Corporate Bond Index, Term Government Bond Index, International Bonds: Salommon Brothers Non-$ World Government Bond Index, Cash: 3 Month Treasure Bill.

Portfolio's rebalanced annually.

FIGURE 7

Aggressive Growth

Stocks	100%
Bonds	0%
Cash	0%

Portfolio Performance (1990-2001)

Average Annual Rate of Return	12.04%
Number of years positive	9
Best Year	34.15%
Number of years negative	3
Worst Year	-12.2%

Annual Portfolio Performance

Year	Weighted Return	Growth of $100,000
1990	-10.81%	$ 89,190
1991	34.15%	$ 119,652
1992	6.22%	$ 127,100
1993	16.57%	$ 148,161
1994	1.29%	$ 150,073
1995	30.98%	$ 196,572
1996	17.59%	$ 231,153
1997	24.32%	$ 287,372
1998	18.99%	$ 341,942
1999	25.30%	$ 428,465
2000	-7.93%	$ 394,477
2001	-12.20%	$ 346,371

Stocks are allocated as follows: 25% Large-Cap Growth, 25% Large-Cap Value, 10% Mid-Cap Growth, 10% Mid-Cap Value, 5% Small Cap Growth, 5% Small-Cap Value, 20% International Stocks. Bonds are allocated as follows: 40% Long-Term Governments, 45% Long-Term Corporates, and 15% International Bonds. Cash is allocated as follows: 100% Cash Equivalents.

Returns are measured from 1990-2001, by the following indexes: Large-Cap Growth: Wilshire Large Growth Index, Large-Cap Value: Wilshire Large Value Index, Mid-Cap Growth: Wilshire Mid-cap Growth Index, Mid-Cap Value: Wilshire Mid-cap Value Index, Small-Cap Growth: Wilshire Small Cap Growth Index, Small-Cap Value Stocks: Small-Cap Value Index, International Stocks: Morgan Stanley EAFE Index ND, Corporate Bonds: Lehman Brothers Long-Term Corporate Bond Index, Term Government Bond Index, International Bonds: Salommon Brothers Non-$ World Government Bond Index, Cash: 3 Month Treasury Bill.

Portfolio's rebalanced annually.

INVESTMENT POLICY STATEMENT

Now that you have determined your asset allocation (Step 1) and diversification mix (Step 2), it's time to develop a written "investment policy statement."

An investment policy statement outlines how much risk and return you should expect from your portfolio. Why take the time to write this down? By having an investment policy statement in place, you've taken an important step in disciplining your own actions. You will avoid surprises when your portfolio goes through a difficult year and doesn't perform at the average return level you anticipated. Your investment policy statement will identify what you should expect from your portfolio on average over different time frames based on the historical performance of the mix of investments you have chosen. In addition, it will identify the best and worst case scenarios; these figures will help set your expectations. Then if your portfolio goes through a difficult period, you won't be tempted to sell investments into a down market. You will understand the downside when you begin investing and accept the inherent risks.

Your financial advisor can help you formulate an appropriate investment policy statement to govern the management of your portfolio.

The purpose of an investment policy statement is to:

1. Establish a clear understanding of your investment objectives.
2. Establish reasonable risk and return expectations.
3. Outline a portfolio framework and structure, including permissible ranges of exposure into different market segments.
4. Outline the investment philosophy being adhered to (buy and hold, rebalancing, etc.).
5. State types of investments that will be used in the portfolio and expectations of each investment (see Chapter 12).
6. Outline your investment time horizon.
7. State income needs.
8. If working with a financial advisor, provide an outline of duties and responsibilities of the advisor and investor.

Diversifying your portfolio will help you obtain more consistent returns and dramatically decrease your overall investment risk. Understanding the pros and cons of different investments and how they perform in particular economic environments can be invaluable in helping you build a portfolio to meet your retirement goals.

CHAPTER 12
STEP 3: CHOOSING INVESTMENTS

Thus far we've taken great care to thoroughly emphasize the first two steps in the investment process, asset allocation and diversification. Can you guess why? Because most investors just skip those steps and go right on to Step 3, choosing investments. As we've already discussed, this is a major mistake. Questions about what to buy should not be asked until you have developed a strategy for diversifying your assets as outlined in the previous chapters. Remember, your asset allocation model and your diversification strategy are even more important than the investments you own.

Now that you've completed Steps 1 and 2, it's time to go shopping for investments in each asset class you've outlined in your diversified portfolio (see the sample portfolio in Figure 1).

FIGURE 1

Sample Portfolio		
Asset Class	**Target Allocation %**	**Investment Choice**
Large-Cap Growth Stocks	15%	_____
Large-Cap Value Stocks	15%	_____
Mid-Cap Growth Stocks	7.5%	_____
Mid-Cap Value Stocks	7.5%	_____
Small-Cap Growth Stocks	2.5%	_____
Small-Cap Value Stocks	2.5%	_____
International Growth	5%	_____
International Value	5%	_____
Corporate Bonds	10%	_____
Government Bonds	10%	_____
Municipal Bonds	10%	_____
International Bonds	5%	_____
Cash	5%	_____

At this stage of the investment process you must make a major decision: Do you want to buy individual stocks and bonds in each asset class and manage them yourself? Or, would you rather outsource the money management responsibilities to professional money managers? If you choose to manage a portfolio of individual stocks and bonds yourself, what will it take for you to be successful?

First, you must develop criteria for identifying individual securities (stocks and bonds) with the most potential in each segment of your diversified portfolio; you will need different criteria for each asset class. Second, in order to be properly diversified, you should purchase 10 to 15 stocks in each asset class (remember a diversified portfolio will include seven to ten asset classes). This means you must purchase between 70 to 150 different securities. Third, after you purchase all these securities, you must consistently monitor each of them and develop a sell discipline to help you determine when to sell each security. And finally, after you sell an investment, you must start the process all over by reinvesting the proceeds into another security that meets your buy criteria.

How successful do you think you will be if you try to be an expert in managing money in every asset class? Attempting to manage a large portfolio of individual securities on your own can be a very daunting task.

Most investors simply aren't equipped to manage a large diversified portfolio of individual securities. A better alternative is to outsource the day-to-day money management responsibilities to professional money managers and to hire a different money manager for each asset class in your portfolio. This way you have several money managers working for you, each of which specializes in managing money within just one sector of the stock or bond markets.

By turning the daily management responsibilities over to professionals, you will most likely improve your investment performance. After all, making your portfolio succeed is a money manager's full-time job. This chapter will explain the process for identifying and hiring the best money managers available so that you will be sure to choose the most successful investments.

SELECTING THE BEST MANAGERS

There are two ways to hire a professional money manager. You can invest in a mutual fund or hire a private or institutional money manager via a "separate account" program. As of the end of 2001, there were over 13,772 mutual funds[1] and thousands of private money managers from which to choose. Regardless of whether you use a mutual fund or a separately managed account, the criteria for selecting the best managers is identical. Before performing a manager search, you will need to determine which approach is best for you. The similarities and differences of mutual funds and separately managed accounts are outlined on the following pages. Once you understand your two options, you can conduct a search for the best managers.

MUTUAL FUNDS

The easiest and most popular way of hiring a professional money manager is by investing in mutual funds. Mutual funds have become increasingly popular over the past 20 years. In 1980, only 4.6 million households in the U.S. owned a mutual fund. By 2000, that number soared to 50 million. Fifteen years ago, there were only 1,180 mutual funds[2] available to investors, but today that number has risen to just below 14,000.[3]

A mutual fund involves investors pooling their money to be managed by a professional money manager. Each fund has a specific investment objective that determines the types of stocks or bonds the manager can purchase (large company stocks, small company stocks, etc.). It's the money manager's responsibility to search for the best securities available, usually stocks or bonds, within the fund's objective and make the day-to-day decisions about what to buy and sell.

A strict "buy" discipline is observed to determine which securities to add to the portfolio. Once purchased, each security is then monitored and eventually sold based on a specified "sell" strategy. Most funds own 50 to 100 different securities. Investors become a fractional owner of each security held by the fund regardless of the size of their investment. If the underlying stocks or bonds held in the portfolio increase in value, the value of the fund shares or net asset value (NAV) will appreciate also.

SEPARATELY MANAGED ACCOUNTS

Hiring a separate account manager (also referred to as private, independent or institutional money manager) is another way to obtain professional money management. Like mutual funds, the market for separately managed accounts has also grown considerably. In 1996, $165 billion was invested in separately managed accounts. By the end of 1999, that number had risen to $425 billion. It is estimated that by 2004, separately managed accounts will be a $1.2 trillion market.[5]

When a separate account manager purchases a portfolio of stocks or bonds, the investor owns each security outright. Rather than a person's money being mingled with thousands of other investors, separate account money is managed exclusively and privately for a single investor. This is different than a public mutual fund, in which investors own a fraction of each security held by the fund and essentially share what is owned. Most separate accounts invest in over 50 different securities.

ACCOUNT MINIMUMS: MUTUAL FUNDS VS. SEPARATELY MANAGED ACCOUNTS

One of the reasons mutual funds have enjoyed so much popularity is due to their ease of access. Many mutual fund companies have minimum initial investment requirements as low as $500. Fund minimums are completely waived in 401(k) and other corporate retirement plans. Minimums this low mean the average investor can easily purchase seven to ten mutual funds and obtain adequate diversification without having to be independently wealthy.

Most private institutional account managers, on the other hand, have account minimums of $1 million to $10 million. Because of this, separate account money management has traditionally been reserved for the very wealthy and large institutional pools of money such as pensions, retirement plans, and endowments. However, in recent years, with the advent of "wrap" programs where large brokerage firms provide money managers with access to many client dollars, the managers have agreed to lower account minimums, making private separate account managers available for minimums of $100,000 to $500,000. This has opened the door of private money management a little wider, making it possible for more individuals to participate.

More people are considering separate account managers as the size of individual investment portfolios in the U.S. increases. There are over 37 million American households with investable assets over $100,000.[6] The higher minimums required for separate accounts buy investors exclusivity and investment planning custom-tailored to each individual's objectives. Although one manager can be hired for as little as $100,000, separate account managers should only be used when investors have enough money to obtain proper diversification while meeting manager minimum entry requirements. To purchase seven to ten managers and gain exposure to each major asset class in the market, over $1,000,000 would generally be needed.

If your portfolio is less than $1 million, and you are interested in the separate account approach, you could employ both separate account managers and mutual funds to build your portfolio. Hire separate account managers to direct the core pieces of your portfolio — those asset categories with the largest allocations, usually large U.S. company stocks. Then, buy mutual funds with the smaller positions.

An example of this combination strategy is shown in Figure 2.

FIGURE 2

Growth Portfolio			
80% Stocks	20% Bonds	0% Cash	
Asset Category	Allocation %	Allocation $	Mutual Fund or Separate Account
Large-Cap Growth Stocks	20%	$140,000	Separate Account
Large-Cap Value Stocks	20%	$140,000	Separate Account
Mid-Cap Growth Stocks	10%	$70,000	Mutual Fund
Mid-Cap Value Stocks	10%	$70,000	Mutual Fund
Small-Cap Growth Stocks	5%	$35,000	Mutual Fund
Small-Cap Value Stocks	5%	$35,000	Mutual Fund
Large-Cap Intl. Growth	5%	$35,000	Mutual Fund
Large-Cap Intl. Value	5%	$35,000	Mutual Fund
Corporate Bonds	0%	$0	N/A
Government Bonds	0%	$0	N/A
Municipal Bonds	20%	$140,000	Separate Account
International Bonds	0%	$0	N/A
Cash	0%	$0	N/A

PORTFOLIO DIVERSIFICATION: MUTUAL FUNDS VS. SEPARATELY MANAGED ACCOUNTS

The average domestic equity mutual fund owns 146 different stocks and has net assets of $386 million, while the average taxable bond mutual fund owns 322 issues and has over $247 million in net assets.[7] When you invest in a fund, you become a part-owner of every security the fund owns. For example, if you invested $100,000 into the Van Kampen Emerging Growth-A fund, you would become a part-owner of all 124 stocks in the fund (see Figure 3).[8] Although you are a fractional owner of all 124 positions, you will not see a list of these securities on your statements. Your statements will report the number of shares and the value of the fund, not the individual stock and bond positions held in the fund and therefore it is not always apparent what you own. Mutual funds send out quarterly reports so investors can see exactly what is owned and what has been added or subtracted from the portfolio. Unfortunately, most investors disregard these reports and never know what stocks and bonds they actually own. However, if you cracked a fund open, you would find your money diversified similar to the fund in Figure 3.

If you own just one fund, your money may be spread out over 100 or more companies. Figure 3 shows the type of diversification available by owning just one mutual fund. However, if you own seven to ten funds, you instantly become an

FIGURE 3

Van Kampen Emerging Growth A

Security Name	% Net Assets	Security Name	% Net Assets	Security Name	% Net Assets
1. Wal-Mart Stores	3.11	51. Symantec	0.72	101. Progressive	0.39
2. Home Depot	2.26	52. Baker Hughes	0.71	102. Accenture	0.39
3. Procter & Gamble	1.91	53. Quest Diagnostics	0.71	103. BEA Sys	0.38
4. First Data	1.72	54. Boeing	0.69	104. Zimmer Holdings	0.36
5. Lockheed Martin	1.70	55. Weatherford International	0.69	105. McKesson HBOC	0.35
6. United Health Group	1.63	56. Lennar	0.69	106. Clear Channel Comms	0.35
7. Lowe s	1.59	57. AmeriSource Bergen	0.68	107. Ball	0.34
8. Wyeth	1.59	58. Office Depot	0.67	108. Bank of America	0.32
9. Intel	1.57	59. BJ Svcs	0.66	109. SunGard Data Sys	0.31
10. Abbott Labs	1.56	60. Apache	0.66	111. Nokia Cl A ADR	0.31
11. Applied Matls	1.52	61. ACE	0.66	112. King Pharmaceuticals	0.31
12. Costco Wholesale	1.45	62. Network Association	0.65	113. Millennium Pharma	0.28
13. Baxter International	1.39	63. Smith International	0.64	114. Arthur J. Gallagher & Co.	0.26
14. Oracle	1.33	64. Fifth Third Bancorp	0.63	115. MBNA	0.26
15. KLA-Tencor	1.31	65. IDEC Pharmaceuticals	0.61	116. NorthFork Bancorp	0.24
16. Tenet Healthcare	1.30	66. Biomet	0.61	117. Limited	0.23
17. Micron Tech	1.29	67. L-3 Comms Holdings	0.61	118. Sabre Holdings Cl A	0.22
18. United Tech	1.28	68. HCA- The Healthcare Company	0.59	119. MGM Mirage	0.22
19. WellPoint Health Networks	1.22	69. Fannie Mae	0.59	120. International Paper	0.22
20. Johnson & Johnson	1.22	70. Centex	0.59	121. Nabors Inds	0.18
21. Concord EFS	1.20	71. Phillips Petro	0.57	122. Tech Data	0.16
22. USA Networks	1.19	72. Amazon.com	0.56	123. Magna Intl	0.14
23. Nike	1.18	73. Genzyme Corporation General Di	0.55	124. Globalsantafe Corporation	0.11
24. Bed Bath & Beyond	1.17	74. General Dynamics	0.54	125. Intuit	0.00
25. Schlumberger	1.17	75. Ross Stores	0.54	126. EMC	0.00
26. Anheuser-Busch	1.15	76. Starwood Hotels & Resorts	0.54	127. Guidant	0.00
27. Dell Comp	1.11	77. Xilinz	0.53	128. Lehman Brothers Holdings	0.00
28. Philip Morris	1.06	78. Gannett	0.53	129. Freddie Mac	0.00
29. Sears Roebuck	1.05	79. Darden Restaurants	0.53	130. Analog Devices	0.00
30. Target	1.05	80. Southwest Air	0.52	131. Genesis Microchip	0.00
31. Pfizer	1.03	81. Walt Disney	0.52	132. Linear Tech	0.00
32. Best Buy	1.01	82. Express Scripts	0.52	133. Polycom	0.00
33. Wells Fargo	0.94	83. NVIDIA	0.51	134. Ubs Securities	0.00
34. Gilead Sciences	0.88	84. Kohl s	0.51	135. TMP Worldwide	0.00
35. H & R Block	0.88	85. Mercury Interactive	0.51	136. Barr Labs	0.00
36. Fedex	0.87	86. International Game Tech	0.51	137. Veritas Software	0.00
37. Microchip Tech	0.86	87. Danaher	0.51	138. Riverstone Networks	0.00
38. Siebel Sys	0.83	88. Southtrust	0.51	139. TJX	0.00
39. Walgreen	0.81	89. Affiliated Comp Svcs A	0.49	140. Broadcom	0.00
40. Starbucks	0.81	90. Emulex	0.49	141. Brocade Comm Sys	0.00
41. Forest Labs	0.80	91. Apollo Group	0.49	142. EBAY	0.00
42. Maxim Integrated Products	0.80	92. AutoZone	0.47	143. Merrill Lynch	0.00
43. Kraft Foods	0.78	93. DuPont De Nemours E.I.	0.47	144. Cisco Sys	0.00
44. St. Jude Medical	0.78	94. SLM	0.46	145. Computer Axxpc International	0.00
45. Harley-Davidson	0.77	95. Marvell Tech	0.46	146. Allergan	0.00
46. PepsiCo	0.76	96. Electronic Arts	0.46	147. Waste Management	0.00
47. Omnicom Group	0.75	97. Immunex	0.43	148. Whole Foods Market	0.00
48. Texas Instruments	0.74	98. Fiserv	0.43	149. Circuit City Group	0.00
49. Rational Software	0.74	99. Federated Department Stores	0.42	150. Celephalon	0.00
50. Microsoft	0.73	100. Harrah s Entertainment	0.41	151. National Semicon	0.00

Source: Morningstar Principia June 30, 2002, Holdings as of February 28, 2002

owner of 600 to 1,000 stocks and bonds. *Mutual funds provide tremendous diversification and enable you to significantly reduce your risks.* If you buy an individual stock, it is possible to lose all the money, if the underlying company goes bankrupt. By contrast, it would be extraordinarily difficult for you to lose all the money you invested in a mutual fund. Essentially, every stock or bond in the fund's portfolio would have to go bankrupt and be deemed worthless at the same time.

Separately managed accounts are commonly more concentrated than mutual funds. Most of these accounts contain approximately 40 to 60 securities. This is usually due to the size of the individual portfolios. Although the manager may be directing as much as $500 million on an aggregate basis, the individual separate accounts are relatively small in comparison to mutual fund assets. For example, if an investor hires a separate account manager and deposits $100,000 into a stock portfolio, the manager would not be likely to buy over 100 different stocks with that money. By contrast, the average mutual fund manager has $386 million available and buys 146 stocks. Figure 4 illustrates a sample $100,000, large-cap growth portfolio managed by Rittenhouse Investments Management Inc., the nation's second largest separate account money manager.[9]

FIGURE 4

RITTENHOUSE INVESTMENT MANAGEMENT LARGE CAP GROWTH - (2001)	
Portfolio Size $100,000	
NAME	**%**
ABBOTT LABS	3.45%
AMER INTL GROUP INC	5.15%
AUTOMATIC DATA PROC	4.93%
BESTFOODS	2.13%
COCA COLA COM	4.33%
COLGATE PALMOLIVE	4.31%
WALT DISNEY COMPANY	2.95%
EMERSON ELEC CO	2.50%
FREDDIE MAC	3.44%
FANNIE MAY (USA) COM	3.83%
GENERAL ELECTRIC	5.84%
GILLETTE CO	1.77%
HEWLETT PACKARD CO	2.03%
HOME DEPOT INC	5.26%
INTEL CORP	3.60%
JOHNSON & JOHNSON	4.75%
LUCENT TECHNOLOGIES	2.31%
MEDTRONIC INC	2.36%
MERCK & CO INC	4.43%
PEPSICO INC	3.79%
PFIZER INC	5.03%
PROCTER GAMBLE	4.77%
STATE STREET CORP	2.72%
SCHERING-PLOUGH CORP.	5.08%
WAL MART STORES INC	2.02%
WALGREEN CO	2.00%
WELLS FARGO & CO NEW	2.62%
MONEY MARKET RESERVES	1.23%
TOTAL	**100%**

Source: Rittenhouse Investment Management, Sample Large Cap Growth Portfolio 2001

Contrary to mutual funds, each statement you receive from a separate account manager will itemize each position you own including the number of shares, share price, purchase price (cost basis), profit and loss per position, and portfolio changes from the previous month.

MANAGEMENT EXPERTISE: MUTUAL FUNDS VS. SEPARATELY MANAGED ACCOUNTS

Money managers of both mutual funds and separately managed accounts often have similar backgrounds. Most receive MBAs, many from prestigious universities, and then go on to obtain the professional designation of CFA (Certified Financial Analyst). After working many years as securities analysts and sometimes as assistant portfolio managers, the best are promoted to a lead money manager position.

RESEARCH & INFORMATION: MUTUAL FUNDS VS. SEPARATELY MANAGED ACCOUNTS

Teams of security analysts who assist in performing research on companies support both mutual fund managers and separate account managers. Usually some form of quantitative, fundamental, and technical analysis is used to identify stocks and bonds for each portfolio. Many managers start with a quantitative screen to narrow down the investment choices to a short list of companies meeting specific criteria as established by each portfolio. Then fundamental analysis is often used to identify companies with solid financial statements and good growth and profitability prospects. To determine when to buy, managers often apply technical analysis to study the historic price movements of the stocks they are considering.

Due to the amount of money in their control, money managers are given access to information the general public would have a difficult time obtaining. This is one of the great advantages of utilizing a professional money manager.

For instance, managers routinely meet with upper-level leadership at the companies they are considering for purchase, visiting with hundreds of corporations each year. How would IBM respond if either the manager of the American Funds Growth Fund ($35 billion in assets) or a manager for Brandes Investment Partners separate accounts ($15 billion in assets) was interested in buying 1 million to 2 million IBM shares for their portfolios? Obviously, because these managers could positively impact IBM's stock price, IBM would roll out the red carpet for them, invite the manager to meet with upper level management at their corporate head quarters and assist in any way possible. In corporate America, quantity speaks volumes.

What do you think might happen if you were considering buying 100 shares of IBM stock and requested a meeting with the chief executive officer or chief financial officer of IBM? You wouldn't stand a chance of getting in to see them. But through a money manager, doors are opened to information that would otherwise not be available to you.

DIVIDENDS, CAPITAL GAINS AND TAXES: MUTUAL FUNDS VS. SEPARATELY MANAGED ACCOUNTS

Separate accounts offer many tax advantages that mutual funds do not. These tax advantages are only applicable to taxable accounts (non-retirement money). There are three ways to make money when owning a mutual fund or a separately managed account: appreciation, dividends and interest, and capital gains. The appreciation of the stocks and bonds in a portfolio, as well as the dividends and interest paid, is similar for both funds and separate accounts. However, a major difference between the two professional money management approaches is how the capital gains and losses are handled in non-retirement accounts. (In retirement accounts, of course, whether using mutual funds or separately managed accounts, all growth, dividends, and interest are tax-deferred.)

Mutual funds present two potentially large tax problems to non-retirement portfolios: capital gains distributions and embedded capital gains. If the fund manager buys a stock low and sells it high, this capital gain will be passed on to the fund's investors in the form of a capital gain distribution. In 1999, approximately $238 billion in capital gains and another $159 billion in dividends were distributed by mutual funds. Fund shareholders paid an estimated $43 billion in taxes on these distributions.[10]

Although most investors choose to reinvest these distributions rather than having the fund send a check, the distributions are still taxable at long- and short-term capital gains rates in taxable accounts. The higher a fund's turnover rate, the more likely investors will have sizable capital gains distributions. While a portfolio with a buy and hold strategy would have a turnover rate of less than 30 percent, representing very little buying and selling, the average U.S. stock fund has an annual portfolio turnover rate of 114 percent.[11] This reflects the active trading strategies employed by many mutual fund managers.

In 2000, many fund investors experienced a decline in their fund values but were still required to pay taxes on capital gains distributions. It's no fun to pay taxes when your funds do well, but it's especially painful to do so when your funds aren't making money. For instance, in 2000 the Fidelity Magellan fund reported a negative 9.29 percent return and fell another 11.65 percent in 2001, but during these two years it paid $4.69 and $.80 per share[12] in capital gains distributions. If you had invested $100,000 in Fidelity Magellan on January 1, 2000, and held on for two years until December 31, 2001, your portfolio dropped to $80,142, a near 20 percent loss. To add insult to injury, you would have been required to pay taxes on a capital gains distribution of $3,565 in 2000, and $615 in 2001.

Capital gains distributions are usually paid out at the end of the year. If you are investing in mutual funds at year-end when these distributions are being made, you should inquire from the fund company whether the fund is going to pay a capital gains distribution. If you buy a fund the day before it pays out its capital gains and other distributions, you will be taxed on the entire amount of the distribution.

How is it possible to experience a drop in your fund's value and be required to pay capital gains taxes? The reason is because many mutual funds often contain significant, embedded, capital gains. That means investors may be required to pay taxes on profits derived when a manager sells a stock that was purchased many years before they even owned the fund. Let's look at an example of how this could happen.

Let's say that early in 1990, Paula Assay, the long-time manager of the Make-Me-Rich-Fund, purchased 100,000 shares of General Electric stock for the fund. The stock has appreciated over 100 percent since being purchased. On June 15, 2001, an investor, Larry Williams, purchased the Make-Me-Rich-Fund in his taxable brokerage account. Later that same year, fund investors began liquidating shares of the fund. In order to meet redemption requests, Ms. Assay sold General Electric out of the portfolio and realized a sizable capital gain (100 percent appreciation). In December, this gain was passed on to all the investors of the fund in the form of a capital gains distribution. Larry, although he had only owned shares of the fund for less than six months, was required to pay taxes on his portion of the General Electric gain as if he had owned it since it was purchased in 1990.

Larry became a victim of hidden, embedded capital gains. This could have been avoided had Larry asked his advisor how much capital gains exposure the fund had. Information about capital gains exposure can be found in a fund's annual report. Morningstar Inc. also reports this information at *www.morningstar.com* or in the Morningstar reference book found at your local library. Morningstar reports each fund's potential capital gains exposure, which is how much of the fund's assets would be subject to taxation if the fund were to fully liquidate today.

In taxable accounts, these tax problems can be solved when investor's use separately managed accounts and own the securities outright. Separate account managers follow disciplined strategies to buy and sell stocks and bonds, just like mutual fund managers. The securities in a separate account, however, are purchased when you open the account and are held in your name. Consequently, there are no embedded capital gains of which to speak. Some separate account managers, of course, actively trade securities in their portfolios, creating taxable capital gains. If you hire a manager to handle some of your taxable money, you should find out how much portfolio turnover to expect. Lower turnover generally means less tax liability.

Regardless of the amount of gains realized during the year, the tax burden can often be reduced or eliminated. Prior to year-end, the separate account investor simply has to request that the manager sell some stocks in the portfolio that are currently trading at a loss. The manager can sell enough shares at a loss to offset any capital gains you may have realized during the year. If you realize enough losses, you can offset all gains and avoid capital gains taxes altogether. After the losses have been realized, the stocks that were sold can be repurchased; the manager, however, cannot buy back these stock shares for at least 31 days. This strategy, of course, does not work with mutual funds simply because you don't have sole ownership of the securities.

CONTROL OVER WHAT IS PURCHASED IN YOUR PORTFOLIO: MUTUAL FUNDS VS. SEPARATELY MANAGED ACCOUNTS

Mutual fund investors cannot exclude specific securities or market sectors from the funds they buy. What is purchased in the portfolio is left completely up to the manager's discretion as long as he or she buys securities within the fund's prospectus objective. If your social conscience objects to the actions of certain companies, you have no power to exclude those companies from your mutual fund holdings.

When you open a separate account, however, you will be asked to complete a questionnaire asking, "Are there any securities you would like to exclude from this portfolio," or, "Are there any portfolio restrictions?" For example, this could be very important to an investor who has lost a loved one to lung cancer due to the extended use of tobacco or someone who has seen alcoholism destroy a family. Investors in these situations could request not to have any tobacco or alcohol stocks in their portfolios.

In some cases, avoiding an entire industry may be warranted. Consider the investor who just retired from a large utility company and has 50 percent of her portfolio invested in company stock. If she is not planning to diversify this position all at once, she may want to request that her money manager not purchase any utility companies that would throw her portfolio even further out of balance.

DEPOSITING SECURITIES INSTEAD OF CASH: MUTUAL FUNDS VS. SEPARATELY MANAGED ACCOUNTS

When you open a separate account, you can do so with a check or wire transfer, or you can deposit securities. Transferring securities directly to a manager may have some advantages, depending on your situation. The manager may keep some of the shares you deposit in the portfolio. If you are trying to diversify out of a concentrated stock position, you can develop a strategy with the money manager to have the shares sold over time (days, months, or years) or at a specific price. Some managers specialize in helping people diversify out of concentrated positions, controlling tax liabilities while doing so. There is no additional cost to sell the shares that you deposit.

COST: MUTUAL FUNDS VS. SEPARATELY MANAGED ACCOUNTS

There are two types of mutual funds: load and no-load funds (sales charge or no sales charge). Both types of funds have expenses associated with them, but often investors can't see many of these costs on the surface. Let's briefly examine the expenses associated with each type of fund.

FIGURE 5

No-Load Mutual Fund

No-load funds, as the name suggests, do not charge investors a "load" or a sales commission when buying or selling a fund. Typically, no-load funds are purchased directly from a no-load mutual fund company or a discount brokerage firm. Often investors must contact the fund companies directly via a toll-free number, request an application and information

NO LOAD FUNDS

Share Class	Up-Front Sales Charge	Contingent Deferred Sales Charge
No-Load	0%	0%

LOAD FUNDS

Share Class	Up-Front Sales Charge	Contingent Deferred Sales Charge
Class A	4-5%	0%
Class B	0%	5% Year One 4% Year Two 3% Year Three 2% Year Four 1% Year Five 0% Year Six and Beyond
Class C	0%	1% Year One 0% Year Two and Beyond

This is a sample sales charge schedule. Each fund company sets its own fee structure.

about the fund(s) they are interested in, and then send back a completed application with a check. In most cases, investors act independently without the aid of a financial advisor. Investors can buy no-load funds with the help of a fee-based financial planner if they are interested in obtaining advice in the process of buying and managing a portfolio of no-load funds.

No-load is often misinterpreted to mean "no cost" — this is not the case. No-load funds do charge internal management fees (see Figure 6).

Load Mutual Funds

Load funds are offered through financial advisors. Historically, when an investor purchased a "load-fund," he paid an up-front commission equal to 4-5 percent of the amount invested. When the fund was sold, there was no cost to sell.

To combat the perception of load funds being expensive and no-load funds being inexpensive, many years ago "load-fund" companies began offering different pricing alternatives to give investors a choice of how they paid for their funds. Most load funds are now offered in three share classes: Class A, Class B, and Class C (see Figure 5). When buying a load fund, investors must choose which share class to purchase. For example, Class A shares charge an up-front sales charge, usually between 2-5 percent. This sales charge or commission is taken right off the top of your initial investment amount. Class B shares do not charge an up-front fee. However, a deferred sales charge or back-end sales charge is applied if you sell out of the fund within a certain time frame (usually four to six years). The deferred sales charge usually declines by about 1 percent each year. For example, if you sold your fund in year one, you may pay a 5 percent deferred sales charge; in year two, you would pay 4 percent; in year three, you would pay 3 percent, and so on, until year six when you could sell the fund with no charges. Finally, there is no up-front charge for Class C shares, only a 1 percent deferred sales charge if sold during the first year, and no sales charge if sold after one year.

In addition to the different sales charge structures, there is a also a difference in the internal management fees these funds charge. Class A shares charge the lowest internal fees but have the highest up front costs, while Classes B and C charge nothing up-front but have higher internal fees. Which fund class should you buy? Although Class A shares are the cheaper alternative if you hold your funds more than seven to eight years, Classes B and C are typically less expensive in the interim. "C shares" offer the most flexibility if you need liquidity or want to make adjustments in your account over time.

Management Fees

All mutual funds, whether load or no-load, charge investors a fee to cover annual operating expenses and management fees.

The fund's expense ratio is the percentage of a fund's assets paid to cover these costs. The expense ratio includes all operating fees with the exception of brokerage or trading costs. This ratio gives you a snapshot of what you are paying each year to have your money managed by a professional. For example, if a fund has a 1 percent expense ratio and manages $10 million, the annual cost to investors would be

$100,000 (1 percent multiplied by $10 million). If you had $10,000 invested in the fund, the amount of the fee attributed to your portfolio would equal $100 (1 percent of $10,000). If the manager is successful and the assets in the portfolio double to $20 million, the fund would collect an additional $100,000 in fees (1 percent multiplied by $20 million is $200,000).

This is good for investors. Your manager has tremendous incentive to make your money grow since his income is tied to the success of the portfolio. Although you are required to pay the management fee, you will never receive a bill requesting payment. The fee is taken out of the fund's assets on a daily basis and is reflected in the daily price of the shares. The price of mutual fund shares is referred to as the Net Asset Value (NAV), meaning the value of each share net of fees. Although most people do not take time to review these expenses, you can determine what they are by looking in a prospectus, an annual report, or by utilizing certain fund research services like Morningstar. The average expense ratios for load and no-load funds are compared in Figure 6. Some funds also charge 12B-1 fees (this fee is included in the expense ratio). These fees also come out of the portfolio on a daily basis and are stated as a percentage of the portfolios total assets. Mutual funds are allowed to charge 12B-1 fees as a way to raise money to promote the fund and pay for advertising. The 12B-1 fees for the average stocks and bond funds are also outlined in Figure 6.

FIGURE 6

LOAD FUNDS	ANNUAL EXPENSE RATIO	12B-1
Domestic Stock Funds	1.64%	.56%
International Stock Funds	2.01%	.57%
Taxable Bond Funds	1.36%	.51%
Tax-Free Bond Funds	1.12%	.44%

NO LOAD FUNDS	ANNUAL EXPENSE RATIO	12B-1
Domestic Stock Funds	1.19%	.16%
International Stock Funds	1.52%	.17%
Taxable Bond Funds	.87%	.13%
Tax-Free Bond Funds	.72%	.09%

Note: The expense ration includes the 12B-1 fee but does not include brokerage trading cost. See footnotes 13 and 14 for fund search criteria.
Source: Morningstar Principia Pro, December 31, 2001

Hidden Fees: Trading or Brokerage Costs

Load and no-load mutual funds include some additional fees, which are even less transparent to investors than the management fees and are not reflected in the expense ratio. These are the fund's trading costs. Each time your manager buys or sells a stock or bond, he or she must pay a brokerage fee to do so. If your manager is very active, these trading expenses could be quite high and may hurt your fund's performance.

You can determine how much a fund is trading by looking at its turnover rate. This rate will tell you how much of the portfolio is bought and sold each year. If the turnover is high, you could be paying an additional 1-2 percent per year in trading fees. It is estimated that it costs a fund between 0.5 percent and 0.8 percent (of the dollar amount of the trade) each time a manager buys or sells a security in a mutual fund portfolio. A fund manager following an active trading strategy may have a turnover rate of 100 percent (selling all the stocks in the portfolio during the year and reinvesting the proceeds into other stocks). If it costs the manager .5 percent ($^1/_2$ of 1 percent) to sell a stock and another .5 percent to buy a stock to replace it, your fund expenses will increase by 1 percent.[15] You can obtain information on mutual fund brokerage expenses by contacting your mutual fund company. You can also visit *www.andrewtobias.com* for this information.

Don't let these costs scare you away from investing in mutual funds. In the end, these fees are not as important as your bottom-line investment returns — what you make after fees are deducted. Most people, for example, would rather make 12 percent, pay 2 percent in fees, and net 10 percent, than make 10 percent, pay 1 percent in fees, and net 9 percent. When you compare the performance of one investment to another, the most important information is net return (return after fees).

Separate Account Expenses

Operating costs for separate accounts are very similar to mutual funds. Separate accounts also charge an annual fee to cover management expenses and other operating costs. Unlike mutual funds, brokerage and trading costs are included in the total annual fee. The fee is calculated as a percentage of the assets being managed. Like mutual funds, the fees generally range from 1-3 percent per year. The management fee is billed quarterly. It can be debited from the portfolio, as is the case with mutual funds, or it can be paid out of a different account.

Unlike mutual funds, however, the fee for separate accounts is not hidden. In addition, management fees are reduced as the amount invested increases. In a mutual fund your internal expenses as a percent of assets are the same whether you invest $1,000 or a $1 million. With a separate account, your management fee can be negotiated. There are no additional costs when you liquidate, and management fees may be tax-deductible if paid from a taxable account.

Comparing Costs

Separate account fees cover portfolio management, operations, and brokerage costs. This is important if you are comparing the cost of a mutual fund to a separate account. For instance, a fund with a 1.5 percent expense ratio may seem like a better cost alternative than a separate account with a 2 percent management fee. However, when an additional 1 percent in brokerage trading expenses are added to the 1.5 percent expense ratio, the fund's total costs now equal 2.5 percent.

Although the mutual fund expenses in this example are higher, most people would rather pay the higher fees. Why? Because they are essentially "painless." With mutual funds, you are never billed for these expenses and consequently never directly feel the impact of the fees. With separate accounts, the fees are usually debited out of your account and are easy to see on your quarterly statement.

PERFORMANCE: MUTUAL FUNDS VS. SEPARATELY MANAGED ACCOUNTS

Many money managers, in addition to managing mutual funds, also manage separate accounts and will manage each with similar investment strategies. If expenses are about the same and there are no tax implications, investment returns should be about the same for separate accounts and mutual funds managed by the same manager. In each asset class, there are very good mutual fund and separate account managers from which to choose, and performance is often very similar.

Theoretically you would expect separate accounts to have better performance for a couple of reasons. First, the separate account manager does not have to keep any money in cash to meet redemptions of other investors. That means more of your money is working for you. Second, the behavior of other investors will not hurt the performance of your portfolio. With mutual funds, a manager may have to sell positions that they otherwise would like to keep if, suddenly, investors decide they want to redeem shares. Unfortunately and unwisely, this usually happens after market downturns and fund managers are forced to sell when they should be buying. With a separate account, no other investors share your securities so your manager will not be forced to sell anything.

MUTUAL FUND OR PRIVATE MONEY MANAGERS? HOW TO IDENTIFY THE BEST MANAGERS

You can hire a mutual fund manager to manage your money in a publicly-offered mutual fund, or you can hire an independent money manager to manage a separate account of stocks and/or bonds for you, exclusive of other investors. To determine which approach is right for you, compare the advantages and disadvantages of each in Figure 7:

FIGURE 7

	Mutual Funds	Separate Account Managers
Managers to choose from	13,772	Thousands
Minimums	$1,000-$2,500	$100,000-$500,000
Total Portfolio Holdings	146 (Avg. Domestic Stock Fund)	50-75
Overall Portfolio Diversification	Investors can own more funds due to lower minimums.	Higher minimums may restrict diversification.
Positions Owned	Securities are pooled and shared by all investors.	Securities are held in your name in a separate account for you alone.
Investments Customization	Investors have no say about securities being purchased.	Portfolio can be customized. Certain limitations can be implemented.
Management Expenses (Management, Operation, Brokerage)	1-3%	1-3%
How expenses are paid	Expenses are hidden. Built into the daily price the funds shares (NAV) .	Expenses are transparent. Usually paid quarterly from portfolio assets.
Capital Gains	Fund may have embedded capital gains .	No embedded capital gains.
Taxes	Investors cannot request securities held by a fund be sold at a loss to offset gains.	Investors can requests securities be sold to control tax liability.
Impact of other investors	The behavior of other investors may hamper managers ability to manage fund .	Because securities are not shared but owned by you alone, the behavior of others does not impact your portfolio performance.
Withdrawals	May be requested at any time.	May be requested at any time.
Portfolio Monitoring	Statements report the number and value of fund shares owned.	Statements report all securities owned and also any changes made to portfolio during statement period. Investors know what exactly they own.

Source: Mutual Fund Data Taken From Morningstar Principia, December 31, 2001

Figure 8 shows that a decision was made to invest 20 percent of the sample portfolio into large U.S. company growth stocks. After conducting a search to determine which large-cap, growth stock manager to hire, similar choices must be made in each of the remaining asset classes. With thousands of mutual funds and separately managed accounts from which to choose, how are you going to make your choice? Whether you are buying mutual funds or separate accounts, you should choose the best managers available in each asset class. Although performance is important, there is more to choosing the best managers than simply comparing last year's returns.

FIGURE 8

Growth Portfolio: 80% Stocks, 20% Bonds and 0% Cash	
Large-Cap Growth Stocks	20%
Large-Cap Value Stocks	20%
Mid-Cap Growth Stocks	10%
Mid-Cap Value Stocks	10%
Small-Cap Growth Stocks	5%
Small-Cap Value Stocks	5%
Large-Cap International Growth Stocks	5%
Large-Cap International Value Stocks	5%
Long-Term Bonds	5%
Intermediate-Term Bonds	5%
Short-Term Bonds	10%
Cash	0%
Other	0%

Many investors, when buying funds, focus on short-term performance rather than multiple factors that will make a difference over the long-term. For example, making it a practice to buy last year's winners usually leads to poor performance and unnecessary volatility.

Let's look at an *extreme* hypothetical example and consider Joan's investment portfolio. On January 1, 2000, Joan decided to invest $100,000 into the funds that had the best returns in 1999. She examined nearly 14,000 funds and then decided to divide her money equally among the ten top-performing funds from the previous year. How did she do in 2000 and 2001? After investing for just two years Joan's $100,000 investment is worth only $35,650, a loss of 64 percent. Figure 9 outlines her results.

Although investors rarely go to this extreme, purchasing ten funds with last year's best one-year returns as Joan did,

FIGURE 9

Hypothetical $10,000 investment made from 1/1/00 - 12/31/01				
Fund Name	Performance in 1999	Performance in 2000	Performance in 2001	Value 12/31/2001
Fidelity Japan Smaller Co.	237.42%	-50.23%	-20.02%	$3,979
PBHG Tech & Commun	243.89%	-43.69%	-52.38%	$2,681
Amerindo Technology D	248.86%	-64.79%	-50.77%	$1,733
Credit Suiss Japan Gr Adv	260.27%	-69.04%	-25.26%	$2,313
Driehaus Asia Pacific Gro	264.49%	-29.61%	-19.54%	$5,663
Nevis Fund	286.53%	-24.94%	-44.37%	$4,175
Van Wagoner Emerg. Gro	291.15%	-20.90%	-59.70%	$3,187
Morgan stan Ins Sm Gr	313.91%	-18.96%	-20.56%	$6,438
Credit Suiss Jpn Sm Adv	329.68%	-72.10%	-19.28%	$2,252
Nicholas-Apple Glb Tech I	493.73%	-36.37%	-49.26%	$3,229

Source: Morningstar Principia Pro, December 31, 2001

164

it is a very common error many investors make with their 401(k) plans. Given the 10 to 20 options available in most 401(k) plans, investors often buy the funds with the best near-term performance. Short-term returns should not be among your priority criteria for selecting a solid money manager.

The following search process will help you determine which money managers to hire by outlining specific criteria that should be met for each investment choice. If you allocated your money as outlined in Figure 8, you must now conduct a search to find the best manager in each asset class. Let's start with the 20 percent of your money you have decided to invest in large company U.S. growth stocks. The use of a financial advisor becomes especially helpful when you get to this stage of developing your investment portfolio. If you are working with an advisor, he or she should conduct a manager search for you and provide you with information supporting each manager choice.

The idea is to start with the whole universe of funds or separate accounts, then narrow them down to those that are among the best and most consistent. Below is an example of some of the criteria you should include in a search for an above-average, large company growth mutual fund.

As of December 31, 2001, there were 13,772 funds available.[16]

- Of these 13,772 funds, 1,035 were large company growth funds.

- Of these 1,035 funds, only 242 have a manager with fund tenure greater than five years.

- Of these 242 funds, only 129 have a 3-year track record above the category average.

- Of these 129 funds, only 82 have a 5-year track record above the category average.

- Of these 82 funds, only 26 have a 10-year track record above the category average.

- Of these 26 funds, only 7 have performed above average in a bear market.

Once you have a short list of funds from which to choose, you can then conduct a detailed check of each to make sure they have a consistent performance history and follow their size and style discipline. Following are a number of criteria that can help you do that.

Criteria #1: Long-term Performance vs. a Benchmark

It is not important that the fund you buy be the best fund out of the almost 14,000 available. You should, however, make certain that it is one of the better funds in its respective investment category. You want to seek investments with above-average performance in their asset class over the last three, five, ten, and 15 years. Looking simply at the last 12 months is not particularly helpful. Managers can fall to the bottom of their asset category in one "off" year, but be well above average in nine others and have a fantastic track record.

Each manager of a fund or separate account is given a performance hurdle. This is a rate of return they are expected to provide investors. The rate is determined by a stock or bond index that replicates the types of stocks or bonds the manager can buy based on the portfolio's objective. For example, large company growth managers generally use the Russell Top 200 Growth Index as their performance benchmark. As the name suggests, the index is made up of 200 large company growth stocks. Whether you are buying a mutual fund or a separate account, you should find out whether the manager has a record of consistently beating the performance index. This will give you a reasonable idea of what to expect from the manager going forward.

Let's use these search criteria to identify the best large company growth mutual funds available. Out of the 1,035 large company growth mutual funds available, how many beat the Russell Top 200 Index?

- For the past one- and three-year periods, 268 out of 656 large growth funds outperformed the index in each period (41 percent).

- For the past one-, three- and five-year periods, 125 out of 420 large growth funds outperformed the index in every period (30 percent).

- For the past one-, three-, five-, and ten-year periods, 21 out of 122 large growth funds outperformed the index in every period (17 percent).

- For the past one-, three-, five-, ten-, and 15-year periods, 11 out of 83 large growth funds outperformed the index in every period (13 percent).[17]

Now that we have narrowed the search, you can hone in on the 10-20 funds that have outperformed the average consistently over the long term.

Criteria #2: Year-to-Year Performance vs. a Benchmark

Once the long-term returns have been examined, you will need to do a quick check of the fund's year-to-year results, versus the benchmark. Figure 10 shows

FIGURE 10

Year	Russell Top 200 Growth Index (ending 12/31/2001)	Large Cap Growth Fund 1	Large Cap Growth Fund 2
1991	39.41%	42.67%	35.85%
1992	3.89%	2.03%	7.35%
1993	-.07%	21.10%	14.54%
1994	4.85%	-1.65%	.02%
1995	38.65%	35.75%	29.75%
1996	25.52%	2.73%	14.84%
1997	33.74%	28.58%	26.86%
1998	45.10%	35.05%	31.78%
1999	29.68%	63.74%	45.70%
2000	-24.52%	19.25%	7.49%
2001	-20.50%	-5.00%	-12.28%

Note: see footnote 18 and 19 for information on fund 1 and 2

how two of the better funds in our long-term search ranked on a year-to-year basis, versus the performance benchmark. You'll notice as you look at each fund's performance on a year-to-year basis that even the best funds will not always beat the index hurdle. Although, both Fund 1[18] and Fund 2[19] were beaten by the index six out of 11 years, their long-term average returns were much higher than the index, thus providing investors with superior performance.

Criteria #3: Manager Tenure

When you buy a fund, make sure your manager has some experience under his or her belt. You don't want a new manager cutting teeth and learning how to invest with your money. Your retirement money is your future, and you don't want someone "practicing" with it.

Preferably the manager you choose should have at least ten years' experience. This will ensure that he or she has been face-to-face with a couple of down markets and has gained experience handling adverse environments. Of the 122 large company growth funds with ten-year track records, only 33 of the funds have managers who have been with the fund for ten or more years. Out of all 1,035 large company growth funds available today, the average manager has been managing the portfolios for only 3.7 years. In our search above, out of the 21 funds that beat the benchmark over the past three, five, and ten years, only nine have managers with more than ten years' experience running their funds.[18]

Criteria #4: Consistent Investment Size and Style

It is important to buy a fund that is true to its investment size and style discipline. This means if you buy a large company growth fund, you can be assured it will still be a large company growth fund in five or ten years. If the manager begins buying small company or international stocks or moves from growth to value stocks, it will change your overall allocation and throw your portfolio out of alignment. The manager is hired as a specialist and to manage money in only one part of the market. You should make sure your manager sticks to his guns.

Criteria #5: Tax-efficiency

If you are investing taxable money (as opposed to tax-deferred money in a retirement account), you should find a fund with low turnover and a high tax efficiency rating. Low turnover means that the fund isn't overactive in its buying and selling. Remember, a 100 percent turnover rate means that every position in the portfolio is sold at least once during the year. The average large company growth fund has a portfolio turnover rate of 130 percent. The top four funds in our search have average turnover rates of only 49 percent. Lower turnover rates equate to lower taxable capital gains distributions. Turnover is not as much an issue in a retirement account in which there are no tax consequences for buying and selling.

Criteria #6: Performance During Down Years

How did the manager do when the market was falling? Checking the fund's performance, versus its index and other funds managed similarly during down years will give you an indication of what to expect if the market heads south. What was the worst-case scenario? Could you have endured the manager's performance during these periods? How much volatility is acceptable?

Criteria #7: Stock and Bond Overlap: How Much Overlap Exists in Your Overall Portfolio?

Do all of your funds or managers buy the same companies? If they do, you may not be as diversified as you think. Many investors own the two most popular funds of the 90's, Janus Twenty and Fidelity Magellan. If you examine the holdings of these portfolios, you will find that they own many of the same positions. Of the top 25 stock positions in each fund, 12 are exactly the same.[19] You are not adequately diversified if you own multiple funds that all buy the same stocks or bonds.

Criteria #8: Size of Fund As Measured By Total Assets Under Management

Many studies have concluded that smaller funds, meaning those with less total money under management, perform better than larger funds. Smaller funds can maneuver and react to changes in market conditions more quickly than their larger peers. The trade-off is that when you buy smaller funds, they will generally be newer and not have a lengthy track record. If you choose to go this route, be sure your money managers have a great deal of experience.

As a general rule, when buying smaller funds, buy when their total net asset size is less than the median market capitalization of the stocks that the fund purchases. For example, if a fund has $10 billion in net assets and buys stocks with a market capitalization of only $5 billion, you should avoid this fund.[20] This rule is not applicable to an index fund whose results are not a consequence of the manager's ability to maneuver in and out of stocks.

Once you've completed a search for one manager, repeat the process for each of the other assets classes in your portfolio. If you work with a financial advisor, it is his or her job to perform money manager searches for you. It is possible, however, to do searches on your own if you have the time and expertise.

In summary, by hiring professional money managers rather than managing a large portfolio of individual securities on your own, you are more likely to enjoy better investment results. Using the information in this chapter, you should now be more prepared to find and hire the best money managers for both mutual funds and separately managed accounts. A strong money manager with the required experience can help you buy the investments that will ensure your portfolio maintains the growth required to help you reach your goals.

CHAPTER 13
STEP 4: ONGOING PORTFOLIO MANAGEMENT

If you've followed the steps outlined in the previous five chapters, you are light years ahead of most investors. You have properly allocated your money, diversified it, and purchased good, consistent investments using the help of professional money managers. Surprisingly, however, the first three steps are the easiest in the investment process. Would you believe that the real work begins after you purchase your investments? That's because it's not easy to adhere to a disciplined investment strategy. This chapter will help you increase your chances of sticking with your strategy by outlining how to best manage your portfolio on an *ongoing* basis.

If you want to make money, you should buy good investments with the intent of holding them for the long-term, making only occasional adjustments. That may sound easy, but it's not. Compared to the hyper trading habits of many investors, making only minor, infrequent changes may feel like you're doing nothing to increase your wealth.

Buying good investments and holding them for the long run requires a tremendous amount of discipline. For example, if a portion of your portfolio is under-performing, your natural instincts will tell you to take immediate action and make changes. The more it lags, the more changes you'll want to make. The investment decisions you make at these points will greatly determine your investment success. Here is where your self-discipline needs to kick in.

Taking too much action too often leads to poor investment results (as explained in Chapter 7). However, by avoiding excessive adjustments to your portfolio and keeping your eye focused on long-term investment results, you're far more likely to enjoy success. Remember, it is not important how your portfolio performs during a one-month stretch or even over a single year, but rather how it does during the next five, 10, 15 and 20 years.

Although this equates to a "buy-and-hold" formula for investing, it is not suggested that you invest your money and then completely forget about it. Your portfolio should be monitored every six months making changes when necessary. Most of the time you will be better off simply being patient with the investments you own. There are times when you'll have valid reasons to sell investments and replace them with others.

Diversification is a key ingredient to long-term investing, and knowing what to expect, from a diversified portfolio will help you maintain your disciplined approach. If you own seven to ten different investments in a diversified portfolio, you can bank on the fact that, at any given time, some of them will be exceeding your expectations while others will be lagging. This is normal and expected. While you may get an intense itch to sell the investments that are performing poorly in order to purchase investments that have recently been on the rise, selling under-performing assets due to problems in short-term performance, as we have already discussed, is short-sighted and leads to selling low and buying high. Each investment you own will naturally experience ups and downs. Again, the goal is not to make short-term profits but rather to achieve solid, long-term performance.

Investors who remain patient with their investments and stay disciplined through market ups and downs will be rewarded for their ability to stay the course.

Semi-Annual and Annual Investment Portfolio Reviews

Every six months you should conduct a review of your portfolio. There is no reason to do this more frequently if you have hired good professional money manager's and are properly diversified. It's your money managers' job to watch your individual investments on a daily basis, so there is absolutely no reason to spend hours each day on the Internet looking at your money. Constant monitoring will only increase the temptation to start tinkering with your investments.

The purpose of a semi-annual review is not to change your allocation or dramatically alter your investments, but rather to do whatever fine-tuning is needed. Annual reviews should be more comprehensive and extensive, while semi-annual reviews can be less formal.

If you are working with a financial advisor, request that he or she review your portfolio with you at least every six months. Don't be afraid to ask for a review if your advisor hasn't already set one up. Semi-annual reviews can often be conducted informally over the phone, particularly if nothing alarming is occurring in the market. Financial advisors have tools that make such reviews an easy task.

During your annual and semi-annual reviews, start by looking at the big picture and updating your retirement analysis to determine if you are still on track. Then evaluate your portfolio as a whole before breaking it down into its individual pieces. Conducted properly, a review will bring to the surface any problems that exist in the portfolio. Once a problem is identified, changes can be made. However, as a general rule, if you can make a case for keeping an investment, you should probably do so. If you can't, then you should sell it and seek a better alternative.

There are a number of questions you should ask when conducting a portfolio review. Your answers to these questions will determine if your portfolio is meeting expectations or if modifications should be made. Use the questions below as a checklist for conducting your reviews:

Retirement Check-Up
- Are you on track to reach your retirement and other financial goals? If not, what adjustments need to be made?

Portfolio Allocation
- Is your portfolio out of alignment? Does it need to be re-balanced?
- Will there be any tax consequences if you do re-balance?
- Will there be any additional costs associated with re-balancing?

(Note: Your target stock, bond, and cash allocations need to be adjusted only every three to five years. You should never alter your allocation due to short-term market gyrations.)

Overall Portfolio Performance
- Is your portfolio meeting performance and risk expectations as outlined in your investment policy statement?

Individual Investments
- Are your money managers meeting performance expectations?
- How are they performing versus their peers (short- and long-term)?
- How are they performing versus their benchmarks (short- and long-term)?
- Has any size or style drift occurred with any of your funds?
- Have there been any money manager changes?
- Are any of the managers causing unwanted tax consequences due to excessive trading within the portfolio? (This question is not applicable for money in retirement accounts.)

Let's take a closer look at each of these questions and why you need to get good answers to each of them.

Are you on track to reach your retirement and other financial goals?
Portfolio reviews are a good time to focus on the big financial picture, making certain that you're still on track to reach your retirement goals. If your portfolio is a little off-track, perhaps you need to increase your savings rate or prepare to work

a little longer than planned. Conversely, maybe you'll find out you're ahead of the game and can retire sooner than planned. If you are already retired, updating your retirement analysis will ensure that you are not headed toward the depletion of your assets. In addition, if you are a retiree, these meetings should also be used to discuss estate planning and long-term care strategies.

Is your portfolio out of alignment?

Your portfolio allocation — how your money is divided between different asset classes — will change over time as a result of individual investments growing at different rates of return. Rebalancing is the process of realigning the portfolio back to its original allocation targets. By re-balancing your portfolio at least annually, it will grow more consistently and often enhance your portfolio returns.

To better understand the need for re-balancing, let's take a look at the mid-cap portion of a portfolio from 1999 to 2001. As you can see from the performance numbers of mid-cap growth stocks and mid-cap value stocks in Figure 1, these two asset classes experienced dramatically different results during this period of time. Because of this variance, a portfolio that was initially divided exactly evenly between mid-cap growth and mid-cap value stocks at the beginning of 1999, would have finished the year with mid-cap growth stocks representing 61 percent of the portfolio pie. At the end of 1999, the portfolio has much more mid-cap growth exposure than was initially intended. To re-balance at the end of 1999, 11 percent of the mid-cap growth positions would be sold and the proceeds used to rebuild the mid-cap value position.

FIGURE 1

Year	Mid-Cap Growth Stocks	Mid-Cap Value Stocks
1999	62.35%	3.69%
2000	-15.38%	24.81%
2001	-12.72%	7.10%

Source: Wilshire Mid-Cap Growth & Value Indexes

It is difficult to re-balance because it requires you to sell some of your investments that have recently done well and buy more of the investments that have recently under-performed. This goes against your natural instincts. Who is excited to sell a recent winner to buy a recent loser? However, by following this course, you are forcing yourself to sell a little bit high (as you shave off 11 percent of your mid-cap growth holdings in our example) and buy a little low as you add to your mid-cap value positions. This process of selling high and buying low will help you increase your returns. As part of a disciplined investment strategy, your portfolio should be realigned in this manner at least annually. Re-balancing should occur with the whole portfolio.

Figure 2 illustrates the growth provided by three different portfolios, 1) 100 percent mid-cap growth stocks, 2) 100 percent mid-cap value stocks, and 3) a blended portfolio consisting of 50 percent mid-cap growth stocks and 50 percent mid-cap value stocks re-balanced annually. As you can see, if you had the foresight to invest 100 percent of your money in mid-cap value stocks, you would have had the best results during this short period. However, if you had guessed wrong and selected mid-cap growth, as many did in 1999, you would have finished with about $10,000 less than the mid-cap value stocks generated during this time. By holding a blended portfolio and re-balancing annually, you would have experienced less volatility and still obtained good solid returns.

FIGURE 2

Year	Mid-Cap Growth Stocks	Mid-Cap Value Stocks	50/50
12/31/1998	$50,000	$50,000	$50,000
12/31/1999	$81,175	$51,845	$66,510
12/31/2000	$68,690	$64,760	$69,679
12/31/2001	$59,953	$69,358	$67,721

Source: Wilshire Mid-Cap Growth Index and Wilshire Mid-Cap Value Index. The 50/50 portfolio is a mix of 50% Mid-Cap Growth and 50% Mid-Cap Value Stocks, rebalanced annually.

Rebalancing also allows you to control your portfolio risk and sustain growth at a more consistent rate. If your portfolio consists of stocks and bonds and is not checked regularly, stocks, because of their higher expected growth, will inevitably outperform bonds and your stock weighting will continue to become a larger piece of your portfolio, while your bond weighting will shrink. This imbalance will make your portfolio more aggressive than you initially planned and put you in a riskier position. By re-balancing your portfolio, risk is controlled.

Once you make the decision to re-balance, there are two additional factors to consider. First, will there be any tax consequences? If so, do your re-balancing in a retirement account where taxes can be avoided. Second, will there be any cost to re-balance? In many cases, you may be required to pay a small transaction fee to move from one fund to another.

Is your portfolio meeting performance and risk expectations as outlined in your investment policy statement?

During your semi-annual portfolio evaluation, take another look at your investment policy statement. It will outline realistic short- and long-term expectations and acceptable levels of risk and volatility. Is your overall portfolio meeting the performance and risk expectations as outlined in your investment policy statement?

For example, your portfolio may be built to provide annual returns between –10 percent and 20 percent annually, with a target long-term average of 10 percent. If your portfolio drops 8 percent or gains 18 percent, you're operating within the range of your expectations. However, if in a given year the portfolio drops 20 percent, some of your money managers may be investing too aggressively or dramatically under-performing their benchmarks. Further examination of each manager is recommended if this occurs.

To monitor your investments, simply go back to the original criteria you established when you bought each investment to see if it is still making the grade (refer to Chapter 12 as needed). If not, find out why.

Are each of your money managers meeting performance expectations?

Are your money managers meeting your performance expectations? To answer this question, you need the correct performance yardstick. For example, you can't compare the performance of a small company stock mutual fund to the Dow Jones Industrial Average or the S&P 500 (large company stock indicators). It's an apples-to-oranges comparison. The correct performance yardstick for small company stock funds is the performance of other small company stock funds or a small company index.

Now let's suppose your money manager, who once had performance numbers in the top of an investment category, slides below average for a year or two. What should you do? This is likely to happen to even the best managers at one time or another. Yes, it's frustrating to see a fund slip from among the best in its category to below average, but your best course of action is still to stay put. A quick study of any of today's top mutual funds will reveal that they don't stay at the very top of their respective categories year in and year out. This would be virtually impossible. Money managers' investment styles will naturally go in and out of favor with the market, outperforming in some years and under-performing in others.

When poor performance occurs, put the money manager on trial and see if you can build a case for continued ownership; if not, make a change. Below are several items to consider as you attempt to make a case for your investment.

How is your manager doing vs. all other managers handling similar portfolios?

Short-Term Performance Versus Peers and Asset Class Index. Let's suppose you owned a small-cap value stock fund that was up 10 percent in 1999. You can't help but notice that the S&P 500 climbed 21.04 percent for the same period. It would be easy to get down on your small-cap value fund, wouldn't it?

Actually, this comparison doesn't provide you with enough information to make a decision with your investment. Remember, it doesn't really matter how your small-cap value fund did against the S&P 500. A far more useful and accurate comparison would be to match your fund's performance versus all of the other small-cap value funds. In this example, you would find that the average small-cap value fund posted only a 5.43 percent return in 1999. If your fund provided you with a 10 percent return, then you should be quite pleased. This performance would have placed your fund in the top 26 percent of all small-cap value funds in 1999.[1] As a general rule, if your fund posts performance numbers that are above the average when compared to its respective category, then you should hold on to it.

The same comparison can be made against a market index. An index measures a representative group of stocks to provide information about how certain sectors of the market are performing. Each money manager uses an index as a benchmark to evaluate their performance. For example, our small-cap value fund provided a 10 percent return in 1999 while the Russell 2000 Value Index posted a –1.48 percent return. This is another indication that your fund did a nice job.

Let's change the scenario and assume that your fund isn't doing well and its performance is below the average of its peer group and respective tracking index. What do you do then? The smart thing is to turn to its long-term performance. If the manager has done a nice job over the long-term but just recently stumbled and had a rough year, then you should hold on. If, however, the manager's long-term numbers are below average, then you should seriously consider another fund.

Every manager is going to have a rough year occasionally. After one such year, flag the fund and watch the performance for yet another year. If the fund still performs in the bottom tier, it is a sell candidate.

Long-Term Performance Versus Peers and Asset Class Index. To examine a fund on a long-term basis, you must compare its returns to its peer funds and a benchmark index over the last three, five and ten years. By looking at the long-term numbers, you can see how your fund did through complete business cycles. Although future performance will not be identical to past years, studying historical returns should provide an indication of the fund's potential.

For example, what would you do with the Weitz Partners Value fund if you owned it when you conducted your 2001 annual review? You may be concerned because, for the previous 12 months, 74 percent of the mid-cap value funds had better one-year performance numbers than the Weitz Partners fund. In addition, the fund posted a -.86 percent return in 2001 while its respective index, the Russell Mid-Cap Value Index, was up 2.34 percent.[2] In 2001 Weitz Partners Value fund under-performed versus its peer group, mid-cap value stocks funds and its respective index. Research tells us that prior to 2001, the fund was considered one of the best-performing mid-cap value funds available; in 2001 it was one of the worst. Should it be held or sold? Further examination is required.

How has the fund done over the longer term? The performance column in Figure 3 outlines the average annual returns for the fund for various periods of time. Although performance was poor in the short-term, the Weitz Partners Value fund has been one of the leading mid-cap value funds over the last three, five, ten and 15 years (ending December 31, 2001). Its rank was in the top 10 percent of its category over the past five-, ten- and 15-year periods. It has also consistently outperformed the Russell Mid-Cap Value index.[3]

FIGURE 3

Weitz Partners Value Fund			
	Performance	% Rank Vs. Category	+/- Index
One Year	-.86%	74	-3.20%
Three Year	13.57%	27	6.76%
Five Year	21.61%	3	10.15%
Ten Year	18.93%	1	4.52%
Fifteen Year	16.42%	1	2.95%

Source: Morningstar Principia Pro, December 31, 2001

What should we do with this fund? Flag it to be watched more closely in upcoming reviews. Hold it for now; it's a good, solid long-term fund.

Manager Tenure and Performance Figures. When reviewing long-term performance numbers, remember to check the length of time the manager has been handling the portfolio. If the term is, say, just two or three years, then the five- and ten-year performance numbers are irrelevant because they were achieved by an entirely different manager. In the case of the Weitz Partners Value Fund, the manager, Wallace R. Weitz, has been managing the fund for the past nine years, meaning the time frames we should use for comparison purposes are the one-, three-, five- and most of the ten-year numbers.

Has any size or style drift occurred with any of your funds?

Is your fund manager staying true to the fund's size and style objectives? If not, it often means the manager is chasing returns and not adhering to the fund's stated investment discipline.

This frequently happened in 1999. Value managers, after enduring several years of poor performance compared to growth managers, began buying growth stocks to get in on the action. These stocks were leading the market at the time. In 2000, when value stocks came back into favor, many value funds didn't do as well as they should have because of this shift in strategy. Many of their portfolios were overloaded with technology growth stocks, and this hurt performance in 2000.

If you have developed a well-diversified portfolio, a manager who suddenly changes the fund's size or style objectives could dramatically throw your portfolio diversification out of balance. For example, if you had allocated your portfolio as outlined in the "Target Allocation" column in Figure 4, what effect would it have on your portfolio if your large-cap value manager began buying growth-oriented stocks and your small-cap value fund began buying mid-cap value stocks?

FIGURE 4

Sample Aggressive Growth Portfolio		
Investment Category	**Target Allocation**	**Portfolio Allocation After Style Drift**
Large-Cap Growth Stocks	22.5%	35.0%
Large-Cap Value Stocks	22.5%	10.0%
Mid-Cap Growth Stocks	12.5%	12.5%
Mid-Cap Value Stocks	12.5%	15.5%
Small-Cap Growth Stocks	5.0%	5.0%
Small-Cap Value Stocks	5.0%	2.0%
International Growth Stocks	10.0%	10.0%
International Value Stocks	10.0%	10.0%
Bonds	0.0%	0.0%
Total	100.0%	100.0%

Your allocation would entirely change and your portfolio would no longer be covering all of the desired bases (see the last column in Figure 4).

The portfolio in the previous example is no longer as diversified, as it should be. If this style drift had occurred sometime in 1999, this portfolio would have suffered dramatically in 2000 and 2001 when growth stocks fell out of favor.

How do you avoid this problem? During each review, check your fund's size and style to make sure the manager is handling your money as you intended. If the manager is not adhering to his or her size and style mandates, consider another fund.

Have there been any money manager changes?

What do you do if one of your fund managers leaves a fund? This is often a signal to sell but don't do so hastily without diligently collecting and reviewing all of the essential information.

How successful was the newly-hired money manager in his or her previous fund management experience? If the manager has handled a similar fund and has been relatively successful, you may want to hold tight and take a "wait-and-see" approach. Give the manager some time to prove himself before deciding to sell the fund. However, if the manager does not have much management experience or has not managed successfully in the past, consider selling the fund immediately.

In most cases, the new fund manager will dramatically alter the portfolio and management discipline. This is typically not a good thing for investors.

Are any of the managers causing unwanted tax consequences?

If you are investing in a non-retirement account, taxes are most likely a concern. Although you should have a rough idea of what taxes to expect from a fund before you purchase it, it is still a good idea to check the fund during reviews to see that its turnover rate hasn't ramped up recently. Increasing turnover rates in funds drive up the chances you will get hit with higher-than-expected capital gains distributions.

If no manager changes have taken place, your managers are staying true to their size and style mandates, the funds are performing in line with their respective indexes, and the overall portfolio performance is within expectations, there is no reason to make any adjustments.

SELLING A FUND

If you do sell a fund, don't repeat the crucial mistake made by so many investors — taking your proceeds and reinvesting them in a fund from the asset class that has recently enjoyed the most success during the last 12 months! This again is a classic way to sell low and buy high. If you sell a large company U.S. growth stock fund, for example, you should go through the process outlined in Step 3 in Chapter 12 to identify the best large company U.S. growth stock fund with which to replace it. By approaching changes this way, you will be able to maintain your asset allocation and diversification targets.

Morningstar.com can be an excellent source when conducting a portfolio review. In addition, Morningstar offers some additional services that are very useful, including e-mail bulletins to alert you to any fund manager changes, performance problems and much more that may help you monitor your portfolio. Most financial advisors have computer programs that allow them to save your investment criteria on their systems when you initially invest. They can call them up easily for you during each semi-annual review.

Remember, reviewing your portfolio is important, but don't confuse regular reviewing with excessive trading. The latter will do little to aid your success as an investor.

If you have followed the first three steps for developing a successful investment strategy as outlined in the last five chapters, you have properly allocated your money, diversified it, and purchased good investments using the help of professional money managers. As was noted at the beginning of this chapter, however, the first three steps are actually the easiest in the investment process. The real work begins *after* you purchase your investments. That's because it's not always easy to stick to a disciplined investment strategy. By following the guidelines outlined in this chapter on how to best manage your portfolio on an *ongoing* basis, you will greatly increase you chances of adhering to a solid investment strategy and obtaining good long-term returns.

Chapter 14
Strategies for Protecting Principal
While Investing in the Stock Market

From March 31, 2000, to June 30, 2002, the U.S. market, as measured by the S&P 500, experienced a deep 35.2 percent downturn. Over the past 50 years, this pullback is second only to that of the 1973-1974 recession, which was marked by a 21-month, 43 percent stock market drop. Investing in the stock market can be risky and there are more than a few skittish investors who won't invest at all unless they can protect their money from market downturns.

While market drops can be unnerving, they can also be viewed as a time of great opportunity. Investors have forever been taught to buy low and sell high. The stock market is cyclical and will naturally go up and down. One would think, then, that it would make the most sense to invest when the market has suffered its deepest drops. However, the pain of watching a stock portfolio drop for an extended period of time, combined with other uncertainties such as military conflict, corporate accounting practices, energy concerns and the like, make it difficult, if not impossible for many people to invest their money in the stock market.

Yes, investors want the higher returns offered by stocks, but many are scared away by the volatility and uncertainty inherent in the market, and although diversification can eliminate a great deal of the risk associated with investing in stocks (as discussed in Chapter 11), it does not guarantee principal. Some investors need an extra layer of protection to sleep well at night.

This raises an interesting question. Is there a way to participate in the stock market while at the same time protecting investment principal? The answer is "yes." In fact, there are three strategies that allow investors this opportunity. In this chapter we will outline these principal-protection strategies and how each can help many would-be, ultra-conservative cash and bond investors begin to tiptoe into the stock market.

Each of the three strategies is appropriate for those who are investing new money. Additionally, these strategies will help the many investors who simply can't stomach any more stock market volatility and want out of their stock investments. For those who have suffered losses, applying these strategies represent better alternatives than selling stocks and realizing losses when markets are down, then reinvesting that money in low-yielding cash alternatives such as Money Markets or certificates of deposits. The fastest way to make back losses is to be invested in stocks when the market rebounds.

Each of the strategies outlined in this chapter allows investors to participate in the stock market on the upside while at the same time protecting investment principal during market downturns.

STRATEGY #1: PRINCIPAL PROTECTION MUTUAL FUNDS

Principal protection mutual funds are probably the simplest approach to protecting principal while at the same time participating in the stock market. These funds invest the majority of their portfolios in large U.S. companies, typically those comprising the S&P 500 and bonds. These funds attempt to mirror the performance of the S&P 500 while protecting and insuring principal.

To provide principal protection the funds purchase portfolio insurance. Large companies like MBIA and New York Life offer the insurance. This insurance is similar to the insurance municipalities purchase when they are interested in guaranteeing their bond debt and increasing their credit ratings.

After investing your money in a principal protection fund, the value of the portfolio will fluctuate up and down with the value of the underlying stocks in the portfolio. However, if you hold onto your fund for five years (perhaps 10 years, depending on the fund) you are guaranteed, at a minimum, to receive your original investment back no matter how poorly the markets may have performed. If the markets provide a good return and your portfolio is worth more than your original investment after five years, then you can sell the fund at the higher market value or hold it for the long run. Of course, you can sell your fund prior to the five-year mark if you wish and, as with any other funds you would receive the market value of the fund at that time.

Currently, there are only a few fund families that offer principal protection funds:
- ING Pilgrim funds (800-334-3444)
- Mainstay funds (800-624-6782)
- Guardian Park Avenue funds (800-221-3253).

CHAPTER 14 – STRATEGIES FOR PROTECTING PRINCIPAL WHILE INVESTING IN THE STOCK MARKET

According to Morningstar, an investment of $10,000 in the Mainstay Equity Index Fund (a principal protection fund) made on January 2, 1992, would have doubled in value after just five years. If held through June of 2002, it would have reached a balance of $26,608 (a 9.77 percent annualized return). Because the market was so strong over this period, the guarantee feature wasn't needed. However, for apprehensive investors, simply knowing the guarantee was in place would have provided great comfort during dramatic stock market pullbacks such as those that occurred in 1994, 1998, 2000 and 2001.

STRATEGY #2: ZERO COUPON BONDS

Let's suppose you have $100,000 to invest and would like to participate in the stock market without risking any principal. One solution is to invest a portion of your $100,000 into a Zero Coupon U.S. Treasury Bond and another portion into a stock portfolio.

FIGURE 1

Amount to Invest In a Zero Coupon Bond at 5% to Insure Principal			
Current Yield	Years to Maturity	Percentage of Portfolio in Zero	Amount of $100,000 Portfolio to Invest in Zero Coupon Bond
5%	15	48.10%	$48,101
5%	14	50.51%	$50,506
5%	13	53.03%	$53,032
5%	12	55.68%	$55,680
5%	11	58.47%	$58,467
5%	10	61.39%	$61,391
5%	9	64.46%	$64,460
5%	8	67.68%	$67,638

To obtain a 10-year guarantee of principal, using a zero coupon yielding 5 percent you would need to invest approximately $61,391 into a ten-year, zero coupon treasury bond. Zero coupon bonds are purchased at a discount ($61,391 in our example), pay no interest during the life of the bond, and mature at face value ($100,000 in our example). The difference between the purchase price and the face value represents your investment return. Because the zero coupon bond will mature at $100,000, you have guaranteed your principal if you hold onto the bond for ten years. Knowing you will receive $100,000 at maturity gives you the peace of mind to place the rest of your money in more volatile investments.

You can invest the remaining $38,609 in a diversified portfolio of stocks or stock funds. Again, regardless of what happens to these stocks, you are guaranteed to receive back your initial investment of $100,000, via the zero coupon bond. The U.S. Treasury backs this guarantee. You could purchase a corporate or municipal zero coupon bond and accomplish the same objective. Your yields, however, would be different and your guarantee not as strong.

`FIGURE 2

Amount to Invest In a Zero Coupon Bond at 10% to Insure Principal			
Current Yield	Years to Maturity	Percentage of Portfolio in Zero	Amount of $100,000 Portfolio to Invest in Zero Coupon Bond
10%	15	23.94%	$23,939
10%	14	26.33%	$26,333
10%	13	28.97%	$28,966
10%	12	31.86%	$31,863
10%	11	35.05%	$35,049
10%	10	38.55%	$38,554
10%	9	42.41%	$42,409
10%	8	46.64%	$46,651

In your own case, what percentage of your portfolio would you need to invest in a zero coupon bond to insure your portfolio principal? The answer depends on the yield on your zero coupon bond and the years until the bond matures. Figure 1 shows that if you obtain a "zero" yielding 5 percent and want to protect your portfolio over a ten-year period, you would need to invest 61.39 percent of your portfolio into the zero. Figure 2 shows you the same results for a 10 percent zero coupon bond.

How good is the guarantee? That depends on the strength of the bond's issuer. If the U.S. Treasury issues the zero, then it's backed by the full faith and credit of the United States government. This is the strongest guarantee in the world today.

STRATEGY #3: VARIABLE ANNUITY WITH LIVING BENEFIT

Insurance companies are continually adding features to their variable annuity contracts to make them more attractive. A little-known feature called a "living benefit" can be added to a variable annuity to provide another way to protect your portfolio.

What's a variable annuity? Think of it as a tax-deferred mutual fund account. You can buy variable annuities through brokerage firms, banks, insurance companies and mutual fund companies. Ultimately, however, they are products of insurance companies that administer the annuity contract — providing tax deferral — while a mutual fund company is hired to perform the day-to-day money management. The insurance company typically hires a number of portfolio managers from different fund companies to manage individual funds (called sub-accounts) within the annuity contract. Most contracts offer between 20 to 30 different investment choices, covering a wide spectrum of asset classes including large company stocks, small company stocks, international stocks, bonds and more.

When you invest your money into some variable annuities, you can opt to have a "living benefit" feature added to the contract. Here's how the "living benefit" works. Regardless of the performance of the investments you choose, you are guaranteed that your principal will grow at a rate of 5-6 percent per year, which varies by contract. You can cash in on this guarantee typically any time after the seventh year. Again, this varies by contract.

Let's assume you deposited $100,000 several years ago into a variable annuity and invested the entire amount into an aggressive NASDAQ stock sub-account. The sub-account performed well and your investment grew to $175,000 by the fourth year. In years six and seven, however, the market takes a tremendous turn for the worse and your portfolio balance drops to $75,000. Under most circumstances, you would be deeply concerned. In this case, however, because of the living benefit feature you know you have two options: 1) ride out the market downturn in hopes of a future rebound, or 2) exercise your living benefit option.

If you elect to exercise your living benefit option in year seven, you would be guaranteed your original investment of $100,000, plus a 6 percent annual rate of return for the previous seven years. This would give you an additional $50,363, making the living benefit value $150,363. The living benefit feature gives you the option of annuitizing this $150,363. Doing so could provide you with income for life, based on this balance. The guarantee is backed by the underlying insurance company, meaning investors should seek reputable companies with high ratings.

Annuitizing your money is much like receiving a traditional corporate pension payout. Your payments are based on your age, life expectancy, and an interest rate assumption. There are many annuity payout options from which to choose. If, for example, you are a 65-year-old male and choose a life-only annuity option, you would receive approximately $13,000 per year for the rest of your life using the assumptions above.

While the living benefit does not exactly guarantee your principal investment, it does guarantee the stream of income that your principal can provide. This makes good sense. The reason you have a retirement portfolio is not to admire the dollars it contains but to provide you with income at some point in time. Why not guarantee that future income?

This strategy has a downside. Once you annuitize, you cannot touch your principal from that time forward. Using our example above, once annuitization has taken place, no additional withdrawals can be made from the $150,363 portfolio, except for the $13,000 that is being paid out annually. Keep in mind, however, that annuitization is optional and typically would be used only if the markets performed very poorly.

Although this feature may seem somewhat restrictive, it makes sense for several reasons. First, if the markets perform as they have historically and provide good solid returns, you will probably never annuitize your contract and exercise the living benefit option. However, having this option provides peace of mind during times of market turmoil. You can be confident that no matter what happens in the market, your future retirement income will not be at risk if there is a severe market downturn. Second, the annuity provides tax deferral which can help your money grow more rapidly.

Investors should be familiar with other annuity features available whenever purchasing variable annuity contracts. Again, the features offered by each annuity contract will vary. For example:

- Many variable annuities will actually pay you to make an initial deposit. In some cases, this can amount to 4-6 percent of the amount you initially deposit. So, if you invest $100,000, the annuity company will add an extra $4,000 to $6,000 to your account.

- Variable annuities also provide a death benefit. Many guarantee a benefit equal to your initial investment or the highest annual market value of the annuity, whichever is greater. This feature protects the portfolio for your heirs in the event of a market drop.

- Some contracts provide an additional payout at death to cover taxes that may be owed from portfolio gains.

- At one time, virtually all annuities had to be held for five to seven years before they could be liquidated without surrender charges. Now, many contracts offer zero to one-year holding periods, providing tax deferral with liquidity.

- Many variable annuities offer special introductory rates of return if you choose to dollar-cost average from a fixed account into the variable accounts over a 6-to-12 month period. In many cases, these fixed accounts yield 7-9 percent.

Before you buy a variable annuity, consider the following important factors. First, the money cannot be withdrawn prior to age 59 $^1/_2$ without a 10 percent IRS early withdrawal penalty, much like the penalties that kick in when you withdraw money early from an IRA. Second, while variable annuities offer additional features, they also carry additional expenses. In addition to the cost of the underlying mutual fund management (approximately 1 percent annually), there is an additional insurance company fee referred to as the M&E (mortality and expense). This fee typically ranges between 1-1.5 percent. Furthermore, if you purchase an annuity and opt for the living benefit, you may pay an additional .25 percent per year. You will not see any of these expenses because they are all built right into the price of each sub-account

So when you purchase an annuity, an important consideration is whether or not the additional benefits are worth the extra expense. Regarding the living benefit feature, if it gives you the peace of mind to stay invested in stocks for the long run instead of pulling your money out of the market, then it is definitely worth the extra cost.

Each of the three strategies outlined in this chapter are worth considering if the volatility of the stock market has the potential to give you heartburn and insomnia. If you're thinking of selling your stocks and getting out of the market entirely, or if you simply want to purchase an investment while the markets are low but are uneasy about market conditions, these strategies will yield peace of mind during uncertain times.

CHAPTER 15
INCREASE YOUR ODDS FOR SUCCESS:
WORK WITH A PROFESSIONAL FINANCIAL ADVISOR

Evidence suggests that investors who work with advisors enjoy better investment performance.[1] Dr. Jerry Buss, owner of the 2000, 2001, 2002 NBA championship Los Angeles Lakers provides a perfect illustration of why advisors can be so important to success, whether in sports, business, or investing.

Dr. Buss certainly has the prerogative, since he's the boss, to hire himself as a player for the Lakers or even as the coach, if he so desired. But Dr. Buss won't do that because he knows he's neither a professional basketball player nor a professional coach. He is, first and foremost, a businessman that wants his franchise to be profitable and win basketball games. As the person ultimately responsible for the success of the franchise, he hires the best available players and coaches to increase the value of his business.

You are much like the owner of a professional sports franchise — you own assets. Your financial advisors — a financial planner, an accountant, an attorney, for example — are your coaches, and the investments you choose are equivalent to the players on your team. The job of your financial advisors, like that of a coach, is to help you develop a winning financial game plan and to manage that plan over time. Just as Jerry Buss counts on his players to win games, you count on your investments to win returns to accomplish your financial goals. You could choose to fill all these roles yourself. But like Jerry Buss, you will enjoy more success by outsourcing the coaching and playing to professionals.

The role of a financial advisor is to help you develop a sound plan for your money. Developing and implementing a solid investment plan is the first part of this process. A good financial advisor will also meet with you regularly for reviews to update your plan, monitor your portfolio, and suggest changes where necessary.

This chapter outlines how working with a professional financial advisor can dramatically increase your odds for success, the roles an advisor can play, and how to best select and hire an advisor.

ADVISORS PROVIDE STABILITY AND DISCIPLINE

Research indicates that investors, left to their own devices, are fickle and rarely disciplined when it comes to sticking with an investment strategy. As Benjamin Graham, the legendary American investor, said, "The investor's chief problem — and even his worst enemy — is likely to be himself."[2]

An advisor can guide you through the turbulence of the financial markets and help you adhere to your strategy. By sticking to a fundamentally sound strategy, you will ultimately increase your chances of obtaining better investment performance.

Let's look at the evidence: Studies show that the majority of investors seek out the assistance of a financial professional once their investment portfolio reaches $100,000. In addition, 64 percent of those with incomes over $100,000 use the services of a financial planner (Figure 1). The more money a person makes, the more complex their planning becomes, thus the more likely they are to need an advisor. For instance, 70 percent of people who make over $150,000 per year rely on financial advisors.[3]

FIGURE 1

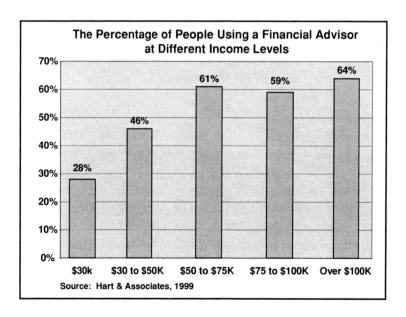

The Percentage of People Using a Financial Advisor at Different Income Levels

Source: Hart & Associates, 1999

Figure 2 illustrates the total returns of various market indexes compared to the total returns achieved by the average investor. If an investor had invested money in the S&P 500 (Large U.S. Companies) from 1984 to 2000, he or she would have earned an annualized return of 16.29 percent. Unfortunately, during this same period, the average investor purchasing equity mutual funds earned just 5.32 percent.

Why did the stock market do so well yet people investing in it so poorly? One reason was their inability to hold investments over the long-term. The job of your advisor is to provide needed encouragement and to help you stick steadfastly to an investment discipline, even when thundering market volatility is tempting you to act out of panic.

FIGURE 2

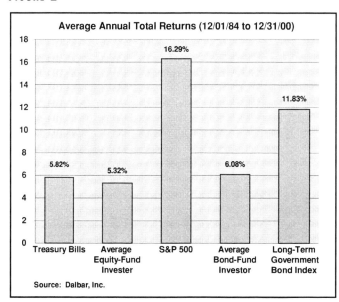

Source: Dalbar, Inc.

Investors are notorious for pouring money into stocks and funds that are hitting all-time highs and selling investments at all-time lows. In other words, the average investor is buying high and selling low, the exact opposite of what they should do. According to a DALBAR study, investors who do not seek advice were more likely to panic and sell when stocks dived.[4] With the advice, knowledge and experience of a financial consultant, investors are more likely to hold onto their investments for the long-run.

THOSE WHO WORK WITH ADVISORS ENJOY BETTER INVESTMENT RETURNS

Studies show that investors who work with financial advisors experience better investment performance and accumulate more money than those who try to do it on their own (see Figure 3).

As the study in Figure 3 indicates, those working with an advisor enjoyed better long-term returns. An advisor can also counsel you on other areas of your financial planning beyond just your investment portfolio.

Let's be clear: Working with a financial advisor does not guarantee better rates of return. However, it does increase your chances of financial success. Even if working with an advisor yields only an extra 1 or 2 percent per year in investment returns, it could be well worth it.

How much difference can that 1 or 2 percent make? Consider that Tiger Woods was the world's number one golfer in 2001 with an average, per-round score of 68.81 and winnings of $5,687,777. Cameron Beckman was the 50th rated golfer in the world. His average score was 70.65, an average of just 1.84 more strokes per round than Woods. Yet, those extra 1.84 shots made a difference of $4,616,434 in earnings. A seemingly small difference in performance can translate into a very large impact on the bottom line.[5]

FIGURE 3

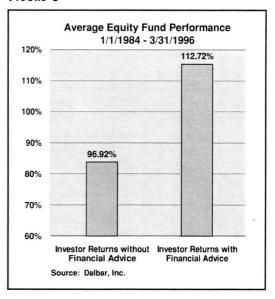

The same holds true for your investment portfolio. Earning just an extra 1 or 2 percent each year can literally put hundreds of thousands of additional dollars into your retirement pocket. For example, an investor with a $100,000 investment portfolio who is planning on retiring in 25 years would have $684,848 by the time he retires if his portfolio grows at 8 percent per year. Increasing that rate of return by just two percentage points would increase the portfolio value to $1,083,471. Add another two points and the balance grows to $1,700,006.

You can see that the difference of an extra percentage point or two is dramatic, over time. If your financial advisor can help you adhere to your strategy and remain invested for the long-term, the benefits to your portfolio could be substantial.

In general, your financial advisor will help you develop realistic expectations by discussing the risks and rewards of investing, match your individual goals and objectives with appropriate investments, continually monitor your portfolio, and conduct regular reviews of your financial status to ensure that you are headed in the right direction.[6]

INDUSTRY COMPLEXITY

You wouldn't consider picking up a scalpel and operating on a patient without first obtaining a medical degree and years of experience gaining an understanding of the complexities of the human body. Likewise, as an investor, you shouldn't consider managing your financial portfolio without a complete understanding of the extremely complex and ever-changing financial services industry.

It is very difficult for an individual who doesn't work in the financial services industry on a day-to-day basis to understand all the nuances surrounding the various financial products and services available. In addition to understanding how thousands of products and services operate, there are also many rules and regulations to which one must adhere.

The following questions are a small sampling of some of the basic things you should know if you are going to attempt to manage your own financial portfolio. If you can't answer these questions with confidence, you should definitely consider using the services of a professional financial advisor:

- What investment assets make up a diversified portfolio?

- What criteria should be used when choosing from among the 14,000 mutual funds available to investors?

- What is the difference between a separately managed account and a mutual fund, and when should a separately managed account be used?

- When should you sell an investment you own?

- What are some tax-advantaged ways to invest in stocks?

- How should you structure your portfolio to provide you with the income you need during retirement?

- What is an appropriate rate to withdraw money from your investment assets during retirement?

- When should you convert your IRA to a Roth IRA?

- If offered, should you take a one-time, lump-sum distribution or annuity payments from your company's pension plan?

- If you decide to retire prior to age 59 $1/2$, how can you take distributions from your retirement plan without being penalized?

- At what age should you apply for Social Security? For Medicare?

If you would like help answering these and many other questions relating to your financial plan, consider hiring an experienced financial advisor.

FIGURE 4

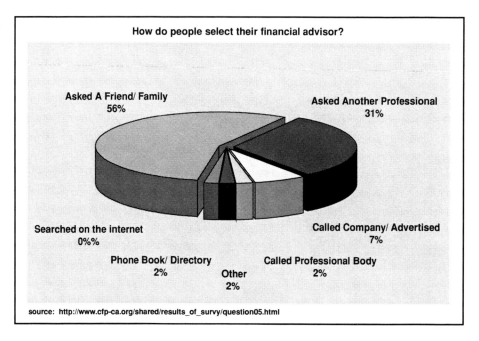

How do people select their financial advisor?

Asked A Friend/ Family
56%

Asked Another Professional
31%

Searched on the internet
0%%

Called Company/ Advertised
7%

Phone Book/ Directory
2%

Other
2%

Called Professional Body
2%

source: http://www.cfp-ca.org/shared/results_of_survy/question05.html

While over half of all investors find a professional financial advisor by taking recommendations from a friend or family member, you should be even more diligent in selecting someone who will play such a major role in shaping your financial future.

Remember, when hiring an advisor, you are the boss, and the financial advisor is the employee. It is important that you interview prospective advisors just as you would if hiring an employee to work at a company you own. There are several steps you should follow.

STEP ONE: KNOW WHAT'S OUT THERE

Seek a financial advisor who is qualified to do the job. Find out what training and certification he or she has. While there are many individuals who use the title "financial advisor;" unfortunately the requirements for carrying that title are minimal. However, there are organizations that provide standards for those in financial advice professions. It is recommended that you work with an advisor who carries one of the following designations:

Certified Financial Planner (CFP): The CFP title is awarded by the International Board of Standards and Practices for Certified Financial Planners (IBCFP). CFP's must undergo two years of intensive training followed by a rigorous, national, two-day examination. CFP's must also have a certain level of education and spend a satisfactory amount of time in the financial services industry. A code of ethics must be followed and participation in a continuing education program is required. CFP's are trained in many aspects of the financial services industry, including investment, insurance, retirement, tax, estate planning, etc.

Chartered Financial Consultant (ChFC): ChFC's are particularly expert in life insurance and receive their designation from the American College in Bryn Mawr, Pennsylvania. To earn this title, the financial planner must pass ten college-level courses on all major topics of personal finance. Recipients must meet specified requirements and adhere to strict ethical standards.

Personal Financial Specialist (PFS): The PFS is a financial planning designation awarded by the American Institute of Certified Public Accountants to people who are already Certified Public Accountants. They must have at least three years of personal financial planning experience and pass a comprehensive examination. They must also complete continuing education requirements and renew their license annually.

Registered Financial Planner (RFP): This title, awarded by the International Association of Registered Financial Planners, goes to planners who have had at least four years experience in planning. RFP's must have a college degree in business, economics or law, and either a CFP, ChFC or CPA designation along with a securities or insurance license.

STEP TWO: LOOK AT EXPERIENCE

Once you have a list of professionally accredited individuals, consider your specific situation and objectives, then look for an advisor who has the kind of experience you need. Ask the potential candidates about their areas of expertise and the types of clients and investments they handle. Ask for copies of plans he or she has done for people with circumstances similar to yours.

STEP THREE: INVESTIGATE ADVISORS THOROUGHLY

Once you have narrowed your selection to a handful of individuals, be sure to undertake an in-depth investigation of each advisor's background and credentials. Remember, this is the person who will be handling your money and your future.

The Forum for Investor Advice recommends, "Spend time to thoroughly check out your advisor's credentials, experience, investment philosophy, specialties and client references to make sure you find someone whom you can trust and will give you valuable advice."

STEP FOUR: FIND OUT HOW THE ADVISOR IS COMPENSATED

Financial advisors are paid either by fee, commission, or by a combination of the two. Fee-based advisors usually charge a flat fee, hourly rates, or a percentage of the assets they manage. Commission-based advisors earn their money through the number of transactions in the stocks, bonds, mutual funds, life insurance, annuities, and other investments they handle. Those who work on a combination fee-and-commission basis typically charge a set fee for their initial planning advice, then a commission on financial products or a yearly charge for assets under management.

How an investment advisor gets paid should be important to you. The Federal Administration on Aging warns investors of the dilemma faced by commission-only advisors:

"A financial planner who collects commissions is open to the criticism that he or she has an incentive to select or recommend investments partly on the basis of the commission offered — not solely on the quality of the investment." It advises, "While competence and performance should be the primary considerations in selecting a planner, compensation should also be considered — especially in cases where commissions are involved."

This is not to say that you should not consider an advisor who works on commissions. The Administration concludes, "The fact that commissions or other payments are made does not necessarily mean the investment is a bad one. Rather, it indicates that your planner may be faced with choosing between what is best for her and what is best for you."

STEP FIVE: INTERVIEW THE FINALISTS

Interviewing candidates is the most important step in selecting your financial advisor. It is no small decision, and a great deal of thought should go into what you ask during your interview.

Be prepared with questions that determine the character, style, and quality of the candidate. Keep in mind that you're the boss, so you want to act as if you are interviewing a potential employee, an employee who will have a huge impact on your success or failure.

THE FORUM FOR INVESTOR ADVICE (FIA) SUGGESTS THE FOLLOWING DETAILED QUESTIONNAIRE:

Qualifications:

1. What is your educational background? College degree and area of study? Financial planning education?

2. What financial planning certifications or designations do you hold?

3. What securities licenses do you hold?

4. What is your professional experience? How many years have you been a financial advisor?

5. How do you keep your financial knowledge base and planning skills current?

Services:

1. How would you prepare my financial plan? Do you recommend specific investments or investment products?

2. Ask to see a sample financial plan. Make sure that the plan is clear and comprehensive.

3. What is your investment philosophy? What types of investments do you favor? Get a sense of the types of investment products and methodology that the advisor would use.

4. Do you have certain areas of expertise: insurance, estate planning, retirement planning, education planning, tax issues?

5. Do you collaborate with professionals in accounting, law, and insurance to offer specialized services?

Clientele:

1. What is the minimum and maximum asset value of your clients? Make sure your assets fall within this range.

2. Do most of your clients have financial situations similar to mine?

Accessibility:

1. Describe how you and I will work together.

2. Will I be working with only you, or do you have an assistant?

3. How often will we meet or talk? Can I reach you by e-mail? Can I view my accounts and research online? How often will I receive reports?

4. How do you help clients implement their financial plans? Do you only give advice or do you also make the transactions? Will you have discretionary power to buy and sell assets in my account?

Compensation:

1. What are your fees? Do you operate on a fee-only, fee-based, commission-only, or fee plus commission basis?

2. If fee only, is the fee based on hourly rate, flat fee, or percentage of assets?

Other:

1. Ask for long-term client and professional associates references.

2. Is your business registered with the SEC? With the state's securities office?

Choosing to work with a qualified financial advisor can dramatically increase your odds of success. Investors who employ the services of a good financial advisor are much more likely to increase the value of their investment portfolio and thus improve the long-term outlook of their retirement future. Use the information included in this chapter on how to select an advisor so you can choose one with confidence.

CHAPTER 16
HANDLING COMPANY STOCK
OR OTHER CONCENTRATED STOCK POSITIONS

Many people do not have complex stock holdings, having invested a majority of their retirement assets in their employer's stock. In some cases, people invest every dollar of their retirement assets in company stock. No matter how solid you perceive your company to be, this much concentration in one stock is not a good idea.

Consider the dramatically reduced retirement lifestyle of an Enron, Worldcom, Lucent or Qwest retiree in 2002, who failed to diversify and got stuck with virtually worthless stock shares. Enron stock dropped 99.78 percent during an 18-month stretch from September 2000 to April 2002, while Lucent stock value fell 94.54 percent over 27 months from December 1999 to April 2002. Each of these companies seemed invincible at one time.

How would a drop of this magnitude affect your retirement planning? Would you be forced to go back to work for a few more years, or perhaps a few more decades to make up these disastrous losses? If you have the lion's share of your money tied up in one company's stock, you're taking huge risks with your future.

While a single stock position can make you very wealthy indeed if your company does well, that stock can also drop abruptly and destroy years of disciplined savings and accumulation — all in a shockingly short period of time. Individual stocks can easily swing up or down by 50 percent or more in a given year. You don't have to look any further than the daily newspaper to find examples of companies that have nose-dived, leaving many retirees with nest eggs that will no longer see them through retirement.

How Much Should You Invest In Company Stock?

What is the maximum percentage of your portfolio that should be invested in a single stock position during retirement? Experts agree that most retirees and pre-retirees who have little time to make back big losses, should generally have no more than 5 percent of their portfolio invested in any one company. By following this guideline, you're protected even if the company's stock value is cut in half. In this case, a 50 percent drop in the price of your company stock would only decrease your portfolio in value by 2.5 percent.

Younger investors, on the other hand, have more time to make up big losses. To determine the maximum percentage of your portfolio to consider investing in any single stock, simply subtract your current age from your retirement age. The result is the maximum percentage you should invest in any one stock (see Figure 1).

Figure 1

Maximum Percentage To Invest In a Single Stock Position		
Retirement Age	Current Age	Maximum % Invested in One Stock
65	30	35%
65	35	30%
65	40	25%
65	45	20%
65	50	15%
65	55	10%
65	60	5%

For example, a 35-year-old who plans on retiring at age 65 wouldn't be wise to have more than 30 percent of his portfolio invested in a single stock. This is the maximum, not the ideal. Most people, even younger investors, shouldn't have more than 5-10 percent of their money tied up in one company.

It's easy to understand the motivation of some investors who rely heavily on the success of one stock. If the stock has performed well in the past, and as an employee of the company you can see its prospects for continued growth look good, then why not ride that train all the way to great prosperity? It does happen. There are many examples of companies that have brought riches to their stockholders. However, if you can reach your retirement goals without taking the risk, then why make such a big gamble on a single stock when a steep decline could be so disastrous for you?

Your company wants you to invest heavily in its own stock. If employees own company stock, they are more likely to work hard to help the company be profitable. Also, it is cost-effective for the company to provide matching contributions in company stock rather than in cash. What's good for the company, though, may not be good for you, the person who stands to be affected most adversely if the stock declines.

Knowing these risks, why do some employees have almost all of their retirement money invested in company stock? Some of it has to do with simple loyalty. Employees want to show support for their company and reinforce their emotional ties by buying stock. As long as those ties stay strong, the stock is seldom sold. Many of these loyal employees also believe the company will never go through a major downturn.

Much of the reason for stock over concentration, however, has to do with the way company benefit plans are set up, with incentives to purchase company stock. Many corporations, for instance, match employee 401(k) contributions with company stock. In addition, some employers won't allow employees to sell the stock until they reach age 55 or leave the company.

Many 401(k) plans offer company stock as one of the many investment options available to plan participants. Not having a great deal of information on other investment choices, many employees simply buy company stock as a default. The advent of stock options gives employees yet another way to accumulate company stock.

Some companies also offer stock purchase plans, which allow investors the ability to buy company stock at discounts as high as 20 percent. While this is usually a pretty good deal, many employees end up with these discounted shares along with the shares in their 401(k) plan and more shares given to them through matching contributions. In the end, they find themselves with too much of their retirement portfolio tied up in their company.

THE RISKS OF A CONCENTRATED STOCK POSITION

If you saved $6,000 diligently each year from age 30 to age 60 and enjoyed a 10 percent growth rate on your savings, you would amass an investment portfolio just shy of $1 million. A million-dollar portfolio could provide a retirement income of over $85,000 per year for 35 years, assuming a steady 8 percent growth rate (we're not taking inflation into consideration in this simple scenario).

Now let's assume your company's stock has been a great performer over the years and has, in fact, been one of the main reasons you were able to build such a substantial nest egg. At retirement, half of your million-dollar portfolio is made up of company stock, while the other half is invested in a money market fund. What would happen to your nest egg and the retirement income it could produce if, during your retirement, your company's stock went through a 50 percent downturn, as has happened to many solid companies over the past five years? The value of your company stock would be reduced to $250,000 and your total portfolio would decline 25 percent to $750,000. This could be even be worse if the other half of your portfolio was placed in investments that dropped as well, rather than the money market fund in our example.

FIGURE 2

Even Big Blue-Chip Companies Can Fall Stock prices from high to low over the past five years	
Company Name	%
The Williams Company	-71%
AOL Time Warner Inc.	-80%
General Electric Company	-48%
The Gillette Co.	-56%
Delta Air Lines, Inc.	-68%
The Proctor & Gamble Co.	-80%
Enron Corp.	-99%
Lucent Technologies, Inc.	-95%
Ford Motor Co.	-60%
Merrill Lynch	-48%
Corning Inc.	-94%
Bristol-Myers Squibb Co.	-62%

Source: Big Charts.com, data from, 4/30/97 to 4/30/02

Assuming the same growth rate you would now have an annual retirement income of only $64,000, or $21,000 less than the $1 million portfolio could have produced. That 25 percent reduction in annual income is a very realistic scenario and presents too great a risk to investors devoting so much of their portfolio to a single stock. Figure 2 illustrates the way prices of some of the country's largest and most respected blue-chip companies have dropped in the last five years. As you can see from this example, even big companies can fall dramatically.

OPTIONS FOR SOLVING THE PROBLEM

If you have too much invested in one stock it's time to develop an exit strategy. You may want to sell your company stock all at once and diversify if the stock is currently selling at a reasonable level. Or you may want to sell a portion of your holdings each year over a one-to-three year period and then reinvest the proceeds into a diversified portfolio. Some investors may even choose to designate a portion of the stock to hold for the long-term, while selling the rest in order to diversify.

In cases in which the stock is owned in a taxable account, there are additional strategies you should consider to reduce your tax burden when you sell. There are several ways to sell a stock held outside a retirement plan in order to diversify without incurring any capital gains taxes. Following are explanations of some of these strategies.

Charitable Remainder Trust

You can contribute your company stock to a charitable remainder trust (CRT). The trustee (you can appoint yourself trustee) can sell the stock and reinvest it in a diversified portfolio of your choice. By making a contribution to a CRT, you will receive an immediate tax credit, avoid all capital gains taxes on the prior appreciation of the stock, and obtain tax-free growth on the investments in the portfolio.

As an income beneficiary, you will receive a lifetime of income from the diversified portfolio. The downside of this strategy, however, is that you give up the right to tap into assets held in the trust. Upon death (typically the death of both you and your spouse), the assets will revert to the charity you have chosen, not to your heirs. This strategy is usually used in conjunction with a second-to-die life insurance policy, which provides for your heirs upon the deaths of both you and your spouse.

Margin or Hypothecation Loan

You can use your stock as collateral to secure a low-interest loan or to obtain margin to purchase other securities. Think of this like a home equity line; however, instead of using your home equity to obtain a loan, you are using your stock position as collateral to obtain a loan. The proceeds of the loan can be invested in a diversified portfolio of stocks and bonds, reducing the risk of being invested in just one company. While you will be required to pay interest on the loan, you will avoid paying capital gains taxes and can reduce your portfolio risk considerably.

Exchange Funds

In an exchange fund, a group of investors deposit their low-basis stock shares into a limited partnership in exchange for a partnership interest in the fund. This is done on a tax-free basis with no capital gains taxes.

As a limited partner, you will have a partnership interest in all the stocks held in the fund and, thus, obtain immediate diversification. Because exchange funds are managed passively, meaning not a lot of buying and selling occurs, the only companies accepted into the fund are those that meet specific requirements crucial to the fund's performance. Consequently, not all stocks are accepted. If you own an obscure company, it will be more difficult or even impossible to find an exchange fund that will accept your shares. When the limited partnership interest is redeemed, usually after at least five years, the investor will receive a diversified portfolio of stocks without having to pay capital gains taxes in the process.

While this strategy works in certain situations, investors must be able to meet strict requirements to participate, such as an initial stock deposit of at least $1 million and a net worth of $5 million.

Zero Premium Collars

There are several option strategies you can use to protect yourself from loss if your company stock nosedives. One strategy, referred to as a "Zero Premium Collar," uses "put" and "call" options to protect an investor from losing too much if the stock turns sour. This strategy is helpful to an investor who is not interested in selling the stock due to potential tax implications but is at too much risk if the stock drops.

To initiate this strategy, an investor sells a call option on his stock and uses the income to buy a put option. The put option protects the stock position on the downside, while the call option provides a source of income to pay for the put. Protection strategies, like the "Collar," are not available for all stocks.

If your portfolio is heavily dependent on the success of one company, it's time to seriously rethink your strategy — if that company falters, it can jeopardize your ability to reach your retirement goals. Just ask those people holding Enron stock who once thought they would be wealthy in retirement and now are resigned to working far beyond age 65.

Opening
the Door
to Retirement

PART 4

OTHER RETIREMENT CONSIDERATIONS:

Chapter 17
Health Insurance During Retirement

Good health is essential to your retirement for reasons both physical and economic. Your retirement years should be some of the most enjoyable of your life, and your health is instrumental in making sure they are all that they should be. In a financial sense, health plays a critical role in your retirement planning.

As you prepare for retirement, you must consider your health insurance needs and your available insurance options. If you don't have insurance, you will be jeopardizing the assets you've built over years of hard work. A serious illness can deplete your resources in the blink of an eye.

Most retirees receive health insurance from Medicare, private insurance, or a continuation of their employer-provided coverage (see Figure 1). This chapter will outline these health insurance options and how understanding them will help protect your nest egg and ensure that you are able to make the most of your retirement years.

Figure 1

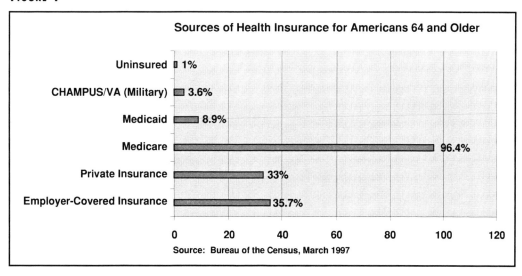

Sources of Health Insurance for Americans 64 and Older

Uninsured	1%
CHAMPUS/VA (Military)	3.6%
Medicaid	8.9%
Medicare	96.4%
Private Insurance	33%
Employer-Covered Insurance	35.7%

Source: Bureau of the Census, March 1997

PRIVATE INSURANCE

- One of every three retirees is covered by private health insurance.
- The average cost of coverage from ages 62 to 64, ranges between $337 and $693 a month.

If you're planning on early retirement, you have some major health insurance decisions ahead of you. Medicare doesn't begin coverage until age 65. That means most people retiring early will need private insurance, and it's a tough market out there for people between the ages of 50 and 64. This age group is largely unprotected by government programs and is most likely to be hit with high insurance premiums. Private insurers hike up premiums for this age group to levels that are hard to swallow due to the likelihood of declining health and vulnerability to disease and disability.

For people ages 62 to 64, health insurance costs range between $300 and almost $700 per month (see Figure 2). If you are planning to retire before age 65, start evaluating your health insurance options as soon as possible. Purchase a private insurance plan early and lock in a guaranteed premium amount, if you can.

FIGURE 2

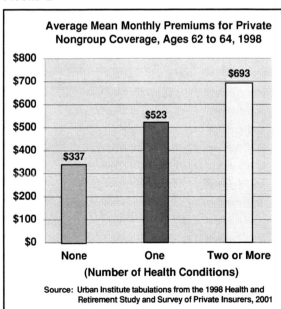

Average Mean Monthly Premiums for Private Nongroup Coverage, Ages 62 to 64, 1998

None: $337
One: $523
Two or More: $693

(Number of Health Conditions)

Source: Urban Institute tabulations from the 1998 Health and Retirement Study and Survey of Private Insurers, 2001

If you have pre-existing conditions (medical problems that exist before you buy an insurance policy) it will be much more difficult to obtain private coverage. An insurance company could reject you for coverage completely or cover you for everything EXCEPT your pre-existing condition, even though that's usually the very reason you need insurance in the first place. If you have a group policy, you're in a better position. Federal law forbids all group health plans from denying coverage due to pre-existing conditions.[1]

CONTINUED EMPLOYEE COVERAGE: GROUP HEALTH INSURANCE

- Group health insurance provides 35.7 percent of retirees with coverage.
- The cost for this coverage could range from zero to $500 per month.

Employer-provided health insurance usually terminates as soon as you retire. There are, however, legal requirements that prevent employers from eliminating health coverage for a certain period of time after an employee is off the payroll.

Under the Consolidated Omnibus Budget Reconciliation Act of 1985, otherwise known as COBRA, employers with 20 or more employees are required to provide continued health insurance coverage to former workers for up to 18 months (or 29 months, if the worker is disabled). COBRA only guarantees you access to coverage, however, not help in paying your premiums. Under COBRA, your employer will not subsidize your monthly premiums; you will be completely responsible for paying the entire amount, plus an administrative fee of up to 2 percent. Your COBRA coverage must be identical to the coverage you had while working. You cannot choose a less expensive plan to save money, although some employers may allow you to drop certain "non-core" benefits like dental and vision care.[2]

Although COBRA costs may seem substantial, especially when you compare them to the employer-subsidized rates you enjoyed while working, your premiums generally will be less than the alternative of buying private health insurance.

Once you retire, you must find some kind of health coverage within 63 days. If you have a gap of more than 63 days you sacrifice your health insurance rights under the Federal HIPAA (Health Insurance Portability and Accountability Act) law. HIPAA guarantees that people who have continuous coverage — without that 63 day gap — can't be denied insurance even if they have a pre-existing condition, such as diabetes or severe arthritis. If you don't have access to COBRA coverage (if, say, you worked for a company with less than 20 employees) or don't take advantage of the COBRA option, then you must find some kind of private coverage within 63 days. If you don't, there could be serious health and financial consequences.[3]

To initiate COBRA, you and your employer must follow proper procedures because if you don't you could forfeit your coverage rights. First, the employer must notify the health plan administrator within 30 days after an employee's "qualifying event" (i.e. death, job termination, reduced hours of employment or eligibility for Medicare). Once notified, the health plan administrator has 14 days to alert you and your family members, in person or by first-class mail, of your right to elect COBRA coverage. The IRS is tough on this point. If the plan administrator fails to act, he or she can be held personally liable for this breach of duty.

You, your spouse and your children have 60 days to decide whether or not to buy COBRA insurance. The 60-day clock starts running on the date your eligibility notification is sent to you or the date you lost your health coverage, whichever is later. As long as you pay the premium, your COBRA coverage will be retroactive to the date you lost your benefits.

If you elect COBRA, you have 45 days to pay your first premium. The first premium is likely to be high because it covers the period retroactive to the date your employer ended your coverage. Successive payments are due according to health plan requirements, but COBRA rules allow for a 30-day grace period after each payment due date.[4]

If you have questions about COBRA or self-insured employer plans (both governed by the U.S. Department of Labor), contact your regional or district office of the Pension and Welfare Benefits Administration of the U.S. Department of Labor *www.dol.gov/pwda/welcome.html.*

Not every company discontinues its insurance for employees who retire. Some, in fact, will not only continue to offer coverage, but will subsidize all or part of the premiums. Be sure to check with your company's personnel department regarding its policy on health coverage. The number of companies that are generous in this respect will continue to diminish as health care costs continue to soar.

MEDICARE

- 96.4 percent of all retirees obtain coverage from Medicare. For those with private coverage or a continued group plan, Medicare becomes a secondary coverage.
- Medicare Part A (hospital insurance) is free while Medicare Part B (medical insurance) costs $59 per month. Additional coverage can be purchased.

Medicare helps provide retired Americans with basic health coverage and, for many people, Medicare is their only source of health insurance during retirement. Since this program is such an integral part of retirement health care planning for so many, it's important that it be covered here in some detail.

Eligibility for Medicare is very similar to Social Security. You or your spouse must have worked 40 quarters (ten years) in Medicare-covered employment to receive Medicare coverage. Additionally, you must be 65 years old and a citizen or permanent resident of the United States. The Social Security Administration recommends applying for Medicare benefits when you turn 65, whether or not you begin collecting Social Security at that time. You can contact the Social Security Administration, toll-free (1-800-772-1213), or visit *www.ssa.gov* if you have questions about your eligibility or want to apply for Medicare.

Medicare consists of two parts: Part A and Part B. Medicare Part A helps pay for inpatient hospital care, skilled nursing facilities, hospice care and some home health care. Part B helps pay for doctors' services, outpatient hospital care and some other medical services such as blood, medical equipment, lab tests and physical and occupational therapy. Part B may also cover preventive services such as mammograms and flu shots.

Medicare Part A (Hospital Insurance)

For most retirees, no premiums are required for Medicare Part A because premiums were taken from your paycheck each month while employed. Even if you or your spouse did not work the required 40 quarters of Medicare-covered employment, you may still be eligible, but you will be required to pay a monthly premium. In 2001, the premium was $300 per month if you worked less than 30 quarters of Medicare-covered employment. If you worked more than 29 but less than 39 quarters, your premium was $165 monthly.

Although the majority of people do not have to pay a premium, there are still expenses involved. For every benefit period, a $792 deductible is required. Also, if you stay over 60 days in the hospital, you will have to pay the following co-insurance rates:

- $198/day, between the 61st and 90th day in the hospital.
- $396/day, between the 91st and 150th day.
- Up to $99/day, between the 21st and 100th day of each benefit period, for skilled nursing facility co-insurance.

Medicare Part B (Medical Insurance)

While Medicare Part B helps pay for doctors' services and outpatient hospital care, Medicare will *not* pay for routine physical exams, eyeglasses, custodial care, dental care, dentures, routine foot care, hearing aids, orthopedic shoes or cosmetic surgery. It does *not* cover most prescription drugs or any health care you receive while traveling outside the United States.[5]

Part B coverage requires a premium of $58.78 per month (2003 rates). If you did not sign up for Part B at age 65 when you first became eligible, the premium may go up 10 percent for each year that you could have had Part B coverage and you will have to pay this extra amount for the rest of your life. Also, as in Part A, you are required to pay a deductible. However, the deductible is significantly less, amounting to only $100 per year.

If you are receiving Social Security benefits prior to age 65, you will be automatically enrolled in both Medicare Part A and Part B, effective the month you turn 65. Your Medicare card will be mailed to you about three months before your 65th birthday. The enrollment package contains information on how to "un-enroll" yourself from Part B coverage if you don't want it.

If you decide to delay receiving Social Security benefits until age 65 or later, you will not be automatically enrolled in Medicare. However, you should still apply for Medicare three months before you turn 65 so your coverage start date will not be delayed.

You can apply using any one of the following three options:

- Visit your local Social Security office.
- Call Social Security at 1-800-772-1213.
- Apply online at the SSA web site at *www.ssa.gov.*

You may want to delay signing up for Medicare Part B if you are receiving medical coverage through either you or your spouse's employer. There's no need to pay that $59 per month if you already have adequate coverage.

The Social Security Administration advises that you should sign up for Medicare Part A even if you keep working past age 65. The Part A coverage carries no premium costs and may help pay some of your health costs not covered through your employer or union group health plan.

Remember, if you plan to join a Medicare managed care plan or a Medicare private fee-for-service plan (more on this later in this chapter), you will need to be a Medicare Part B participant.

If you didn't sign up for Medicare Part B when you were first eligible because you were still enrolled in a group plan, you can sign up for Medicare Part B during a Special Enrollment Period, thus avoiding the 10 percent penalty for late enrollees.

Special enrollment allows you to sign up within eight months of when your employer health plan coverage ends, or when your employment ends, whichever comes first.

Medicare enrollees must use a doctor, specialist or hospital that accepts Medicare, accessing services by presenting your Medicare card. Medicare pays the fee charged for each visit or service after you have met the annual deductible and paid the monthly Part B premium of $59. To pay for medical costs not covered by Medicare, you can:

- Keep or obtain employer or union health coverage.
- Buy a Medigap policy (a private Medicare supplemental insurance).
- Join one of the other Medicare health plans.

Medigap

You might feel that Medicare doesn't provide you with the sufficient coverage you desire. Who could blame you? With a whole array of services not covered by Medicare, you could still be looking at a substantial sum of out-of-pocket health costs if you wind up needing one of these uncovered services.

Medigap plans are private health insurance policies that cover some of the costs and services basic Medicare does not cover, such as prescription drugs. You can contact your state insurance department for information about Medigap policies sold in your area.

In 1992, Congress mandated that Medigap plans be categorized into ten types (lettered A through J) to make it easier for consumers to shop for coverage and avoid scams.[6] The ten plans differ in areas such as deductibles, coverage for eyeglasses, prescription drugs, or medical care received while in foreign countries. Insurance companies must sell at least "A" plans, which offer basic benefits, but not all offer the full range of Medigap plans, and some plans might not be available at all in your state.

Another type of Medigap coverage is the Medicare SELECT policy. These policies use specified hospitals and doctors, except in emergencies, and generally cost less as a result.

Premiums can vary by hundreds of dollars, so it pays to shop around. You can contact your state insurance department (call 1-866-350-6242 to learn how to reach your state's office) or visit Weiss Ratings *(www.weissratings.com)*, a well-respected company, to obtain ratings on insurance companies. Weiss will even provide you with a list of recommended companies. Additionally, the government's Medicare

Web site contains a service called Medigap Compare *(www.medicare.gov/mgcompare/home.asp)* to help you compare policies.

Insurance companies may charge a fixed premium for all participants, based on your age at time of purchase. Other companies charge a variable premium based on how old you are each time you renew the policy, meaning that your premiums will increase as you get older. Again, it is necessary to shop around.

Other Medicare Health Plans

Medicare offers two other health plan choices within the program: the Medicare managed-care plan, sometimes called an HMO, and the private fee-for-service plan. Even if you choose one of these options, you must still pay the Medicare Part B premium. However, you will receive all of the Medicare Part A and Part B covered services. For both types of plan, Medicare pays a set amount of money each month to a private insurance company. Study your options carefully and choose the one that best fits your personal circumstances.

There are many plans of varying quality from which to choose. Fortunately, Medicare will help you assess the quality of the plans. Call 1-800-MEDICARE (1-800-633-4227) or visit *www.medicare.gov/mphcompare/home.asp* for information on health plan quality.

Medicaid

Medicaid helps pay medical costs for people with low incomes. Because state governments rather than the federal government administer these programs, benefits can vary depending on the state in which you live. Medicaid can help pay for nursing home care and outpatient prescription drugs not covered by Medicare. Some states also have programs that help subsidize Medicare's premium, deductibles, and co-insurance.

THE INFLATION OF HEALTH CARE COSTS

Looking at the pace of health care costs and the future of the Medicare program, all retirees would do well to give considerable thought to their health insurance plans. With the post-war baby boomers reaching retirement age, the projected population of Americans over 65 is expected to reach 60 million in 2005. That's an increase of 25 million in just four years (see Figure 3). This is going to put an enormous strain on the Medicare program, to continue operating without reducing benefits, increasing retirees' out-of-pocket costs, or cutting payments to doctors and hospitals. This could further limit the health care options available to Medicare

FIGURE 3

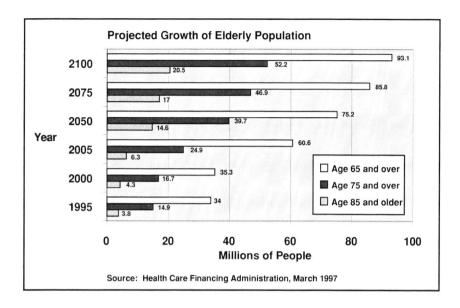

beneficiaries. Because of the expenses associated with health care, approximately 15-17 percent of Americans are currently without insurance coverage.[7] The Health Care Financing Administration predicts that the amount of money America spends on health care will double every 10 years (see Figure 4). This means health costs will continue increasing rapidly for individuals, employers and the government.

FIGURE 4

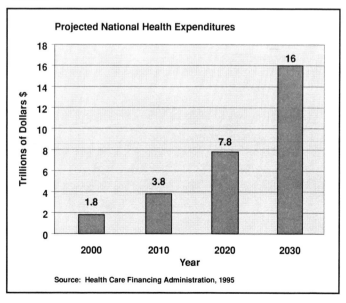

The best way to protect yourself from rising health care costs is to accumulate a substantial retirement nest egg that will enable you to afford whatever insurance coverage you require. Don't let health care costs ruin the retirement you've worked so hard your entire life to achieve.

CHAPTER 18
LONG-TERM CARE INSURANCE

What are the chances you could be afflicted with a chronic illness or disability that would leave you unable to care for yourself for an extended period of time during retirement? The answer might surprise you.

The vast majority of Americans (72 percent) don't believe they will ever enter a nursing home or need any long-term care services.[1] However, according to the U.S. Department of Health and Human Services, if you're age 65, you have a 40 percent chance of entering a nursing home and a 10 percent chance of being there for more than five years. Those odds, of course, increase with age. Women, because they live longer than men, have a 50 percent greater likelihood of needing long-term care at some point[3]. In 1997, there were 1.3 million people in nursing homes; three-fourths of them were women (see Figure 1).

Long-term care is not just a health issue, but also financial concern of tremendous significance. The average cost for a one-year stay in a nursing home is currently $46,000, and home health care can easily run $12,000 per year.[4] You can see the impact these costs can potentially have on reaching your retirement goals. Large long-term care expenses could deplete your assets prematurely.

 FIGURE 1

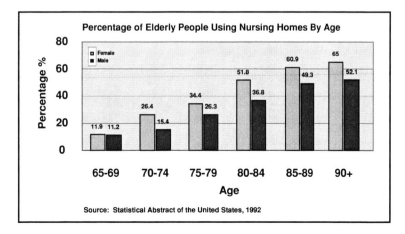

Percentage of Elderly People Using Nursing Homes By Age

Source: Statistical Abstract of the United States, 1992

Over one-half (55 percent) of those who enter nursing homes stay for more than one year, while one out of five (21 percent) remain for five years or longer.[5] The average stay is 2 $^1/_2$ years[6] (see Figure 2). At $46,000 per year, a person would need to set aside $115,000 for nursing home costs alone (at today's average costs). What will it cost for a 2 $^1/_2$ year stay when you turn age 80? If you are 60 years old today and wind up in a nursing home 20 years from now, it is likely that costs will at least double from today's rates, reaching as high as $230,000. Will your retirement nest egg be sufficient to cover this cost in 20 years, while at the same time, providing for your spouse who may be healthy, living at home and also needing income to cover living expenses?

FIGURE 2

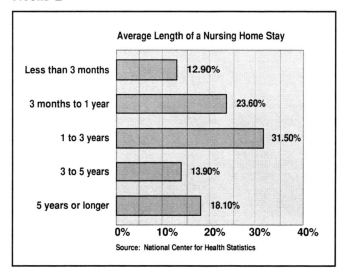

As part of your retirement planning, you should examine several hypothetical scenarios that involve the need for long-term care. This will help you realize the impact a nursing home stay could have on your retirement plans. If admittance into a nursing home for an extended period of time would seriously deplete your assets, you should consider purchasing a long-term care insurance policy. On the other hand, if you have the assets to handle an extended nursing home stay, then there is no reason for the coverage unless you are interested in leaving a larger inheritance to your heirs.

In this chapter, we will examine who pays for long-term care, who should purchase long-term health care coverage, what this coverage pays for, and the costs and issues associated with buying a policy.

WHO PAYS FOR LONG-TERM CARE?

Long-term care leads to poverty for a disturbing number of retired Americans. Of those receiving long-term care, 37 percent pay for it out-of-pocket. Within a year of admission, over 90 percent of these private-pay residents are impoverished.[7] Medicare and health insurance coverage typically pay nothing for long-term care nursing home facilities. Medicaid, a government welfare program, will pay but only after you have depleted all other financial resources. The government currently pays about 57 percent of all nursing home costs.

According to these statistics, if you don't own a long-term care policy, the odds are very high that a lengthy nursing home stay will eat away your assets

FIGURE 3

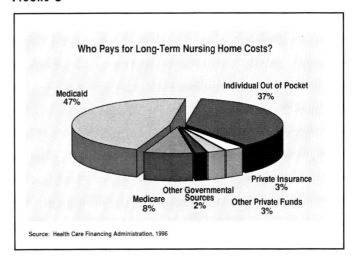

Source: Health Care Financing Administration, 1996

and leave you dependent upon Medicaid. Although long-term care coverage is affordable, only 3 percent of nursing home costs are funded this way. Figure 3 summarizes who gets stuck with the long-term care bill.

WHO SHOULD PURCHASE LONG-TERM HEALTH CARE COVERAGE?

Long-term care insurance is not for everyone but very essential for some. The following table will help you decide if you should buy a long-term care policy:

LTC is for you if:	LTC is not as important for you if:
☐ You would like to insure your independence and not become a burden to your family.	☐ You have health conditions making the cost of LTC coverage too expensive compared to the benefit you may receive.
☐ You family has a history of ailments requiring long-term care (e.g. Alzheimer's, diabetes, strokes).	☐ You are likely to cancel policy because your fixed income won't keep up with increasing annual premiums payments.
☐ You have sufficient money to pay premiums every year until death.	☐ Your only source of income is a Social Security benefit or Supplemental Security Income (SSI).
☐ You want to preserve assets for family members.	☐ Buying a LTC policy stretches your budget to the point of having to forego other financial needs (e.g. paying for utilities, buying food or medicine.)
☐ If having to pay for long-term care for one spouse would seriously hamper your ability to accomplish your retirement plan.	
☐ You are in good health and qualify for lower premiums.	☐ You're self-insured due to the size of your financial portfolio.
☐ You are between 45 and 60 and can lock in lower premiums for life.	☐ You are 79+ (although you may need coverage, premiums may be too high.)

AGE AND COST

Long-term care coverage, like life insurance, is cheaper if you purchase it when you are younger and healthier. A policy purchased at age 55 will generally cost twice as much if you buy it when you're 65. A 50-year-old can plan on paying between $500 and $1,000 per year for a policy that will cost a 65-year-old between $1,000 and $2,500. Those in their late seventies may be required to pay as much as $3,000 to $8,000 for similar coverage, depending on the policy features. If you buy coverage when you are younger, your premiums will be lower but obviously you will be paying them over a longer period of time.

HOW MUCH COVERAGE DO YOU NEED?

You can purchase coverage that will provide a daily benefit of anywhere from $50 to $400. To determine how much long-term coverage you need, first decide how much long-term care you can afford to cover out of your own pocket. For example, if the average nursing home cost is $126 per day, and you can afford to pay $50 per day, then you would need a policy to cover the $76 difference. You should plan on needing this benefit for at least 2 $1/2$ years, the average nursing home stay.

Estimating what you can pay out-of-pocket can be a difficult process. You must predict your future financial status and the future cost of long-term care. The best method for doing this is to re-visit the retirement section of your financial plan and enter some additional hypothetical situations. For example, how would it affect your retirement assets if you or your spouse entered a nursing home at age 75, 80, or 85, and had to pay a cost of $46,000 per year, adjusted for inflation? Would this eat up all of your assets? Would the spouse living outside the nursing home have enough money to meet living expenses? Your retirement plan can help you answer all these questions. Be more exact in your planning by contacting nursing homes in your area and base your estimates on local costs, rather than the $46,000 national average.

WHAT DOES LONG-TERM HEALTH CARE COVER?

Nursing home coverage is just one of several types of long-term care. If you purchase a policy, make sure you understand exactly what is covered and what is not. In addition, speak to a local nursing home to discuss the conditions they require before accepting a patient — this will protect you from buying a policy that is absolutely useless to you. For instance, you may become incapacitated and unable to perform simple household chores. If this occurred, you would want to make sure that your policy will pay for non-skilled nursing care.

Figure 4 lists the different types of long-term care and their definitions:

FIGURE 5

Type of Care	Definition
Nursing Home Care	Nursing homes serve as permanent residences for people who are too frail or sick to live at home or as a temporary facility during a recovering period.
Home Health Care	Home health care ranges greatly in it's definition and can cover a broad range of needs both temporary and permanent. Often times people require only minimal assistance, a couple of hours each in the morning and evening. Some clients require morning and evening. Some clients require only a couple brief visits per week, while others need someone available around the clock because of either physical or mental disabilities. Home health care and homemaker services can also cover needs ranging from help with meals and home maintenance to supervision as well as medication administration.
Assisted Living Facility	The assistance you need may not require the round-the-clock, skilled health care a nursing home provides, yet your needs cannot be met living by yourself, such as eating, the ability to get around in one's home, dressing and bathing oneself. The goal of assisted living is to help you continue living as independently as possible.
Adult Day Care	A planned program that includes a variety of health, social and supportive services in a safe, protective environment during daytime hours. It is a community-based service designed to meet each individuals's needs.
Alternate Care	Non-conventional care and services developed by a physician.
Respite Care	Short term, temporary care provided to people with disabilities in order that their families can take a break from the daily routing of care giving.
Other	Various, such a modifications to home (wheelchair ramps, etc.)

What is Not Covered by Long-term Care Insurance?

Long-term care policies do not cover a number of items and the exclusions in each policy differ. Treatment that was under way or recommended prior to obtaining long-term coverage is usually not covered. In addition, the following ailments are often excluded:

- Mental disorders
- Nervous disorders
- Alcoholism
- Drug abuse
- Care necessitated by an act of war
- Intentional self-inflicted injury

How Long Will Benefits Be Paid?

Most policies provide a maximum dollar amount, or ceiling, on the number of covered days. Often, benefits will last two to six years or a lifetime. In addition, some policies have various limits for different types of coverage — nursing homes, assisted living facilities, home health care, etc.

Policy Features

Avoid the serious blunder made by so many when purchasing a long-term care policy: focusing on the premium more than the benefits you may need.

Inflation

Many people save a lot of money on premiums by purchasing a policy without a feature to adjust the daily benefit for inflation. While this lowers the cost of premiums, it's not likely to provide you with nearly enough benefits if you eventually enter a nursing home.

For instance, one plan that pays a $150-per-day benefit for two years of nursing home coverage would cost a 55-year-old approximately $600 annually without an inflation feature. With inflation protection, the same policy would cost $900 yearly. Trying to save a little in premiums may bankrupt your financial portfolio if nursing home costs double to $300 per day by the time you need care.

Home Health Care

No one wants to leave their home any sooner than necessary, even when their health conditions begin to deteriorate. The best way to ensure you can remain in your home as long as possible is to hire a home health care agency to provide you with the level of help you need. Non-skilled help, which can assist with dressing, bathing, preparing meals, and other household duties, can easily cost $1000 per month. Skilled help provided by a physical therapist or health care professional can cost much more. Home health care averages about $16 per hour[8]. Most long-term care policies will offer home health care provisions, which can be added to the policy. This is an option you should seriously consider.

Elimination Periods

An "elimination period" represents the number of days you must be in a nursing home before your policy kicks in and begins paying benefits. Most policies offer a range between zero and 100 days. Not surprisingly, the longer the elimination period you select, the lower your premium will be.[9] You can determine your optimum elimination period by looking again at your retirement plan to estimate whether or not your investment resources are sufficient. If you have plenty of assets, you may want to opt for a policy with a longer elimination period.

SHOPPING FOR A POLICY

The following is a comprehensive checklist you can use as you shop for a long-term care policy.[10] It's always a good idea to collect quotes from several solid insurance companies.

Long-Term Care Check List

1. What services are covered?
   A) Nursing home care
   B) Home health care
   C) Assisted living facility
   D) Adult daycare
   E) Alternate care
   F) Respite care
   G) Other

2. How much does the policy pay, per day, for nursing home care? For home health care? For an assisted living facility? For adult daycare? For alternate care? For respite care? Other?

3. How long will benefits last in a nursing home? At home? In an assisted living facility? Other?
4. Does the policy have a maximum lifetime benefit? If so, what is it for nursing home care? For home health care? For an assisted living facility? Other?
5. How long must I wait before pre-existing conditions are covered?
6. How many days must I wait before benefits begin for nursing home care? For home health care? For an assisted living facility? Other?
7. Are Alzheimer's disease and other organic, mental and nervous disorders covered?
8. Does the policy require an assessment of activities of daily living? An assessment of cognitive impairment? Physician certification of need? A prior hospital stay for nursing home care? Home health care? A prior nursing home stay for home health care coverage? Other?
9. Is the policy guaranteed renewable?
10. What is the age range for enrollment?
11. Is there a waiver-of-premium provision for nursing home care? For home health care?
12. How long must I be confined before premiums are waived?
13. Does the policy have a non-forfeiture provision?
14. Does the policy offer an inflation adjustment feature? If so, what is the rate of increase? How often is it applied? For how long? Is there an additional cost?
15. What does the policy cost per year?
    A) With the inflation feature?
    B) Without inflation feature?
16. Is there a 30-day free look?
17. What is the insurance company rated?
18. Is the policy tax-qualified or non-tax qualified?

Is long-term care coverage worth the cost? That depends, of course, on whether you wind up needing long-term care. Let's assume you purchase a policy at age 65 to cover the average cost of a five-year stay in a nursing home. The premium is $2,500 per year. Let's also assume your policy has an inflation feature so your benefits will increase as long-term care costs escalate.

At age 80, you incur a chronic illness that requires your admission into a nursing home for the average stay of 2 ½ years. Was this a good investment? For 15 years, you paid $2,500 per year in premiums for a total of $37,500. The total cost of your 2 $^1/_2$-year nursing home stay, adjusted for inflation, is $183,500. By having the coverage in place, you avoid having to withdraw $183,500 from your investment accounts to pay for your stay. The ability to keep this money invested may prove vital if your spouse is using it as a source of retirement income. In this scenario, buying a long-term care policy was a very wise investment decision. However, if you never used the coverage, you would have spent $37,500 on a policy you didn't need.

It's not pleasant to consider a future where you might need others to care for you, either in your own home, in a nursing home or in a assisted living facility. Nonetheless, this is an eventuality you need to factor into your retirement planning, because without adequate preparation in the form of a long-term care policy, the cost of care could be devastating to your retirement portfolio.

Opening the Door to Retirement

PART 5

RETIREMENT PLAN DISTRIBUTION GUIDE

CHAPTER 19
RETIREMENT PLAN DISTRIBUTION OPTIONS

Next to a home, a 401(k) plan is often the largest asset people own. The average 401(k) participant has an account balance of $58,774[2] and most will have to make decisions about what to do with that money over a half dozen times during their working years (since the average person in the U.S. changes jobs eight times during 40 years[1] in the workplace). These decisions will have a serious impact on the success or failure of an entire retirement plan.

Such decisions are made every day in the U.S. with billions of dollars flowing from one financial institution to another. In an 18-month period from 1999 to mid-2000, over 10 million people had the option to withdraw money from a qualified retirement plan, and many of them used that option, impacting assets totaling more than $400 billion.[3] Were the decisions made by these individuals wise? Did they make the right choices to ensure a comfortable retirement? Sadly, many people do not make smart decisions when it comes to 401(k) distributions.

How are you going to handle your 401(k) money at retirement? Two out of every three people automatically roll their money into a Rollover IRA.[4] But is this the best option? And what if you aren't ready to retire but are in the process of changing jobs? You may be enticed by the appeal of taking your 401(k) cash and "running" with it, but this could prove detrimental to you in the long run. By understanding and carefully considering all of your distribution choices, you will be able to avoid unnecessary taxes and penalties and ultimately reach your retirement goals.

The final section of this book, which includes this chapter and chapters 20 and 21, is intended to be a distribution guide, outlining retirement plan distribution options, company stock distributions, and how to make final decisions using a distribution analysis. You should use this chapter and the two that follow it to help make wise choices about how to get the most out of the money you have worked so hard to accumulate during your working years.

Accomplishing your retirement goals is not only a function of good savings habits and sound investing (as has been explained in previous chapters) but also how you handle your money at financial milestones such as job changes and retirement.

Whether you're retiring or changing jobs, you will usually have five to seven different distribution options from which to choose. Each, of course, has its own advantages and disadvantages, and you should know how each affects you before deciding what to do with your retirement funds.

These options include:

- Taking a lump-sum cash distribution
- Rolling the money into a "Rollover IRA"
- Rolling the money into your new employer's retirement plan
- Leaving the money in your former company's retirement plan
- Rolling the money into a traditional IRA, then converting it to a Roth IRA
- Receiving an annuity payout
- Utilizing a combination strategy: Net Unrealized Appreciation (NUA) and an IRA Rollover. (NUA is complex and will be discussed in greater detail in Chapter 20).

OPTION 1: A LUMP SUM/CASH DISTRIBUTION

FACT
Cash distributions account for 18 percent of retirement plan distributions.[5]

TIP
Consider a lump sum/cash distribution *only* under very extreme circumstances:

- You are faced with a financial emergency and have absolutely no other source of money.
- You have ownership of highly-appreciated company stock (Net Unrealized Appreciation or NUA), to be discussed in Chapter 20.
- It is advantageous for you to use 10-year forward averaging (see discussion later in this chapter).

Quick cash does have its appeal. If you choose a lump-sum cash distribution of your 401(k) funds, your employer will simply send a check to you for the vested balance in your plan, minus the 20 percent required tax withholding. Think of what you could do right now by withdrawing all the money in your retirement plan. A rapid cash infusion like this could be used to purchase a luxury car, a boat, or an exotic vacation. Doesn't sound too bad, does it?

But taking a cash distribution is *usually* a grave mistake. Although having cash in hand may be an appropriate option in some limited circumstances, such as emergencies, choosing this option is usually shortsighted because it opens you up to penalties and severe tax consequences. Your employer is required by law to withhold 20 percent of the amount distributed to you; this is a prepayment of taxes the government anticipates you will owe as a result of the distribution. You could get some of this refunded if you're in a tax bracket less than 20 percent. If, however, you're in a higher bracket, Uncle Sam will take additional taxes.

The 20-percent withholding does not apply to company stock distributed to you in shares. In this case, the company will send you a stock certificate often referred to as an "in-kind" distribution. All other cash and securities you own in your plan upon distribution are subject to the 20-percent tax withholding.

FIGURE 1

2002 Federal Income Tax Rates		
Tax Rate	**Single Filers**	**Joint Filers**
10%	$0-6,000	$0-12,000
15%	$6,001-27,950	$12,001-46,700
27%	$27,951-67,700	$46,701-112,850
30%	$67,701-141,250	$112,851-171,950
35%	$141,251-307,050	$171,951-307,050
38.6%	$307,051+	$307,051+

Additionally, the entire withdrawal is considered ordinary income for the year in which you take the distribution. When you add the distribution amount to your earned income, you may find yourself thrust into a much higher federal income tax bracket (see Figure 1). If your state imposes local taxes, you will also be required to pay those. And if you are not yet age 59 1/2, you will be subject to an additional 10 percent penalty for taking a premature distribution.

When you add up penalties and taxes, depending on your bracket, you could lose almost one-half of your retirement savings by taking a cash distribution — and that's not even the worst aspect of this distribution method. You'll feel an even bigger headache years later when you realize how large your retirement plan could have grown with years of compound interest and tax-deferral.

Let's assume a 40-year-old man gets the urge to cash out $100,000 from his retirement plan to buy a car and take a trip. He will be required to pay 37 percent in taxes (assuming a 30 percent federal tax bracket and 7 percent state tax bracket.) In addition, because he's not yet 59 $^1/_2$, he gets hit with the 10-percent early withdrawal penalty. Instantly, he has turned 47 percent, or $47,000, of his hard-earned retirement savings over to federal and state governments, leaving only $53,000 to spend as shown in Figure 2.

FIGURE 2

Cash Distribution

$100,000	cash distribution
Taxes and Penalties	
$30,000	30% federal taxes
$7,000	7% state and local taxes
+ $10,000	10% early withdrawal penalty
= $47,000	total taxes and penalties
$53,000	amount left over

Now, let's take a closer look at his retirement decision. If he had not "donated" $47,000 to the government because of his early withdrawal and let that money grow, tax-deferred at 10 percent instead, it would be worth $509,231 in 25 years. The $53,000 he spent on a car and a trip would have grown to $574,239 over the same period. Retiring at age 65, he would have had an additional $1,083,470 in his account (see Figure 3). Instead, he chose a $100,000 lump sum at age 40. Making these kind of choices can make it difficult, if not impossible, to reach your retirement goals. Was that new car worth a million dollars in retirement funds? Even if you are over 59 $^1/_2$ and beyond the age of early withdrawal penalties, it's better to take the money out of your retirement accounts over time so you can control your tax burden and keep the power of tax deferral working to your advantage as long as possible.

Remember, one of the reasons you initially made pre-tax contributions to your retirement account was to obtain much-needed tax advantages. In most cases, by making these contributions, you avoided paying taxes while

FIGURE 3

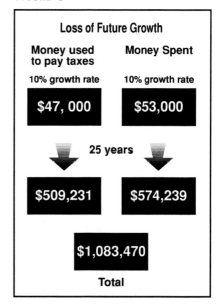

Loss of Future Growth

Money used to pay taxes	Money Spent
10% growth rate	10% growth rate
$47,000	$53,000
25 years	
$509,231	$574,239
$1,083,470	
Total	

working and in a higher tax bracket. When you retire and drop to a lower bracket, you can begin taking distributions. In addition, if taking a cash distribution vaults you into a higher tax bracket, you may have just deferred paying taxes until you have to pay them out at a higher rate.

As long as your funds remain in a retirement plan, the money grows tax-deferred. This privileged status ends as soon as the money is withdrawn from the plan. Preserving this tax shelter is another reason you shouldn't withdraw the funds.

Some people take cash distributions if they lose their job, if they choose to buy or start a business, to get rid of unwanted debt, or to pay off their house. In each of these cases, dipping into your retirement funds is still a bad idea. It would usually be better to obtain a loan, home equity or otherwise, rather than tap into retirement funds for a purpose other than retirement. This also holds true even for emergencies.

If you absolutely must take a cash distribution, there are ways to control and in some cases, minimize the tax burdens associated with early withdrawal:

100 Percent IRA Rollover

If you rollover 100 percent of your vested plan balance to an IRA, no taxes or penalties will be withheld upon this transfer. Once your money is deposited into the IRA, you can take a distribution and request that no money be withheld for taxes *at that time*. Keep in mind that you will still have to pay all of the taxes you owe on the IRA distribution when you file your 1040 at year's end.

Ten-Year Forward Averaging

Ten-year forward averaging allows the lump-sum cash distribution to be taxed as if it were taken out of the retirement plan over a ten-year period, rather than all in one year, to minimize the tax liability. The tax is paid entirely in the year of distribution, but the lump sum qualifies for a lower tax rate.

Forward averaging is available only to individuals who reached age 65 during or prior to 2000, and have been participating in their company's retirement plan for at least five years. Your distribution must qualify as a lump-sum and be due to separation of service, retirement, disability or death. Some additional criteria apply in order to receive this special tax treatment.

While these options do help ease tax burdens, it is still better to spread your withdrawals, and thus the taxation, over the 20 to 30 years you are in retirement.

STEPS FOR OBTAINING A CASH DISTRIBUTION

1. Obtain distribution paperwork from your former employer which usually includes the following items:

   - *Special Tax Notice Regarding Plan Payments* packet, which outlines the tax consequences of each distribution option.
   - *Election for Distribution of Benefits* form, which allows you to choose a distribution option (see Figure 4).

2. Complete the paperwork.

   - Indicate that you would like to take a cash distribution.
   - Indicate what you would like to do with any company stock you may own. You can choose to have the stock sent to you in shares, in which case you will receive a stock certificate that you can either hold or deposit into a brokerage account (this is referred to as a "transfer-in-kind"). *Remember, there will be no withholding on the distribution you take in company stock shares.* (See Chapter 20 on Net Unrealized Appreciation.) You can also choose to have the stock sold and the cash proceeds sent to you.

3. Return the paperwork to your employer.

4. Allow approximately 2-4 weeks for the distribution to be sent to you.

OPTION 2: ROLLOVER TO AN IRA

FACT

Sixty-seven percent of all retirement plan distributions are rolled over to IRAs.[6]

TIP

Consider rolling your money to an IRA if:

- You want additional flexibility
- You are interested in working with a financial advisor
- You wish to sell company stock without restrictions

FIGURE 4

Sample: Distribution of Benefits Election

Name of Plan: ABC Corp. 401 K
Plan Participant: John Smith
Social Security Number: 522-22-2221

I select the following distribution option:

__X__ I elect a LUMP SUM DISTRIBUTION of $400,000. I am entitled to a distribution of $500,000, but understand that this is reduced by $100,000 because it is subject to the 20% mandatory withholding rules. I read the Special Tax Notice Regarding Plan Payments, and I understand the tax consequences of this election.

        COMPANY STOCK
_____ Please issue a stock certificate for all company stock in my plan.
__X__ Please liquidate all shares of company stock held in my plan.

_____ I elect a DIRECT ROLLOVER of _____ % of my benefit (insert the percentage you wish to be rolled) into an Individual Retirement Account (IRA) or another qualified retirement plan. If you select his option you must also complete the Direct Rollover Instruction form.

        COMPANY STOCK
_____ Please transfer all company stock in-kind to my IRA.
_____ Please liquidate all shares of company stock held in my plan.

Signed:

_____   _____
John Smith   Date

Two out of every three people eligible to take a withdrawal from a company-sponsored plan roll their money into a Rollover IRA (also referred to as a conduit IRA). These plans are popular and worth examining closer to see if they may be right for you.

IRA is an acronym for Individual Retirement Account. IRAs are tax-deferred retirement programs designed by the federal government to encourage retirement savings. An IRA is a type of account; it is not an investment. Think of an IRA as a personal storage unit. It's a place where you store your money, on a tax-deferred basis, while investing it in virtually any legitimate investment you choose. In many IRAs you can buy stocks, bonds, mutual funds, annuities, certificates of deposit and money market mutual funds. The rate of return your IRA produces is determined by the investments you select.

There are two types of IRAs into which you can roll your money: Traditional and Rollover. You can rollover your retirement plan money into either type, but there are definite advantages to selecting a Rollover IRA. A Rollover IRA can only contain money previously invested in a qualified company-sponsored retirement plan. Because the money came from a qualified plan it can, at a future date, be rolled back into a qualified company-sponsored plan. It's a good idea to leave this option open by choosing a Rollover IRA because at some point it may be advantageous to transfer the money back into a qualified plan. If you're having a financial crisis, for instance, obtaining a loan from your employer-sponsored retirement plan is preferable to taking a taxable withdrawal from your IRA. Assuming your plan allows for loans, this could be accomplished by transferring your Rollover IRA (money from a past employer) into your new employer's plan and then taking a loan.

You can open an IRA at a bank or a self directed IRA through a brokerage firm or a mutual fund company. Let's look a these options:

Self-directed IRAs, which allow virtually unlimited investment options and flexibility, are distinctly different from bank IRAs, which generally pay a low, fixed rate of return. Bank IRA's are indeed one of many IRA choices, but there are better places to invest long-term retirement money. The rates for most bank IRAs are comparable to the rates for one-to-five year certificates of deposit (CDs). If you invest in a bank IRA, you are essentially limiting yourself to one investment option: a fixed interest rate account.

It's true that a bank IRA does offer FDIC insurance, which protects your principal up to $100,000. However, it doesn't protect you from one of the most serious retirement risks: inflation. Investing long-term retirement money in short-term, low-interest accounts can be a costly mistake. If you keep your funds from growing, it may be difficult to reach your retirement goals. By contrast, a self-directed IRA held at a brokerage firm or a mutual fund company offers almost endless investment choices and more opportunities to increase the value of your savings.

Although there is a limit on the amount of new money you can contribute annually to an IRA, these limits do not apply to rollovers or transfers. Any amount can be rolled over from a qualified retirement plan or from another IRA. If you leave your company, you can have the entire balance of your retirement plan rolled into an IRA. Your money will continue to grow on a tax-deferred basis without any taxes or penalties.

Once you open an IRA account, each year you can add to that account to increase your retirement savings. However, there are limits on the amount you can add each year to your IRA. The annual contribution limit in 2002 was $3,000 per person. This contribution amount is being increased due to recent tax law changes (see Figure 5). In order to contribute to an IRA, you must have earned income or have a spouse who has earned income. If you participate in a company-sponsored retirement plan, your IRA contribution may or may not be deductible depending on your income level.

FIGURE 5

Traditional IRAs: Annual Contribution Limits		
Year	Contribution Limit (Under Age 50)	Contribution Limit (Over age 50)
2001	$2,000	$2,000
2002	$3,000	$3,500
2003	$3,000	$3,500
2004	$3,000	$3,500
2005	$4,000	$4,500
2006	$4,000	$5,000
2007	$4,000	$5,000
2008	$5,000	$6,000
2009 and thereafter	Increases for inflation in $500 increments	$1,000 more than the under age 50 limit

Rolling your money into a self-directed IRA has a multitude of advantages. It provides the enhanced ability to diversify in order to reduce investment risk, and it opens up a panorama of investment choices. In a self-directed IRA, you can choose from approximately 14,000 mutual funds, thousands of stocks and bonds, hundreds of fixed or variable annuity contracts and more. This lets you uncover better investments than those available in a bank IRA or in your former company's retirement plan. With additional investment options, you can also further diversify your portfolio and build a successful investment strategy. Recent corporate failures have highlighted the risk of not diversifying and leaving your retirement savings in your company's stock. Moving the money to a self-directed IRA and creating a diversified investment portfolio is the best way to protect against such risk.

The flexibility of a self-directed IRA allows you to control how much money you want to withdraw from your IRA and how frequently you make withdrawals. You can take a distribution from your IRA at any time you choose, in any amount, and for any purpose. The same early withdrawal penalty applies to distributions taken prior to age 59 $^1/_2$, unless the distribution qualifies for an exception to this penalty. Withdrawal flexibility will prove essential if you decide to take early withdrawals (before age 59 $^1/_2$) from your IRA under the penalty exception of Section 72T of the IRS Code (see Chapter 4).

If you own company stock in your plan, you can roll it into your IRA without having to sell it. This is called an "in-kind" transfer. Your company will issue a stock certificate for the number of shares you own and send it directly to the institution handling your IRA, presuming the institution can hold individual securities. If you decide to sell the stock at a later date, you can do so anytime.

The ability to sell company stock when you wish is an important element of IRA flexibility. Many companies place restrictions on selling company stock in an employer-sponsored retirement plan. For example, if you sell company stock while it's being held inside your company's plan, you will usually receive the closing price of the stock on that trading day, not the price at the time you requested the stock be sold. This could result in costly losses to you if the stock drops dramatically between the time you call and the end of the trading day.

In a self-directed IRA, you can use "limit orders" to ensure that a stock is sold before it goes into free fall and seriously erodes your retirement savings. This mechanism is invaluable in protecting your hard-earned nest egg. For example, you may want to protect your stock from loss by entering a stop-loss order and having your stock sold automatically if it falls below a specified price. In addition, you may want to enter a limit order to have your stock automatically sold when it reaches a certain target price. However, specifying a price to sell usually cannot be done in a company-sponsored plan.

Many investors prefer self-directed IRA's due to the amount of personal control they can exercise over their own money. If you are unhappy with your IRA provider, simply transfer your account to another firm. You can do this as often as you like as long as you have the money transferred directly from one institution to another without it ever touching your hands along the way. You are limited to one transfer per year if you physically receive the IRA money, and then re-deposit it in a new IRA at another institution. This is called a "60-day Rollover" since 60 is the number of days you have to deposit the money into another IRA once you have received it. If you do not re-deposit the money within that 60-day window, you will of course, be taxed and penalized (if applicable).

IRAs also give you the flexibility to make changes to your investments immediately, if you're not happy with their progress. Also, it is very easy to set up a withdrawal plan from your IRA. Most people at retirement establish a system of regular withdrawals from their IRAs to provide the necessary additional income desired during retirement.

With IRAs, you can also hire a financial advisor to help you develop and maintain an investment strategy. If you have IRAs at other institutions, you can consolidate them together for ease of management. IRAs are much more flexible than company-sponsored plans.

ROLLOVER METHODS

There are two ways to take a distribution from your employer's plan and roll the money into an IRA account. Method 1 is cumbersome while Method 2 is easy:

Method 1: Lump-Sum/Cash Distribution and 60-day Rollover

To initiate this method, you must request that your plan balance be sent directly to you just as if you were taking a lump-sum cash distribution.

Upon receiving the money, you have 60 days to deposit it into an IRA to avoid penalties. Be advised, however, that there is a major hitch to this method. Distribution rules mandate that your employer withhold 20 percent of all cash distributions — the prepayment of income taxes that may be owed if the money doesn't get rolled into an IRA. Since the IRS has no idea whether your retirement plan money is going to be rolled over or spent, the withholding is applied to every cash distribution.

This presents a huge problem. How can you roll the full distribution amount to an IRA if 20 percent is taken off the top before you even receive the distribution? You know the IRS is not going to be able to refund that money to you within 60 days. Let's do the math: Say you decide to take a $100,000 cash distribution from your company's 401(k) and roll it over into an IRA within 60 days. Your company will send you a check for $80,000 and withhold $20,000. You then have 60 days to deposit the full $100,000 into an IRA to avoid taxes and penalties. This means you will have to withdraw $20,000 from your savings account or elsewhere to make up the difference (when you file your income taxes at year-end, you will get back the

$20,000 initially withheld).

As you can see, the whole process is fairly complicated and an inefficient way to move money from your company's retirement plan to an IRA. Utilizing a direct rollover will enable you to reach the same end result with fewer headaches.

Method 2: Direct Rollover

To avoid the problems that come with taking direct receipt of your retirement money, instruct your employer to transfer the entire vested balance of your plan directly to a previously established IRA. This way, you will never receive a check made payable to you for the balance of your plan, and the aforementioned tax-withholding problem never arises. Because the check is made payable to your IRA institution, the IRS knows the money was transferred directly to an IRA account — no taxes are withheld in the process.

Some plans will mail the rollover check directly to your IRA provider, and others will mail the check directly to you. In either case, it will be made payable to your IRA provider for and in behalf of you (FBO). In cases where the check is mailed to you, don't be alarmed. Simply forward it to your IRA provider to deposit in your account.

At year's end, you will receive a 1099R form from your former employer showing that a distribution was made. You will also receive a statement from your IRA provider showing the money was deposited into your IRA. As long as these transfer balances match, there will be no tax consequences or penalties.

STEPS FOR INITIATING AN IRA ROLLOVER

The rollover process is very simple. First, open a Rollover IRA account at the financial institution of your choice. After completing the necessary paperwork, you will be assigned an IRA account number. (Double-check to make sure you set up your account as a Rollover IRA so you have the option of transferring the money back to an employer-sponsored retirement plan in the future.) You will need your IRA account number and the IRA provider's address to complete the rollover.

Retirement plan administrators usually process distributions in one of two ways. Some will provide you with retirement distribution forms (see the sample forms in Figures 6 and 7). If this is the case, complete these forms and return them to your employer. The second method processes the rollover via the telephone. When phone distributions are available, simply contact your 401(k) provider directly (usually a mutual fund company or brokerage firm) and request your money be rolled into an IRA account. Distributions processed by phone usually speed up the

FIGURE 6

Sample: Distribution of Benefits Election

Name of Plan: ABC Corp. 401 K
Plan Participant: John Smith
Social Security Number: 522-22-2221

I select the following distribution option:

_____ I elect a LUMP SUM DISTRIBUTION of $400,000. I am entitled to a distribution of $500,000, but understand that his is reduced by $100,000 because it is subject to the 20% mandatory withholding rules. I read the Special Tax Notice Regarding Plan Payments, and I understand the tax consequences of this election.

      COMPANY STOCK
    _____ **Please issue a stock certificate for all company stock in my plan.**
    _____ **Please liquidate all shares of company stock held in my plan.**

__X__ I elect a DIRECT ROLLOVER of __100__ % of my benefit (insert the percentage you wish to be rolled) into an Individual Retirement Account (IRA) or another qualified retirement plan. If you select his option you must also complete the Direct Rollover Instruction form.

      COMPANY STOCK
    __X__ **Please transfer all company stock in-kind to my IRA.**
    _____ **Please liquidate all shares of company stock held in my plan.**

Signed:

_____   _____
John Smith   **Date**

FIGURE 7

Sample: Direct Rollover Instructions

Name of Plan: ABC Corp. 401 K
Plan Participant: John Smith
Social Security Number: 522-22-2221

FOR A DIRECT ROLLOVER TO AN IRA:

Name of IRA Trustee: _____

IRA Account Number: _____

IRA Trustee Address: _____

FOR DIRECT ROLLOVER TO COMPANY SPONSORED QUALIFIED PLAN:

Name of New Company Plan: _____

Plan Account Number: _____

Plan Address: _____

_____

Signed:

_____   _____
John Smith   Date

process. In either case, you will likely be asked for the following:

1. Your Social Security number (and Personal Identification Number, PIN, if processing the transaction over the phone).

2. Your IRA account number and the address of your IRA provider.

3. If you would like to sell your company stock or transfer it to your IRA in-kind. (If you transfer stock to your IRA, you will have more control of the price at which it is eventually sold, but you will probably have to pay some commission fees to do so. If you request that your employer sell the stock for you, you will usually receive the closing price on the day of your request and won't pay any trade commissions. Before making a final decision about your company stock, read Chapter 20 on Net Unrealized Appreciation (NUA). You may be able to obtain favorable tax treatment upon selling your stock if you own highly appreciated shares.)

4. Whether or not you would like taxes withheld; indicate that you do not.

5. If you have received and read the *Special Tax Notice* explaining the tax considerations associated with each retirement plan distribution option. *If you haven't read this notice, your rollover request will not be processed.*

Allow approximately two to four weeks for the distribution to be sent to your IRA.

When you request an IRA rollover, the investments in your employer's plan will be liquidated, and a check for the balance will be sent to your IRA provider. New investments will need to be purchased in the IRA. The process for developing a successful investment strategy was discussed in Chapters 8-13.

Have you borrowed any money from your retirement plan? If you have an outstanding loan balance at the time you retire, you should repay it prior to taking a distribution. Plan loans must typically be repaid within 30-60 days from the time you leave the company. If the loan is not repaid and you leave money in your former employer's plan, or choose to roll over money to an IRA without repaying it, the loan amount will be treated as a distribution and be subject to taxes and possible penalties.

If you have stock in your company's retirement plan, you can choose to have the shares sent directly to you and roll the balance of the plan into an IRA. This combination distribution method is used when utilizing the Net Unrealized Appreciation strategy and may allow you to qualify for favorable tax treatment.

There are other considerations you should keep in mind. If you are over age 55, once your money transfers into an IRA, you are no longer eligible to take a penalty-free, lump-sum distribution (see Chapter 4), nor will you be eligible for ten-year forward averaging. In addition, depending on your IRA provider, you may be required to pay an IRA custodial fee and commissions to purchase investments in your IRA. While invested in your company's retirement plan, your employer pays these fees.

A substantial majority of those who change jobs or retire choose to roll their retirement money into an IRA and take advantage of the unlimited investment options, enhanced control and tremendous flexibility that IRAs provide.

OPTION 3: ROLL YOUR RETIREMENT MONEY INTO YOUR NEW EMPLOYER'S PLAN

FACT
Only 3 percent of all distributions are rolled into a new employer's plan.

TIP
Consider rolling your retirement plan money into a new employer's plan if:

- You would like to keep your accounts consolidated.
- Your new employer's plan offers many good investment choices.
- You anticipate needing a retirement plan loan in the near future.

If you are changing jobs, you may have the choice of moving your retirement money into your new employer's retirement plan. Some employer plans will not accept a rollover from a previous employer's plan — check with your new employer to see if this option is offered. If you do roll your money into the new company's plan, you will not encounter any taxes or penalties and your money will continue to grow tax-deferred.

Consolidating your money into one employer-sponsored retirement plan may be advantageous for at least four reasons. First, if you have a small balance in a former company's plan, you may want to consolidate your accounts to make managing your portfolio easier. Second, if you transfer the money into your new employer's plan, you will still be eligible to obtain a loan if that option is available (loans are not available from IRAs). Third, if you are eligible, you may still take advantage of ten-year forward averaging when you eventually take a distribution from your account (this is not available from IRAs). Fourth, after reaching age 55, you could request a penalty-free lump sum distribution from your company-sponsored plan upon separation from service (this is not available for distributions from IRAs).

The biggest disadvantage to rolling your money into your new company's plan is the limitations on investment choices. As mentioned in other chapters, limited investment options generally mean less portfolio diversification and an increased possibility of mediocre investments. This option leaves you with limited flexibility to take withdrawals or move money to other investments, especially when compared to an IRA. If you own company stock in your former employer's plan, it must be sold in order to transfer your money to the new plan.

The process for rolling money directly from a previous employer's plan to one managed by your new employer is identical to performing a direct rollover to an IRA (see instructions on page 240). Additionally, you could roll your money into a Rollover IRA and, at some future date, transfer it into your new employer's retirement plan.

OPTION 4: DEFER DISTRIBUTION — LEAVE THE MONEY IN PLACE

TIP
Consider deferring distribution if your former employer's plan:
- Offers numerous investment choices
- Offers investment choices that are above average
- Offers flexibility of investment changes
- Allows participants to sell company stock

Deferring distribution and leaving your money in your former company's retirement plan is the simplest thing to do because it does not require you to do anything — there are no forms to fill out and no additional investment decisions to make. Because you are not taking a distribution, there are no taxes or penalties to pay, and your money will continue to grow tax-deferred. In addition, there are no fees or commissions. Although the mutual funds you own in your 401(k) charge annual management fees, you don't actually pay anything out of pocket. Many employers cover account and transaction-related costs and will continue to do so if you defer your distribution.

Leaving money in your former employer's plan does have its downside. Most company-sponsored retirement plans have limitations, primarily concerning the number and quality of the investment choices offered. This inhibits your ability to properly diversify. The average retirement plan only offers 12 investment choices.[7] Although a dozen investment options could easily provide an acceptable level of diversification, many retirement plans lack important components of a well-balanced portfolio, such as a combination of both growth and value stocks, mid-cap and small-cap stocks, and international positions.

In addition to diversification limitations, it is highly unlikely that each of the 12 investments offered is among the best available, compared to the thousands accessible outside the plan. If your plan offers a large company growth stock fund, for example, is it among the best in its category and, if not, do you have any other options?

Another potential downside is stock concentration. Many plan participants are too heavily invested in their own company's stock (as covered in Chapter 16). Matching contributions often come in the form of company stock and unfortunately, many companies will not allow employees to sell company stock to diversify into other investments.

This is a serious dilemma. Take an extreme case like Enron, for example, in which over 57 percent of the cumulative 401(k) money was invested in company stock. After corporate fraud was discovered, Enron's share price quickly lost over 98 percent of its value.[8] Employees ended up not only losing their jobs, but also a huge chunk of their retirement savings.

If you leave a company, but choose to keep your money in the company's retirement plan, you may still be saddled with the problem of stock concentration. However, if you request a stock distribution, you can sell it immediately or transfer it to a brokerage account and sell at a later time. After reducing your company stock exposure, you can reinvest in other positions and gain desired diversification.

Leaving your money in place also costs you some control and flexibility. Once you're off the company payroll, you can no longer make contributions, and you cannot obtain a loan from the plan. Some plans may limit how often you can make changes to your investments. Also, you may be unable to set up a systematic withdrawal program to supplement your other retirement income.

In some plans, deferring distribution may not even be an option. Not all employers allow former employees to keep money invested in the retirement plan and may mandate that you take a distribution from the plan by a certain date. This is almost always the case for accounts with balances of $5,000 or less. Let's look at an example. Recently, Edward Harrison and his wife Martha, both age 62, retired — Edward from a local accounting firm, Martha from her job as a reservations manager for a major airline. Edward's 401(k) offered only six investment options. To obtain more choices, he rolled his money into a Rollover IRA at a large brokerage firm. He and his financial advisor searched for investments from over 14,000 mutual funds and thousands of individual securities. They developed a diversified investment strategy using eight highly ranked stock funds and created a bond ladder with six carefully selected, high-grade corporate and government bonds.

Martha, on the other hand, saw advantages in leaving her money in the much larger plan operated by her former airline employer, which allowed participants to invest in any mutual fund available at a national discount brokerage firm. The plan even allowed participants to sell company stock without restriction.

Do the limitations presented by leaving your money in your former employer's plan concern you? The choice is clear. If the limitations are insignificant and the plan offers plenty of good investment choices, consider deferring distribution and leaving your money in place. If, however, you don't feel comfortable with the constraints of your former employer's plan, look at other choices.

OPTION 5: ROLL YOUR RETIREMENT MONEY INTO AN IRA AND THEN CONVERT TO A ROTH IRA

TIP

Consider converting your IRA to a Roth IRA if:

- You are in a low tax bracket now and anticipate being in a higher bracket at retirement.
- You would like to withdraw some retirement funds prior to age 59 ½ without penalty (applies to principal only).
- You would like to be "tax diversified" at retirement.
- Your adjusted gross income is less than $100,000.

A Roth IRA is very similar, in many respects, to a traditional IRA when it comes to annual contribution limits, investment choices and flexibility. It differs, however, when it comes to the way taxes are applied.

Money contributed to a Roth IRA is done on an after-tax basis as opposed to conventional IRA's or company-sponsored plans that consist of pre-tax contributions. Money invested in Roth IRA's grows tax-free, not tax-deferred like traditional

IRAs. This means that you can withdraw money from your Roth IRA, tax-free, upon reaching age 59 ½.

For many Americans, it makes sense to take advantage of these tax differences. In order to deposit your retirement plan money into a Roth IRA, you must initially transfer it to a traditional IRA and then convert the IRA to a Roth. This conversion option is only available to those who have adjusted gross incomes under $100,000. The amount of the IRA conversion, while taxable as ordinary income, is not included in this figure.

Does tax-free growth coupled with tax-free withdrawals sound too good to be true? You think there has to be a catch?

In a sense, there is: You will be required to pay income taxes (federal and state) on any amount converted from a Traditional IRA to a Roth IRA (see tax brackets below in Figure 8.) The entire amount converted will be added to your taxable income in the year of the conversion; you pay taxes now to avoid paying taxes later.

FIGURE 8

2002 Federal Income Tax Rates		
Tax Rate	Single Filers	Joint Filers
10%	$0-6,000	$0-12,000
15%	$6,001-27,050	$12,001-46,700
27%	$27,051-67,700	$46,701-112,850
30%	$67,701-141,250	$112,851-171,950
35%	$141,251-307,050	$171,951-307,050
38.6%	$307,051+	$307,051+

You can control the way you make this transfer. Because taxes are due in the year of conversion, you may want to convert money from your traditional IRA to a Roth IRA a little at a time to avoid having your tax bracket ratcheted higher. You can convert any amount from an IRA to a Roth IRA and do so as often as you choose; the 10 percent early withdrawal penalty does not apply when making a conversion from an IRA to a Roth.

Should you convert your IRA to a Roth? You need only ask one question: Do I want to pay my taxes now or later? Determining whether to convert or not depends on your current tax bracket compared to your future bracket when you begin withdrawing the funds (retirement). For example, if you are in the highest tax bracket now, 38.6 percent, and you anticipate being in a lower bracket, say 15 percent, when you retire, converting to a Roth IRA wouldn't make much sense — you would pay high taxes now to avoid paying lower taxes later.

On the other hand, if you are in a 15 percent tax bracket now and anticipate being in a higher bracket during retirement, then it makes perfect sense to convert your IRA to a Roth. Pay taxes now when they are low and avoid paying them later when they are higher. This is often the case for younger investors who are not yet in their peak earning years. If your tax bracket doesn't change between now and retirement, both options will yield the same result (see Figures 9, 10 and 11).

FIGURE 9

FIGURE 10

FIGURE 11

If you are in a tax bracket that is neither very high nor very low, there is a middle ground you can pursue. Convert some of your IRA to a Roth IRA. At retirement you will be "tax diversified." Some of your money will be invested in before-tax accounts while your Roth IRA money will have already been taxed. If tax rates are higher at retirement, you can take money out of your Roth IRA and not pay any taxes. If tax rates are lower at retirement, you can take money from your traditional IRA. This diversified approach makes sense for people who are in the mid-range tax brackets.

Another benefit of the Roth IRA is liquidity. Unlike a Traditional IRA, you can withdraw your principal without penalty or taxes prior to age 59 $^1/_2$. To avoid a premature withdrawal penalty, withdrawals cannot take place for five years after the Roth conversion. For those retiring prior to age 59 $^1/_2$, the ability to tap some retirement funds without penalty may be very helpful.

The process for rolling your money to an IRA and then converting to a Roth is identical to that for rolling your company retirement plan over to an IRA except for one additional step. Once your retirement plan money has been rolled over into a traditional IRA, your financial institution will provide you with an *IRA/Roth Conversion Form* on which you indicate the amount of your IRA you would like converted to a Roth. At year-end, you will receive a 1099R form from your IRA provider indicating the taxable conversion amount.

OPTION #6: ANNUITY DISTRIBUTION

FACT
Only 12 percent of plan distributions are taken as annuity payments.

TIP
Consider annuity payments if:

- You don't want to be involved in the management of your own portfolio.
- You want to guarantee your income for life.

When you choose to take annuity payments, your vested account balance is used to buy an immediate annuity. Many annuity payout options are usually available. Annuity payments will be made to you for your entire lifetime and possibly your spouse's as well, depending upon the payout option you choose. With annuity payments, you do not have to worry about the management of the balance in your plan or the stock market's ups and downs. Although the annuity payout is generally lower than what could be produced by an investment portfolio moderately invested, the freedom of not having to manage the money or worry about market downturns makes this option a nice fit for some.

The various annuity payout options are usually the same as those offered to people receiving company pensions. These annuity options are outlined in detail in

Chapter 6, "Company Pensions and Pension Maximization Strategies."

The downside of annuity payments, in addition to a possible lower payout rate, is the inability to reverse your decision. Once the decision is made to annuitize, it is irrevocable. You are guaranteed a lifetime income; however, you can never again tap into your total retirement plan balance.

MAKING A FINAL DISTRIBUTION DECISION

Which distribution option should you choose? It's not a decision to take lightly because of the impact it will have on your retirement years. Before choosing, look at your options side-by-side, comparing the long-term effects of each. Chapter 21 looks at several case studies and provides examples showing how a distribution analysis can help you determine which is the best fit for you.

By making educated decisions about your money during job changes and at retirement, you can ensure that one of your largest and most critical assets is managed properly.

CHAPTER 20
COMPANY STOCK DISTRIBUTIONS
(NET UNREALIZED APPRECIATION)

Upon withdrawal, the money you've invested in mutual funds within a 401(k) and other types of employer-sponsored plans must be liquidated. Most people choose to roll this money into individual retirement accounts (IRAs). Rolling money into an IRA is often the best distribution method for plan money invested in mutual funds. It may not, however, be your best choice for the portion of your plan that is invested in company stock.

According to research, 401(k) participants invest about one-third of their retirement savings in their company stock.[1] In fact, in some corporations, company stock represents over half of the total plan balance. One usually finds this over-concentration in plans where employers provide matching contributions in their own stock. If you own company stock in your employer-sponsored retirement plan, you may be able to save thousands of dollars upon distribution by utilizing a little-known and all-too-rarely considered IRS tax strategy. It's called Net Unrealized Appreciation (NUA).

This strategy works best in situations in which an investor is in a high tax bracket, has very low-cost basis stock in his or her plan, and desires to hold on to the stock for many years after distribution.[2] It also works extremely well in combination with the IRA Rollover distribution method covered in Chapter 19.

It's inevitable that the money in your retirement plan is going to get taxed at some point. The NUA strategy allows you some control over how it is taxed. If you sell your company stock while in the 401(k) plan or after rolling it into an IRA, you will be required to pay income taxes on the entire balance when you withdraw the proceeds, whether that occurs immediately or during retirement. The NUA strategy allows your company stock gains to be taxed at capital gains tax rates, which are generally lower than income tax rates.

Compare your income tax rate to the capital gains rates in Figures 1 and 2. You will probably see a significant difference.

FIGURE 1

2002 Federal Income Tax Rates		
Tax Rate	Single Filers	Joint Filers
10%	$0-6,000	$0-12,000
15%	$6,001-27,950	$12,001-46,700
27%	$27,951-67,700	$46,701-112,850
30%	$67,701-141,250	$112,851-171,950
35%	$141,251-307,050	$171,951-307,050
38.6%	$307,051+	$307,051+

FIGURE 2

Capital Gains Rate	
Long-Term Capital Gains (longer than one-year holding period)	20%
Long-Term Capital Gains Rate for those in 15% tax bracket	10%
Short-Term Capital Gains (less than one-year holding period)	Ordinary Income Tax Rates

What is Net Unrealized Appreciation or NUA? It is the value of company stock upon distribution from the plan, compared to the value of the stock when originally contributed (cost basis). For example, let's say your employer contributed $10,000 of company stock to your plan (this is the cost basis), and it is now worth $60,000 — you have NUA of $50,000. When you retire or separate from your company, you must decide what to do with the company stock held in your retirement plan. You have four options, as listed below. Three of these options were covered extensively in Chapter 19.

1. Sell the stock and take a cash distribution. Income taxes are due immediately as well as applicable penalties.

2. Sell the stock and rollover the cash balance into an IRA. Income taxes are due when you eventually take a withdrawal from your IRA.

3. Don't sell the stock, but roll it over "in-kind" into an IRA. Again, you must pay income taxes when you eventually sell and take a withdrawal.

4. Don't sell the stock, take a stock distribution "in-kind" and deposit the shares into a non-retirement account . Capital gains taxes are due when you eventually sell shares.

The last option is referred to as the "Net Unrealized Appreciation" (or NUA) strategy. A quick comparison of each of these options shows the value of the NUA strategy: Option 1 triggers immediate income taxation upon distribution. In Options 2 and 3, income taxes must be paid when withdrawals are taken in retirement. But the fourth option, the NUA strategy, allows you to pay capital gains taxes upon selling your company stock, rather than income taxes. Using the NUA strategy defers taxation on the appreciation of the stock until it is eventually sold, at which point capital gains taxes are imposed only upon the *appreciation*.

Let's take a closer look at this strategy.

How the NUA Strategy Works

To initiate this strategy, you must request a lump-sum distribution and have the "qualifying" company stock in your plan sent directly to you in-kind. Stock shares will be sent to you in certificate form from your employer-sponsored retirement program. These shares can then be deposited into a taxable brokerage account (a non-retirement account). Money that is not invested in your company's stock can be rolled into a Rollover IRA. Mutual fund shares, for example, will be liquidated and distributed to you in cash; the cash portion of the distribution can subsequently be rolled into a Rollover IRA.

Some plans will allow you to split your plan distribution. If this is the case, your eligible stock shares will be sent to you in-kind while the remaining balance of your account can be directly rolled to a Rollover IRA.

Qualifying shares are those contributed to your plan by your employer and those non-deductible shares purchased by you (to the extent that they are both part of a lump- sum distribution from your plan.)[3] Deductible shares purchased by you do not qualify for this favorable tax treatment.[4] A lump-sum distribution is defined as a payment of your entire plan balance occurring in one taxable year that takes place after a "qualifying event" which is: separation from service (including retirement), attaining age 59 $\frac{1}{2}$ or death.

Sound complicated? It is. Therefore, it's recommended that you contact your financial advisor or a tax advisor before you take a distribution of your employer's stock.

The distribution of the stock is subject to immediate taxation since you are moving money from a retirement account to a non-retirement account. This may set off some alarms in your mind, but don't worry, you're going to save money in the long run.

Upon taking a stock distribution, you will be required to pay taxes (at income tax rates) on only the cost basis of the stock — the average value of the shares at the time they were initially purchased in the plan — NOT the stock's total current value. Your employer will not withhold any tax upon distribution of stock shares. The 20 percent mandatory withholding tax applies only to cash distributions. If you are not yet age 55, you will also be required to pay a 10 percent premature withdrawal penalty. Again, though, this is imposed only on a cost basis, not the entire value of the stock distribution. This is a sticky point for many people who are simply unwilling or unable to pay any taxes now, even if it will save them money in the long run. However, if your cost basis is very low, the tax and penalty will not be a heavy burden.

You are not required to pay any tax on the appreciation of the stock, it's net unrealized appreciation (NUA) until you eventually sell it. At that time, any appreciation is subject only to capital gains taxes, not income tax. This means you have a built-in 20 percent capital gains ceiling, a far-cry cheaper than the maximum income tax bracket of 38.6 percent.

WHO SHOULD CONSIDER THE NUA STRATEGY?

Those with low-cost basis stock and who are in the highest tax brackets will gain the greatest benefit from the NUA strategy. As a general rule, the current value of the stock should be at least double, and probably three or four times the cost basis for the strategy to make sense.[5]

NUA VS. IRA: WHICH STRATEGY IS BEST WHEN YOU WANT TO SELL STOCK IMMEDIATELY AND SPEND THE PROCEEDS?

If you have low-basis stock, are in a higher tax bracket (usually over 27 percent) and would like to sell your stock upon distribution and spend the proceeds, it's generally advantageous to use the NUA strategy.

Let's look at an example: Robert Stewart accumulates 5,000 shares of company stock in his 401(k) plan. The average purchase price (cost basis) is $5 per share for a total of $25,000. When he retires in the near future, he is planning to sell the stock and use the proceeds to buy some property. He is trying to decide between a stock distribution to a taxable account (NUA) or a rollover to his IRA. Which should he choose?

If he requests a stock distribution and deposits the shares into a taxable, non-retirement account, he will owe income tax on the cost basis ($25,000). In Robert's 27 percent tax bracket, that amounts to $6,750. Robert is over age 59 ½ so there are no early withdrawal penalties applied to his distribution. He plans to sell his stock shares at $60 per share. Multiplying that price by his 5,000 shares will give Robert $300,000. His net unrealized appreciation (NUA) will be $55 per share, or $275,000. (This is calculated by subtracting the $25,000 cost basis from the total value of the stock.)

When he sells those shares, he will owe capital gains tax (20 percent) on the $275,000 of appreciation, for a total of $55,000 in taxes. This $55,000 is due in the year he sells the stock. If he never sells the stock, he will never have to pay the tax. Assuming he does sell, however, his total tax bill will equal $61,750 ($6,750 of income tax on the cost basis, plus $55,000 in capital gains taxes when the stock is sold). After taxes, Robert is left with $238,250.

Now let's say Robert chose to roll his stock shares directly into an IRA account, realized the same appreciation, sold the shares at the same time, and then took a distribution from his IRA to buy the property. In this case, he would owe $81,000 in federal income taxes (in his 27 percent bracket) and possibly some additional state income taxes, leaving him with just $219,000. Even worse, if he took the entire $300,000 out of his IRA all in one year, he would find himself in the highest income tax bracket (38.6 percent) and would be left with only $184,200 after taxes.

Robert could maintain his tax bracket at 27 percent if he chooses simply to take distributions over a period of years rather than all at once. This won't help him, however, if he needs a large sum of money now to buy property. In this scenario, the Net Unrealized Appreciation strategy actually saved Robert $19,250 (if he stayed in a 27 percent tax bracket) or $54,050, if the distribution had launched him into the highest bracket.

Saving this amount of money makes the effort to set up a separate taxable account highly worthwhile. The higher the tax bracket and the greater the net unrealized appreciation, the more valuable the NUA tax break becomes. See Figure 3 for a summary of this example.

FIGURE 3

Sell stock immediately and spend proceeds.

Low Basis Stock	NUA	IRA Rollover
Total value of shares at time of distribution.	$300,000	$300,000
Cost basis of shares.	$25,000	$25,000
Net unrealized appreciation of shares at time of distribution (27%).	$275,000	$275,000
Income tax on cost basis of shares paid at time of distribution (27%).	$6,750	N/A
Growth of stock in 10 years.	N/A	N/A
Gain on stock over cost basis.	$275,000	$275,000
Capital gains tax on stock when sold (20%).	$55,000	N/A
Income tax on IRA distribution (27%).	N/A	$81,000
Total Tax	$61,750	$81,000

Advantage to NUA	$19,250

Assumptions: No dividends, capital gains rate 20%, income tax rate 27%; employee is over age 59 1/2, so there are no early withdrawal penalties upon the distribution of the company stock.

WHO SHOULD NOT CONSIDER THE NUA STRATEGY?

If you are planning to sell your stock immediately upon distribution and reinvest and diversify the proceeds into other investments, the tax advantages are lessened. Also, the NUA strategy will not yield as many benefits if you own high basis stock in your plan or are currently in a low tax bracket.

When you sell stock immediately to reinvest into a diversified portfolio, you will have to immediately pay income taxes on the cost basis of the stock and capital gains taxes on the appreciation. The money left over can be reinvested; however, in a taxable account, some of your portfolio growth will be lost to taxes each year. If your objective is to diversify your stock position, it is generally wiser to sell the stock in a retirement account and let the proceeds continue to grow tax-deferred.

Let's look at another example: William is age 55 and about to retire. His primary objective is to sell his 5,000 shares of company stock ($5 per share basis) and reinvest the proceeds into a more diversified portfolio. He doesn't plan on spending any of this money for 20 years. Which strategy should he choose?

Following the NUA strategy, he would transfer 5,000 shares of low-basis stock into a taxable brokerage account. If he sells the stock at $60 per share ($300,000) and pays the $61,750 in taxes (income and capital gains), he would have $238,250 after taxes to reinvest in a taxable portfolio. William is considering what his portfolio will be worth if he averages a 10 percent pre-tax growth rate. Now that his money is in a taxable account, some of that growth (interest, dividends and capital gains) is subject to taxes each year. Assuming that 15 percent of his return goes to pay the taxes, he will average just 8.5 percent growth after taxes have been paid.

Because William's objective is to diversify and invest for the long-term, it would make far more sense for him to rollover his money to an IRA. This will allow his growth to take place in a tax-deferred account (see Figure 4). Most people do not withdraw money from their IRA's all at once. If, for instance, money is withdrawn over a 20-year period during retirement, the tax rate may be reduced even more.

FIGURE 4

Sell immediately and diversify into other investments.

Low Basis Stock	NUA	IRA Rollover
Total value of shares at time of distribution.	$300,000	$300,000
Cost basis of shares.	$25,000	$25,000
Net unrealized appreciation of shares at time of distribution.	$275,000	$275,000
Income tax on cost basis of shares (paid immediately 27%	$6,750	N/A
Capital gains tax on stock (paid immediately 20%).	$55,000	N/A
Balance of portfolios in 20-years (after tax).	$1,217,944	N/A
Balance of IRA (before tax)	$1,217,944	$2,018,250
Income tax on portfolio upon withdrawal (27%).	N/A	$565,110
Ending Balance After Tax	$1,217,944	$1,453,140
Advantage to IRA		**$255,378**

Assumptions: Capital gains rate 20%, pre-tax growth rate for diversified portfolio is 10%, after tax-rate is 8.5%, employee is over age 59 1/2, so there are no early withdrawl penalties upon the distribution of the company stock. Tax rate applied to IRA distribution is 27%. The rate would be higher if the investor took a distribution all in one year rather than spreading it out over several years.

This makes the rollover strategy even more advantageous. Also, if you own high-cost basis stock, it is usually better to keep the stock in a retirement account. In this case, if you did utilize the NUA strategy, you would pay income tax on most of the value of the stock due to its high cost basis. Capital gains tax would only be applied to a small portion of the stock's value (the amount above the cost basis).

In addition, if you are not yet age 55, the NUA strategy may not be as effective. In this case you will be required to pay a 10 percent early withdrawal penalty on the original cost basis of the stock. Again, this is money that won't be compounding toward your retirement. The good news is that no penalties are owed on your stock appreciation.

NUA AND "STEPPED-UP" COST BASIS FOR HEIRS

If you roll your stock into an IRA, you not only face paying income taxes whenever you take a withdrawal, but income taxes must be paid upon your death.

When you pass away, your spouse can transfer your IRA balance to his or her IRA and avoid taxation. However, upon your spouse's death, your heirs must pay ordinary income tax on the entire balance of the IRA. Let's go back to the case of Robert Stewart. Assume when he passes away (and his spouse, if married) that the stock he owns is worth $100 per share and has a total value of $500,000. His heirs would be required to pay income taxes on the entire $500,000 if it was held in an IRA. This would inevitably place Robert in the highest tax bracket (38.6 percent) when computing the final income tax owed. Before his heirs received anything, the government would take $193,000.

If, however, he utilized the NUA strategy and transferred his 5,000 shares of company stock into a non-retirement account, his heirs would enjoy some tax advantages. They would be required to pay capital gains tax on the net unrealized appreciation of the shares while they were in the employer-sponsored retirement plan. This is referred to as "income in respect of the decedent." In Robert's case, he had $275,000 of net unrealized appreciation at the time he took an in-kind distribution from the plan. However, any appreciation that occurred after the stock was distributed from the plan will receive a "stepped-up basis" and will be tax-free following death.

If Robert dies when his stock is selling at $100 per share, the $100 price would become the new cost basis for the heirs. The appreciation from $60 (value of stock at the time of distribution from the plan) to $100 (the value of the stock upon death) is tax-free. In Robert's case, this amounts to $200,000. If the heirs subsequently decide to sell the stock, they will pay capital gains tax on the difference between

$100 and the price at the time they sell. If, for example, they sold the shares for $105, they would pay capital gains tax only on the appreciation since Robert's death, and only $5 per share would be taxed. Also, unlike with the IRA, no income tax is due at death.

No Mandatory Distributions

Another general disadvantage associated with an IRA, when compared to the NUA strategy, has to do with mandatory distributions.

If you own an IRA, you must begin taking mandatory distributions at age $70^{1}/_{2}$ whether you need the money or not. Mandatory distribution is synonymous with mandatory taxation. If you opt for the NUA strategy and deposit your company stock in a taxable account, you are not required to take any distributions at any age. Having funds in different types of accounts (both retirement and non-retirement) can help you stretch your nest egg and provide more money to your heirs.

What Is the Process for Initiating the NUA Strategy?

Your first step should be determining the cost basis of your employer's stock. This will help you determine how much the stock has risen in price (the NUA) since being purchased in your retirement plan and whether or not it makes sense to pursue this strategy. Next, you need to determine if your company stock shares are eligible for the NUA strategy. It may take several phone calls or letters to acquire this information. You'll need to contact your benefits department or the company that administers your employer's retirement plan. Because this information is sometimes difficult to obtain, you should start requesting it at least six months before you expect to retire or separate from service. Due to the technicalities involved, it may be advantageous to hire a tax professional. IRS Tax Code Section 402(e)(4) may also be helpful.

You will need to complete the necessary distribution paperwork. If you are going to take advantage of the NUA strategy, you must request a lump-sum distribution with the stock shares being sent directly to you. If your employer allows split distributions, you can roll the remaining balance of your plan directly into an IRA. If it does not allow for split distributions, you will receive your stock shares and a check for the balance of your plan (non-employer stock). Of course, your company must withhold 20 percent from the money distributed that was not invested in stock. You will have 60 days, upon receiving the check, to roll it into an IRA to avoid taxes and penalties. (See 60-day rollover section in the Chapter 19.) At year-end after distributing the stock, your employer will provide you with a copy of Form 1099R and will report the transaction to the IRS.

Prior to deciding what to do with your company stock, obtain a retirement plan distribution analysis (discussed in Chapter 21) so you can compare each of your options side-by-side (see also Figure 5). Chapter 21 also reviews some helpful case studies and gives several examples showing what information is available in a distribution analysis.

Depending on your goals and objectives, you may be able to save a lot of money in taxes by utilizing the NUA strategy.

FIGURE 5

IRA Rollover	In Kind Distribution (NUA)
No Taxes at time of rollover	Cost Basis taxed at income tax rate upon distribution. Potentially lower taxes overall.
Tax-Deferred Growth	Partial tax-deferment
When stock is sold and distributed from the IRA, ordinary income taxes must be paid (maximum tax rate 38.6%).	When stock is sold in taxable account capital gains taxes are paid on appreciation only (maximum tax rate 20% for long term gains).
Non-spouse heirs must pay income tax upon death of IRA owner.	Heir will receive a step in cost basis upon inheriting shares. All gains between holder's retirement and death are tax free. Capital gains taxes are due on appreciation of shares while in plan (income in respect of decedent).

CHAPTER 21
MAKING A FINAL DECISION USING A DISTRIBUTION ANALYSIS

Having come this far in the book, your mind is undoubtedly swimming with information. Do you feel ready to put your new knowledge to use, choosing the distribution option that makes the most sense for you, your circumstances and your objectives?

The pressure is on to make the right decisions. You're about to make choices that will profoundly affect your financial security and your lifestyle for the next 20 to 30 years. Because so much is at stake and many of your decisions are going to be irrevocable, it makes sense to obtain what's called a "Retirement Plan Distribution Analysis" from a qualified financial advisor so you can compare each of your options side-by-side (after tax). You don't want to make decisions of this magnitude without all essential information at your fingertips. This chapter shows you an easy way to determine which distribution method is right for you using this analysis.

In making the important decisions associated with a retirement distribution, seven out of every ten investors seek the advice of a professional financial advisor. This is a wise step on their part because an experienced professional can make certain you're not overlooking anything that can influence your choices.

Typically, the distribution analysis report is eight to ten pages and consists of at least the components outlined in Figure 1. Let's examine three realistic scenarios to see the value of a retirement distribution analysis. We'll call our hypothetical investors Mary Ann, Richard and Curtis. For the purposes of this exercise we'll focus only on the sections of the analysis that summarize the investor's options.

FIGURE 1

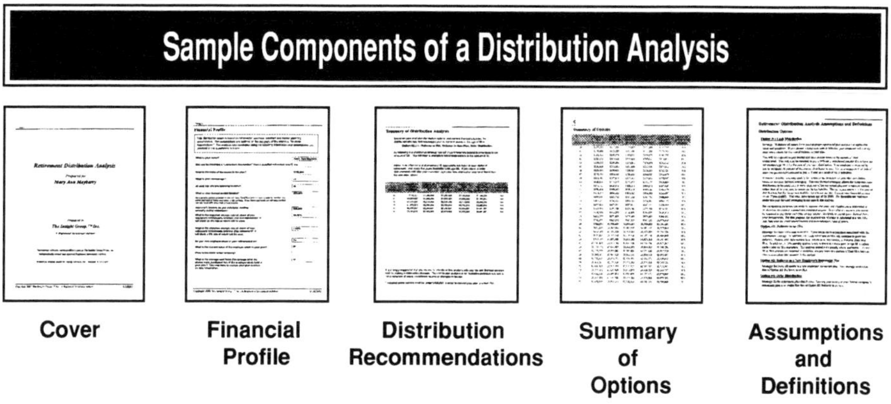

Sample Components of a Distribution Analysis

| Cover | Financial Profile | Distribution Recommendations | Summary of Options | Assumptions and Definitions |

Case Study #1: Mary Ann and the IRA Rollover

Mary Ann is a 40-year-old who just changed jobs. She wants to take a distribution from her employer-sponsored retirement plan without having to pay taxes or penalties. She also wants to develop a more diversified investment strategy and seek better mutual funds than those offered in her former employer's 401(k).

Mary Ann is planning on retiring at age 60. She is in a 27 percent tax bracket now but anticipates her tax bracket dropping at retirement. She is confident that her retirement money will grow at a 10 percent annual rate between now and retirement and 7 percent throughout retirement. Based on these assumptions, her financial advisor has prepared a retirement distribution analysis for her.

Mary Ann's distribution analysis helps her realize that she can maximize her retirement goals by rolling the entire balance of her plan into a Rollover IRA at a brokerage firm or mutual fund company that offers thousands of investment choices (see Figure 2). By choosing a Rollover IRA and deferring all taxes and penalties now, she will have $196,321 (after tax) more than she would have received from a Roth IRA at retirement, and $604,381 (after tax) more when compared to a cash distribution.

Making the wrong choice would have cost Mary Ann roughly $200,000 to $600,000 at retirement (see Figure 3). By transferring the money to a brokerage firm or a mutual fund, she gets the dramatic increase in investment choices she desires.

Notice that the calculations in the analysis shown in Figures 2 and 3 are the same for three of the distribution choices: rolling to an IRA, deferring distribution, and rolling to a new employer's plan. The calculations are the same because each of these options is treated the same for tax purposes: no immediate taxes or penalties and continued tax deferral. The analysis assumes that the investment returns for each of these options will be the same each year and, as a result, the balance will be identical each year. Although each of these options is treated the same for tax purposes, Mary Ann is hoping that rolling her money into a Rollover IRA and expanding her investment options beyond the mere 14 choices offered in her former employer's plan will result in better investments and greater long-term returns.

Also, by using a Rollover IRA rather than a Traditional IRA, Mary Ann keeps her future options open. At a later date, if she wishes, she can move her money back to an employer-sponsored plan. This may prove valuable for a number of reasons. She could qualify for a larger loan from her employer's retirement plan or elect a one-time lump-sum distribution available to those over age 55, avoiding the 10 percent early withdrawal penalty.

FIGURE 2

Summary of Distribution Analysis

Based on your available distribution options and current financial situation, the distribution strategy that maximizes your retirement assets at the age of 60 is:

Option #2,3,4 - Rollover to IRA, Rollover to New Plan, Defer Distribution

By following this distribution strategy you will incur immediate federal income taxes in the amount of $0. You will incur a premature withdrawal penalty in the amount of $0.

Below is an after-tax and after-penalty (if applicable) summary of each option at retirement, and every five years thereafter until age 85. If you intend to delay disbursement until after your retirement age your best distribution may be different than the one listed below.

Client Age	Option #1 Cash Distribution	Option #2 Rollover to IRA	Option #3 Rollover to New Plan	Option #4 Defer Distribution	Option #5 Convert to a Roth IRA*	Option #6 Combination Strategy
60	$786,224	$1,390,605	$1,390,605	$1,390,605	$1,194,284	N/A
65	$1,049,667	$1,950,396	$1,950,396	$1,950,396	$1,675,045	N/A
70	$1,401,381	$2,735,530	$2,735,530	$2,735,530	$2,349,338	N/A
75	$1,870,945	$3,792,314	$3,792,314	$3,792,314	$3,295,068	N/A
80	$2,497,847	$5,244,601	$5,244,601	$5,244,601	$4,621,503	N/A
85	$3,334,806	$7,193,906	$7,193,906	$7,193,906	$6,481,897	N/A

It is strongly suggested that you review the results of this analysis with your tax and financial advisors prior to making a distribution decision. The distribution analysis is for illustration purposes only and is not a reflection of actual investment returns or changes in tax law.

* Adjusted gross income must be under $100,000 in order to convert your plan to a Roth IRA.

FIGURE 3

Summary of Options

Client Age	Option #1 Cash Distribution	Option #2 Rollover to IRA	Option #3 Rollover to New Plan	Option #4 Defer Distribution	Option #5 Convert to a Roth IRA	Option #6 Combination Strategy
40	$157,500	$157,500	$157,500	$157,500	$157,500	N/A
41	$170,888	$173,250	$173,250	$173,250	$175,747	N/A
42	$185,413	$190,575	$190,575	$190,575	$193,323	N/A
43	$201,173	$209,633	$209,633	$209,633	$212,655	N/A
44	$218,273	$230,596	$230,596	$230,596	$233,919	N/A
45	$236,826	$253,656	$253,656	$253,656	$257,312	N/A
46	$256,956	$279,021	$279,021	$279,021	$312,435	N/A
47	$278,797	$306,923	$306,923	$306,923	$343,679	N/A
48	$302,495	$337,615	$337,615	$337,615	$378,047	N/A
49	$328,207	$371,377	$371,377	$371,377	$415,850	N/A
50	$356,105	$408,514	$408,514	$408,514	$457,436	N/A
51	$386,374	$449,366	$449,366	$449,366	$503,179	N/A
52	$419,216	$494,302	$494,302	$494,302	$553,497	N/A
53	$454,849	$543,733	$543,733	$543,733	$608,846	N/A
54	$493,511	$598,107	$598,107	$598,107	$669,732	N/A
55	$535,460	$657,917	$657,917	$657,917	$736,706	N/A
56	$580,974	$723,708	$723,708	$723,708	$810,377	N/A
57	$630,356	$796,079	$796,079	$796,079	$891,413	N/A
58	$683,937	$875,687	$875,687	$875,687	$980,555	N/A
59	$742,071	$963,255	$963,255	$963,255	$1,075,610	N/A
60	**$786,224**	**$1,390,605**	**$1,390,605**	**$1,390,605**	**$1,194,284**	**N/A**
61	$833,005	$1,487,947	$1,487,947	$1,487,947	$1,277,884	N/A
62	$882,569	$1,592,104	$1,592,104	$1,592,104	$1,367,336	N/A
63	$935,081	$1,703,550	$1,703,550	$1,703,550	$1,463,049	N/A
64	$990,719	$1,822,800	$1,822,800	$1,822,800	$1,565,463	N/A
65	$1,049,667	$1,950,396	$1,950,396	$1,950,396	$1,675,045	N/A
66	$1,112,122	$2,086,922	$2,086,922	$2,086,922	$1,792,298	N/A
67	$1,178,293	$2,233,008	$2,233,008	$2,233,008	$1,917,759	N/A
68	$1,248,401	$2,389,318	$2,389,318	$2,389,318	$2,052,003	N/A
69	$1,322,681	$2,556,571	$2,556,571	$2,556,571	$2,195,643	N/A
70	$1,401,381	$2,735,530	$2,735,530	$2,735,530	$2,349,338	N/A
71	$1,484,763	$2,907,717	$2,907,717	$2,907,717	$2,513,791	N/A
72	$1,573,106	$3,109,029	$3,109,029	$3,109,029	$2,689,757	N/A
73	$1,666,706	$3,323,073	$3,323,073	$3,323,073	$2,878,040	N/A
74	$1,765,875	$3,550,580	$3,550,580	$3,550,580	$3,079,502	N/A
75	$1,870,945	$3,792,314	$3,792,314	$3,792,314	$3,295,068	N/A

CASE STUDY #2: RICHARD AND A CONVERSION TO A ROTH IRA

Richard, age 50, is in a situation that often happens to a large number of people during difficult economic times. He has been downsized out of a corporate management position and has been unemployed for most of the year. He is trying to decide what to do with the $40,000 in his former employer's 401(k) plan.

Because he is jobless, his tax rate will drop dramatically this year, placing him in the 15 percent bracket. When he was working, he was in the highest tax bracket, 38.6 percent, and he anticipates returning to that bracket when he rejoins the workforce. Based on his savings and retirement income sources, Richard also anticipates being in the highest tax bracket during his retirement.

His goal is to take advantage of his current unemployed status by capturing some tax benefits while he is in a lower bracket. Richard's goal is to achieve a 10 percent pre-retirement rate of return and a 7 percent post-retirement rate on his investments. Review the distribution analysis in Figures 4 and 5 to determine which option will help him meet his goals and provide him with the most money at retirement.

Based on Richard's unique circumstances, he should consider rolling his employer-sponsored plan money to an IRA and then converting it to a Roth IRA. Although he will be required to pay $6,000 in income taxes immediately on the entire balance, he will be doing so while in a low 15 percent tax bracket. The $40,000 he is converting to a Roth IRA will be added to his taxable income but penalties are avoided. When Richard retires, he can begin withdrawing money from his Roth IRA, tax-free, since he's already paid taxes on the amount at the 15 percent level.

When Richard retires at age 65, the balance — if he chooses to convert his plan balance to a Roth IRA — will be over $30,000 more than if he had used an IRA or taken a cash distribution.

In addition to the advantage of being able to access his Roth money tax-free, he won't have to worry about mandatory IRA distributions at age 70 $1/2$. If he chooses to retire early before reaching 59 $1/2$, he can withdraw up to the amount initially converted to the Roth IRA without any premature withdrawal penalties. However, he must wait five years from the time of conversion before he can take a withdrawal to avoid the penalty on the converted amount.

In addition to the tax advantages, Richard gains a great deal of flexibility from this approach. From his Roth IRA account, he can invest in any stock, bond, mutual fund, variable annuity, unit investment trust or other investment vehicles he chooses. Richard can build a nicely diversified portfolio from the best options available to him.

FIGURE 4

Summary of Distribution Analysis

Based on your available distribution options and current financial situation, the distribution strategy that maximizes your retirement assets at the age of 65 is:

Option #5 - Roll to an IRA and then convert to a Roth IRA

By following this distribution strategy you will incur immediate federal income taxes in the amount of $6,000. You will incur a premature withdrawal penalty in □ the amount of $0.

Below is an after-tax and after-penalty (if applicable) summary of each option at retirement, and every five years thereafter until age 85. If you intend to delay disbursement until after your retirement age your best distribution may be different than the one listed below.

Client Age	Option #1 Cash Distribution	Option #2 Rollover to IRA	Option #3 Rollover to New Plan	Option #4 Defer Distribution	Option #5 Convert to a Roth IRA*	Option #6 Combination Strategy
65	$99,595	$99,795	$99,795	$99,795	**$138,153**	N/A
70	$132,967	$139,968	$139,968	$139,968	**$193,757**	N/A
75	$177,520	$190,960	$190,960	$190,960	**$271,768**	N/A
80	$237,003	$264,500	$264,500	$264,500	**$381,168**	N/A
85	$316,416	$362,656	$362,656	$362,656	**$534,608**	N/A

It is strongly suggested that you review the results of this analysis with your tax and financial advisors prior to making a distribution decision. The distribution analysis is for illustration purposes only and is not a reflection of actual investment returns or changes in tax law.

* Adjusted gross income must be under $100,000 in order to convert your plan to a Roth IRA.

FIGURE 5

Summary of Options

Client Age	Option #1 Cash Distribution	Option #2 Rollover to IRA	Option #3 Rollover to New Plan	Option #4 Defer Distribution	Option #5 Convert to a Roth IRA	Option #6 Combination Strategy
50	$30,000	$30,000	$30,000	$30,000	$30,000	N/A
51	$32,550	$33,000	$33,000	$33,000	$33,150	N/A
52	$35,317	$36,300	$36,300	$36,300	$36,465	N/A
53	$38,319	$39,930	$39,930	$39,930	$40,112	N/A
54	$41,576	$43,923	$43,923	$43,923	$44,122	N/A
55	$45,110	$48,315	$48,315	$48,315	$48,534	N/A
56	$48,944	$53,147	$53,147	$53,147	$58,864	N/A
57	$53,104	$58,462	$58,462	$58,462	$64,751	N/A
58	$57,618	$64,308	$64,308	$64,308	$71,225	N/A
59	$62,516	$70,738	$70,738	$70,738	$78,348	N/A
60	$67,830	$88,188	$88,188	$88,188	$88,187	N/A
61	$73,595	$97,006	$97,006	$97,006	$97,006	N/A
62	$79,851	$106,706	$106,706	$106,706	$106,707	N/A
63	$86,638	$117,377	$117,377	$117,377	$117,377	N/A
64	$94,002	$129,115	$129,115	$129,115	$129,115	N/A
65	**$99,595**	**$99,795**	**$99,795**	**$99,795**	**$138,153**	**N/A**
66	$105,521	$106,781	$106,781	$106,781	$147,824	N/A
67	$111,800	$114,256	$114,256	$114,256	$158,171	N/A
68	$118,452	$122,254	$122,254	$122,254	$169,243	N/A
69	$125,500	$130,812	$130,812	$130,812	$181,090	N/A
70	$132,967	$139,968	$139,968	$139,968	$193,767	N/A
71	$140,878	$146,390	$146,390	$146,390	$207,330	N/A
72	$149,261	$156,532	$156,532	$156,532	$221,844	N/A
73	$158,142	$167,318	$167,318	$167,318	$237,373	N/A
74	$167,551	$178,781	$178,781	$178,781	$253,989	N/A
75	$177,520	$190,960	$190,960	$190,960	$271,768	N/A
76	$188,083	$203,898	$203,898	$203,898	$290,792	N/A
77	$199,274	$217,659	$217,659	$217,659	$311,147	N/A
78	$211,131	$232,243	$232,243	$232,243	$332,927	N/A
79	$223,693	$247,748	$247,748	$247,748	$356,232	N/A
80	$237,003	$264,200	$264,200	$264,200	$381,168	N/A
81	$251,104	$281,650	$281,650	$281,650	$407,850	N/A
82	$266,045	$300,157	$300,157	$300,157	$436,400	N/A
83	$281,875	$319,776	$319,776	$319,776	$466,948	N/A
84	$298,646	$340,570	$340,570	$340,570	$499,634	N/A
85	$316,416	$362,656	$362,656	$362,656	$534,608	N/A

By comparing his options side-by-side with a distribution analysis, Richard avoided simply rolling his money into an IRA account, an option that could have cost him about $38,000 during retirement.

CASE STUDY #3: CURTIS AND THE COMBINATION STRATEGY (IRA & NUA)

Curtis just turned 65 and has decided to retire. He has a $500,000 401(k) balance, 80 percent of which is invested in his former employer's stock ($400,000). Curtis, who is in the highest tax bracket (38.6 percent) is looking for strategies to help him reduce his overall tax burden once he sells his stock. He plans to sell the company stock sometime during the next couple of years, using the proceeds to purchase a vacation home. His stock shares were originally purchased for just $10,000, his cost basis for tax purposes.

Curtis should, as the distribution analysis indicates in Figures 6 and 7, consider using the combination strategy. To start this process, he will simply request that his stock shares be transferred in-kind to a non-retirement account. He will have to pay income taxes on his $10,000 cost basis, which will amount to $3,860 in his tax bracket. However, when he sells his shares in the near future, he will be required to pay 20 percent capital gains taxes on the appreciation of his shares ($390,000), rather than the income taxes (38.6 percent) he would have paid had he transferred his shares to an IRA and then taken a withdrawal.

The $100,000 that is not invested in company stock can be transferred to a Rollover IRA. Curtis can defer taxes on this portion of the distribution until he begins taking withdrawals. By taking advantage of the Net Unrealized Appreciation tax strategy and transferring company stock in-kind into a non-retirement brokerage account, Curtis saved himself a great deal of money in taxes.

The advantages to Curtis are clear. The combination strategy will provide him with $146,680 more than the Rollover IRA strategy if he sells his stock and takes a withdrawal at age 65, and $93,801 more if he sells his stock at age 75 (after tax). (See Figures 6 and 7.) The reason for the gain is that the 20 percent he will pay in capital gains taxes when he sells the stock is much less than the 38.6 percent income tax rate he would pay had he taken a withdrawal from an IRA. A Roth IRA is not a feasible option for Curtis because his adjusted gross income is over $100,000.

Heading toward retirement is not unlike traveling down a major highway and facing a number of possible exit ramps, only a few of which will take you where you want to go. Having a retirement plan distribution analysis at hand will help you make the right choices and avoid wrong turns. To obtain your own distribution analysis contact your financial advisor.

FIGURE 6

Summary of Distribution Analysis

Based on your available distribution options and current financial situation, the distribution strategy that maximizes your retirement assets at the age of 65 is:

Option #6 - Combination Plan

By following this distribution strategy you will incur immediate federal income taxes in the amount of $3,860. You will incur a premature withdrawal penalty in □ the amount of $0.

Below is an after-tax and after-penalty (if applicable) summary of each option at retirement, and every five years thereafter until age 85. If you intend to delay disbursement until after your retirement age your best distribution may be different than the one listed below.

Client Age	Option #1 Cash Distribution	Option #2 Rollover to IRA	Option #3 Rollover to New Plan	Option #4 Defer Distribution	Option #5 Convert to a Roth IRA*	Option #6 Combination Strategy
65	$307,000	$307,000	$307,000	$307,000	N/A	**$453,680**
70	$461,623	$494,427	$494,427	$494,427	N/A	**$577,412**
75	$694,122	$773,384	$773,384	$773,384	N/A	**$867,185**
80	$1,043,721	$1,221,917	$1,221,917	$1,221,917	N/A	**$1,293,925**
85	$1,569,398	$1,909,454	$1,909,454	$1,909,454	N/A	**$1,915,471**

It is strongly suggested that you review the results of this analysis with your tax and financial advisors prior to making a distribution decision. The distribution analysis is for illustration purposes only and is not a reflection of actual investment returns or changes in tax law.

* Adjusted gross income must be under $100,000 in order to convert your plan to a Roth IRA.

FIGURE 7

Summary of Options

Client Age	Option #1 Cash Distribution	Option #2 Rollover to IRA	Option #3 Rollover to New Plan	Option #4 Defer Distribution	Option #5 Convert to a Roth IRA	Option #6 Combination Strategy
65	$307,000	$307,000	$307,000	$307,000	N/A	$453,680
66	$333,095	$337,700	$337,700	$337,700	N/A	$413,390
67	$361,408	$371,470	$371,470	$371,470	N/A	$449,371
68	$392,128	$408,617	$408,617	$408,617	N/A	$488,511
69	$425,459	$449,479	$449,479	$449,479	N/A	$531,091
70	$461,623	$494,427	$494,427	$494,427	N/A	$577,412
71	$500,861	$531,861	$531,861	$531,861	N/A	$621,355
72	$543,434	$584,486	$584,486	$584,486	N/A	$671,047
73	$589,626	$641,994	$641,994	$641,994	N/A	$724,622
74	$639,744	$704,807	$704,807	$704,807	N/A	$782,370☐
75	$694,122	$773,384	$773,384	$773,384	N/A	$844,605
76	$753,122	$848,221	$848,221	$848,221	N/A	$911,661
77	$817,138	$929,948	$929,948	$929,948	N/A	$983,951
78	$886,594	$1,018,958	$1,018,958	$1,018,958	N/A	$1,061,796
79	$961,955	$1,116,089	$1,116,089	$1,116,089	N/A	$1,145,693
80	$1,043,721	$1,221,917	$1,221,917	$1,221,917	N/A	$1,236,077
81	$1,132,437	$1,337,171	$1,337,171	$1,337,171	N/A	$1,333,441
82	$1,228,695	$1,462,643	$1,462,643	$1,462,643	N/A	$1,438,308
83	$1,333,134	$1,599,178	$1,599,178	$1,599,178	N/A	$1,551,245
84	$1,446,450	$1,747,696	$1,747,696	$1,747,696	N/A	$1,672,863
85	$1,569,398	$1,909,454	$1,909,454	$1,909,454	N/A	$1,803,965

Conclusion

As you get ready to retire, you will face changes that will profoundly affect your lifestyle for many years to come. No doubt you have many pressing questions that must be answered in order to make proper decisions about the way your money will be distributed and invested at retirement. After reading *Opening the Door to Retirement,* many of those questions should now be answered. Even though the pressure is on to make the right decisions, and many of those choices will be irrevocable, the strategies outlined in this book can give you the knowledge you need to make those decisions with confidence. You should now be ready to:

- Assess your retirement goals and determine whether you are on track to reach them.
- Develop a *written* financial plan and implement strategies that will help you reach your goals.
- Choose a safe portfolio withdrawal rate.
- Tap into retirement savings early without incurring premature withdrawal penalties.
- Incorporate your Social Security benefits into your overall retirement plan.
- Maximize company pension benefits.
- Avoid the 10 most common investor mistakes.
- Effectively allocate your assets within your investment portfolio.
- Properly diversify your portfolio.
- Choose successful investments through hiring competent money managers.
- Adhere to a disciplined investment strategy through ongoing portfolio management.
- Properly handle company stock or other concentrated stock positions
- Apply investment strategies that will help protect your principal while investing in the stock market.
- Protect your hard-earned nest egg through purchasing the proper amount of health care coverage and long-term care insurance.
- Properly take a distribution from an employer-sponsored retirement plan.

Opening the Door to Retirement is your guide to making the right decisions for the future. Use it as an ongoing reference as you maneuver through the complex financial decisions you must make in order to achieve the retirement lifestyle you've been dreaming of. Good luck and remember, the best is yet to come!

Opening the Door to Retirement

*Successfully Transitioning from
the Workforce Into Retirement*

End Notes

INTRODUCTION

1. New York Life web page, www.newyorklife.com, "When It's Time to Rollover...," (July 5, 2002).
2. Marcella DeSimone, "Baby-Boom Retirees Want Advice On High-Balance IRA Rollovers," National Underwriter/Life & Health Financial Services, June 25, 2001, 37.
3. The Cerulli Report, www.cerulli.com/report-mu-401k.htm, Market Update: The 401(k) Industry, (June 20, 2002).
4. *Ibid.*
5. *Ibid.*
6. Kristin Adamonis, "Roll Out an Effective Rollover Strategy," FRC Monitor, (December 2001).
7. Spectrem Group, www.spectrem.com, "High Balance IRA Rollovers," (September 16, 2002.)

PART TWO: RETIREMENT PLANNING

Chapter 1:   Retirement Planning: Are You on Track?

1. Americans Savings Education Council ASEC, "The 1999 Retirement Confidence Survey (RCS) Summary of Findings," http://www.asec.org/rcssummary.pdf, 1.
2. www.medicarewatch.org/2001basic/reform-proposals-1.html

3. http://www2.homefair.com/calc/citypick.html
4. Sharon E. Epperson , "Death and the Maven," Time Magazine, 18 December 1995), 61.
5. U.S. Department of Labor, Past Annual Inflation (C.P.I.) Rates.
6. Lynn O'Shaughnessy, Retirement Bible (New York, Hungry Minds, Inc., 2001), 11.

Chapter 2: Importance of a Comprehensive Financial Plan.
1. Office of Investor Education and Assistance, Securities and Exchange Commission, "The Facts On Savings and Investing," (April 1999), 18.
2. Jack Sirard, "Confused? Written Financial Plan Helps," The Sacramento Bee,   14 March 2000, D1.
3. Barbara Epstein, "Advanced Life Design Yields Powerful Results…," http://www.lifestrategycoach.org/whatis.htm, (September 16, 2002).

Chapter 3: Determining a "Safe" Portfolio Withdrawal Rate
1. Scott Burns, "Dangerous Advice from Peter Lynch, "www.scottburns.com, (October 1, 1995).
2. Scott Burns, "The Trinity Study," http://www.scottburns.com/wwtrinity.htm, (May 17, 2002).
3. The Retire Early Home Page, "What's the "Safe" Withdrawal Rate in Retirement?," http://www.geocities.com/WallStreet/8257/safewith.html, (May 16, 2002).

Chapter 4: Early Retirement Strategies (prior to age 59$^1/_2$)
1. IRC, Section 72 (T).
2. *Ibid.*
3. This is based on IRS private letter ruling #8946045.
4. Oppenheimer Funds, IRA Section 72(t) Distributions, (July 30, 1997), 10-11.
5. College for Financial Planning, Certified Financial Planner Professional Education Program, Retirement Planning Book #7, (Denver, College For Financial Planning, 1998), 19.

END NOTES

PART TWO: SOURCES OF RETIREMENT INCOME

Chapter 5:   *Social Security: How much will you receive?*
1. Much of the information from this chapter was obtained from the Social Security Administration's web site: www.ssa.gov.

Chapter 6:   *Company Pensions and Pension Maximization Strategies*
1. This calculation assumes the portfolio is depleted in the thirtieth year.
2. See note 1 above.
3. Standard and Poors 500 Index.
4. Lehman Brothers Govt/Corp. Index.
5. Hypothetical Illustration, $500,000 hypothetical investment made from 12/31/1975 to 12/31/00. Assumes all interest and dividends are reinvested and $35,000 withdrawn from the portfolio annually.

Chapter 7:   *Savings and Investments: Avoiding the 10 Most Common Investor Mistakes*
1. Humberto Cruz, "Bad Timing Plagues Many Investors," *Orlando Sentinel*, www.orlandosentinel.com, 26 July 2001.
2. Terrance Odean and Brad Barber, "You Are What You Trade," *Bloomberg Personal Finance*, May 2000, 1.
3. Mark Hulbert, "The Blinding Power of Data," *New York Times*, www.nytimes.com, 8 April 2001.
4. Brian O'Reilly, "Why Johnny Can't Invest," *Fortune Magazine*, www.business2.0.com, 9 November 1998, 1.
5. S&P 500 Index, Lehman U.S. Aggregate Bond Index from 12/31/89 to 12/31/01.
6. SEI Investments. The average return of top ten mutual funds in 1999 was 67.2% while the Wilshire 5000 returned 23.82%. In 2001 the average return of those same ten funds was a dismal –24.97% while the Wilshire 5000 returned 10.89%.
7. Morningstar Principia for mutual funds, (12/31/01).
8. Morningstar Principia for mutual funds, (12/31/01), 376 Technology Funds Measured.
9. Stocks: 50% Large-Cap, 20% Mid-Cap, 10% Small-Cap and 20% International stocks with equal exposure to both growth and value in each market segment. Bonds: 40% Long-term governments, 45% Long-term

Corporate Bonds and 15% International Bonds.

10. Michael Pretzer , "Men Behaving Badly ," Investment Advisor, www.djfpc.com, (October 1999).

11. *Ibid.*

12. Morningstar Principia for mutual funds, (12/31/01).

13. Sharon E. Epperson , "Death and the Maven," *Time Magazine*, (18 December 1995), 61.

Part Three: Developing a Successful Investment Strategy

Chapter 8:   Step One: Asset Allocation

1. Frank Armstrong, CFP, Excerpt from Investment Strategies for the 21st Century, Chapter Six: The Asset Allocation Decision, found at www.fundsinteractive.com on September 16, 2002.

Chapters 9, 10 and 11: Step Two: Diversification

1. Wilshire Mid-Cap Value Index
2. Wilshire Small-Cap Value Index
3. Lehman Brothers Long-Term Government Bond Index
4. Lehman Brothers Municipal Bond Index
5. Morningstar Principia Pro for mutual funds, (December 31, 2001).
6. Ibbotson Associates, (March 1, 2001).
7. Morningstar Principia Pro for mutual funds, Funds measured for the ten years ending March 31, 2002, (December 31, 2001).
8. S&P/Barra Growth Index.
9. *Ibid.*
10. EBRI/ICI Participant-Directed Retirement Plan Data Collection Project, "401(k) Plan Asset Allocation, Account Balances, and Loan Activity in 2000," EBRI Issue Brief no. 239, (November 2001).

Chapter 12:   Step Three: Choosing Investments

1. Morningstar Principia Pro for mutual funds, (December 31, 2001).
2. Investment Company Institute, *Mutual Fund Factbook 2001 Edition*, excerpts taken from www.ici.org, 44.
3. Morningstar Principia Pro for mutual funds, (December 31, 2001).
4. Investment Company Institute, (2001).

5. Separate Account Solutions, www.separate.com, "About Separate Account Solutions," (June 20, 2002).

6. *Ibid.*

7. Morningstar Principia Pro for mutual funds, (December 31, 2001).

8. *Ibid.*

9. The Cerulli Report, "Asset Management: The State of Separate Account Consultant Programs," from www.cerulli.com, (June 20, 2002).

10. Securities and Exchange Commission, "Final Rule: Disclosure of Mutual Fund After-Tax Returns," www.sec.gov, (2001), 3.

11. Morningstar Principia Pro for mutual funds (December 31, 2001), 7494 Domestic Equity Funds.

12. Morningstar Online, www.morningstar.com

13. Morningstar Principia Pro for mutual funds (December 31, 2001), Load funds: 3008 domestic stock funds, 806 international stock funds, 890 taxable bond funds, and 993 tax-free bond funds measured, front-end load greater than 1%, or back-end load greater than 1%, minimum initial purchase of 10k of less.

14. Morningstar Principia Pro for mutual funds (December 31, 2001), No-Load funds: 2255 domestic stock funds, 484 international stock funds, 616 taxable bond funds, and 342 tax-free bond funds measured, front-end load equal to 0% and back-end load equal to 0%, minimum initial purchase of 10k of less.

15. John C. Bogle, *Common Sense on Mutual Funds*, (New York, John Wiley & Sons, Inc.,1999), 269.

16. Morningstar Principia Pro for mutual funds (December 31, 2001).

17. Morningstar Principia Pro for mutual funds (June 30, 2002).

18. Smith Barney Aggressive Growth A, Morningstar Principia Pro for mutual funds (December 31, 2001).

19. American Funds Growth Fund A, Morningstar Principia Pro for mutual funds (December 31, 2001).

20. Morningstar Principia Pro for mutual funds (December 31, 2001).

21. www.morningstar.com, February 12, 2002, comparison of top 25 positions. The information reported for Fidelity Magellan is dated 9/30/01 and that of Janus Twenty is dated 10/31/01.

22. Brendan Boyd, Desert News, http://deseretnews.com, "Use the 4 P's to Grade Portfolio, Ditch Losers," 19 May 2002.

Chapter 13:   Step Four: Ongoing Portfolio Management.
1. Morningstar Principia Pro for mutual funds (December 31, 2001).
2. *Ibid.*
3. *Ibid.*

Chapter 15:   Increase Your Odds for Success: Work with a Professional Financial Advisor
1. DALBAR Inc., DALBAR Issues 2001 Update to "Quantitative Analysis of Investor Behavior" Report, "More Proof that Market Timing Doesn't Work for the Majority of Investors," www.dalbarinc.com/content/showpage.asp?page=2001062100, (June 21, 2001).
2. Nationwide Financial 2002 High-Income Survey, www.nationwide.com
3. Christopher Farrell, "Mutual-Fund Investors' Enemy: Themselves," Business Week Online, www.businessweek.com, (March 1, 2001).
4. Retirement Planning Associates RPA, "No-Load Versus Load," www.retirement-planning.com/loadvsnoload.html, (August 8, 2002).
5. http://www.pgatour.com/stats/
6. Source: Forum for Investor Advice http://pub.franklintempleton.com/public/welcome/inv_prof/what_to_expect.htm

Chapter 16:   Handling Company Stock or Other Concentrated Stock Positions
1. EBRI Special Report—Company Stock in 401(k) Plans: Results of a Survey of ISCEBS Members, Introduction, 2000.

PART FOUR: OTHER RETIREMENT CONSIDERATIONS

Chapter 17:   Health Insurance During Retirement.
1. www.insure.com, "The HIPAA law: Your Rights to Health Insurance Portability," (September 16, 2002).
2. www.insure.com, "Know Your COBRA Rights," (September 16, 2002).
3. www.insure.com, "The HIPAA law: Your Rights to Health Insurance Portability," (September 16, 2002).

4. www.insure.com, "Know Your COBRA Rights," (September 16, 2002).
5. www.medicare.gov, "Does Medicare Pay For Prescription Drugs?" FAQ, (September 16, 2002).
6. www.medicare.gov, "What is a Medigap Policy?" FAQ, (September 16, 2002).
7. Robert Kuttner, "The American Health Care System—Health Insurance Coverage," *New England Journal of Medicine*, Vol. 340, No. 2., 14 January 1999. Note: "The proportion of Americans without insurance increased from 14.2 percent in 1995, to 15.3 percent in 1996, and to 16.1 percent in 1997, when 43.4 million people were uninsured."

Chapter 18:   Long-term Care Insurance.

1. Public Attitudes on Long Term Care: "The EBRI Poll": A National Public Opinion Survey Conducted by The Gallup Organization, Inc., Released August 1993, 15.
2. Health Insurance Association of America, www.hiaa.org/cons/guideltc.html#likely, "What is Long-Term Care?" 2002.
3. *Ibid*.
4. *Ibid*.
5. *New England Journal of Medicine*, 1991; 324(9), 595.
6. James Palma, "Long-Term Care Insurance Revisited," National Center on Women and Aging, http://heller.brandeis.edu/national/ltcr499.htm, (April 1999).
7. David Braze, "The Spectre of Long Term Care," www.Fool.com, (January 31, 2000).
8. Ellen Hoffman, "Long Term Care Policies That Will Last," *Business Week*, http://www.businessweek.com, 20 November 2000.
9. Health Insurance Association of America, www.hiaa.org/cons/guideltc.html#likely, "What is long-term care?" 2002.
10. National Association of Insurance Commissioners LTC standards (NAIC), the Health Insurance Association of America (HIAA), and the Association for Aged and Retired Persons (AARP)

PART FIVE: RETIREMENT PLAN DISTRIBUTION GUIDE

Chapter 19:   Retirement Plan Distribution Options
1. 2000 U.S. Department of Labor Statistics
2. CNN Money, "401(k)s Down, But Not Out," http://money.cnn.com/2001/08/13/investing/retirement/, (August 13, 2001).
3. "Targeting High-Balance Rollovers, 2001," Pension Benefits, July 2000, 6.
4. The Cerulli Report, www.cerulli.com/report.rollover.htm, The Rollover IRA Market: Retirement Markets in Transition, (June 20, 2002).
5. *Ibid.*
6. *Ibid.*
7. Lynn O'Shaunessy, www.money.msn.com, "What's Wrong with Your 401(k)—and How to Fix It," http://money.msn.com/articles/retire/basics/9092.asp?special=msn, (April 1, 2002), 4.
8. EBRI Special Report, "Company Stock in 401(k) Plans: Results of a Survey of ISCEBS Members", Information compiled at year-end 2000, 2.

Chapter 20:   Company Stock Distributions (Net Unrealized Appreciation)
1. Jack L. VanDerhei, "Company Stock in 401(k) Plans: Results of a Survey of ISCEBS Members," Employee Benefit Research Institute (EBRI) Special Report (January 31, 2002).
2. Vern Hayden, "Looking for a Great 401(k) Tax Break? Try Your Employer's Stock," TheStreet.com, (June 28, 2000).
3. IRC § 402 (e) (4) (A) and (B)
4. IRC § 402 (e) (4) (D)
5. Dan Kadlec, www.time.com

ABOUT THE AUTHOR

Ray E. LeVitre is a financial advisor and Certified Financial Manager (CFM). He began his career in the financial services industry in 1987 while working for Fidelity Investments and later managed an office for Merrill Lynch, one of the nation's largest brokerage firms. Ray now runs a successful independent financial planning practice with an emphasis on transition management, helping people properly handle their retirement plan distributions upon separation from a company at retirement. He has been invited by many Fortune 500 companies to teach financial management seminars to their employees, and has been published in *Bank Investment Representative* magazine.

Ray can be contacted to answer questions, to arrange speaking engagements, or to obtain a Retirement Plan Distribution Analysis:

By mail: Net Worth Advisory Group, LLC
4505 Wasatch Blvd., Suite 330B
Salt Lake City, Utah 84124

By e-mail: networth@networld.com

By Phone: (801) 277-6280